Pragmatism,

Feminism,

and

Democracy

Pragmatism, Feminism, and Democracy

Rethinking the Politics of American History

James Livingston

Routledge
New York and London

Published in 2001 by
Routledge
29 West 35th Street
New York, NY 10001

Published in Great Britain by
Routledge
11 New Fetter Lane
London EC4P 4EE

Copyright © 2001 by Routledge
Routledge is an imprint of the Taylor & Francis Group.

Typography: Jack Donner

Library of Congress Cataloging-in-Publication Data

Livingston, James 1949–
    Pragmatism, feminism, and democracy: rethinking the politics of American history / James Livingston.
        p.   cm.
    Includes bibliographical references and index.
    ISBN 0–415–93029–4 (alk. paper)—ISBN 0–415–93030–8 (pbk. : alk. paper)
        1. United States—Politics and government—1865–1933. 2. United States—Historiography. 3. United States—Intellectual life—1865–1918. 4. Progressivism (United States politics)—History. 5. Pragmatism—History. 6. Feminism—United States—History. 7. Capitalism—United States—History. 8. Socialism—United States—History. I. Title.

E661 .L78 2001
973'.07'2—dc21

                                                                00–067375

Printed in the United States of America on acid-free paper
10 9 8 7 6 5 4 3 2 1

This book is for my children,
Vincent James Livingston and Julia Rossi Livingston

Contents

Acknowledgments

This book got started, more or less inadvertently, as I was finishing the last one. I was then noticing that pragmatists and feminists asked similar questions about the sources of the self, the uses of epistemology, and the embodiments of knowledge. So I designed an undergraduate seminar that examined the historical and theoretical intersections of pragmatism and feminism in the twentieth century. That was back in the amazing winter of 1994. The seminar was great fun, and it taught me a great deal—much more than I bargained for. My originary debts are to its members, and particularly to four students who later wrote honors theses that emerged from their research in the seminar: Robert Genter, Venita Jethwani, Andrew Kessler, and Barbara Schweiger.

As usual, my principal debts are to my friends from the Rutgers English department, John McClure and Bruce Robbins, who are always willing to disagree with me. I've learned more from my endless arguments with them than from anything I've ever read. Other members of the English department who have given me good advice and valuable comments are Richard Poirier, Marc Manganaro, Elin Diamond, Richard Dienst, Kurt Spellmeyer, and Harriet Davidson. In my own department, Mia Bay, Paul Clemens, Belinda Davis, Nancy Hewitt, Jackson Lears, Jan Lewis, Jennifer Morgan, James Reed, and Bonnie Smith have helped me by reading, discussing, and criticizing chapters in draft. So have several graduate students in history at Rutgers. My thanks to Rosanne Currarino, Andrea Volpe, David Nack, J. Allen Douglas, Rob Nelson, Jennifer Pettit, April de Stefano, Christopher Fisher, Brian Connolly, Curt Cardwell, and Sarah Gordon for stimulating conversation or useful comments, and to the "Gang of Four"—Gary Darden, Sara Dubow, Justin Hart,

and Peter Lau—for its intensity, inspiration, and intellectual com-
radeship. Thanks also to the former Dean of the Faculty of Arts and
Sciences at Rutgers, Richard Foley, who granted me two semester-
length leaves, one in 1995, the other in 1999, which gave me time to
write the first and the last chapters.

I have many outside agitators to thank for their help in completing this book. For warm encouragement and strong criticism, often
enough in equal doses from the same person, I am grateful to Patri-
cia A. Rossi, Alice Kessler-Harris, David Hollinger, George Cotkin,
Thomas Haskell, Michael Merrill, Thomas Bender, Mary Lawlor,
Mike Fennell, Alec Marsh, James T. Kloppenberg, Richard Teich-
graeber III, Marc Chandler, Martin J. Sklar, Richard Schneirov,
Louis Ferleger, Keith Haynes, Robert Johnston, James Giarelli,
Eliza Jane Reilly, Dorothy Sue Cobble, Jeff Sklansky, John
Cicchino, Paul Buhle, William Connell, and Bert Weltmann. Once
again I am deeply indebted to Eliza Reilly for long-distance con-
versations about the limits and implications of my arguments; and
this time she helped with the cover art, too.

Except for the last, all the chapters that follow were written as
an invited lecture, a conference paper, or a contribution to an
edited volume. So I am also grateful to those who allowed me to
participate in their projects, and who followed up with insightful
comments on what I wrote for the occasion. Chapter 1 was written
for a conference on consumer cultures organized in 1995 by
Charles McGovern, Susan Strasser, and Matthias Judt; it appeared
four years later in the published proceedings of the conference.
Chapter 2 was originally a paper delivered in 1995 at Purdue's
annual American Studies symposium, where my hosts were Harold
Woodman, Leonard Neufeldt, Susan Curtis, Leonard Harris, and
Charlene Haddock-Seigfried. This paper was published in *Social
Text* in 1996, when Andrew Ross and Bruce Robbins were still co-
editors. Chapter 3 was written for presentation at the 1998 meeting of the Organization of American Historians, where my fellow
panelists were Mary King, Barry Shank, and Casey Nelson Blake.
Our panel showed up two years later in *Radical History Review*, in
a special issue I helped Van Gosse coordinate—but he did all the
real work, so he gets all the credit. Chapter 4 was also written in
1998, at the request of John Pettegrew, who was editing a volume
on Richard Rorty which has since been published by Rowman &
Littlefield. And the original version of chapter 5 was a paper deliv-

ered at an American Studies conference organized by Jonathan Arac at the University of Pittsburgh in 1997, then revised and presented at MIT at the request of Bruce Mazlish. It appeared later that year in *Raritan*, when Dick Poirier was still the editor. Most of these chapters have, then, been published before now. But I have rewritten chapters 1 and 2 and have radically revised and substantially enlarged chapters 4 and 5.

I wrote the Introduction and the Afterword at the suggestion of my editors at Routledge, who have consistently expressed confidence in the book's ecumenical appeal. My thanks to Derek Krissof, Deirdre Mullane, and especially Vikram Mukhija for keeping the faith through many changes in their professional lives.

My children have put up with a lot from me over the last five years. I hope I can make it up to them over the next five. This book is dedicated to them.

James Livingston

Introduction

Attitudes
Toward History

Only in the United States do the losers, deviants, miscreants, and malcontents get to narrate the national experience—not, mind you, as exiles or émigrés such as Leon Trotsky or Aleksandr Solzhenitsyn, but as accredited professionals boring from within their own cultures and disciplines. In histor*iographi*cal time, for example, coming to terms with the second American republic codified in the Fourteenth Amendment took almost a century, because the formative moment known as Reconstruction was originally defined by historians who identified with the good old causes of southern honor and white supremacy. But an even better example is the historiography of the Progressive Era, which qualifies, by all accounts, as an equally formative moment in the making of the nation. Here, too, historians who have proudly identified with the good old lost causes (especially but not only Populism) have been able to define the moment in question, and to shape research agendas accordingly. In this sense, coming to terms with the *third* American republic—the one that resides in the emergence of corporate capitalism between 1890 and 1930—has been no less difficult than coming to terms with the second.[1]

Several years ago, in a graduate reading seminar that covered the period 1880 to 1930, I was reminded of just how difficult it has been for historians to acknowledge the legitimacy of this third republic, to accept it as the horizon of political expectation in the twentieth century and after. I assigned Richard Hofstadter's *Age of Reform* (1955) as a matter of course—as a key text in the making of the discipline as well as an important interpretation of the Progressive Era from which we can still learn a great deal. I knew that the graduate students would be suspicious of a so-called consensus historian who was agnostic on the "democratic promise" of Populism. But I was not prepared for their refusal to consider the possibility that Hofstadter wrote from the Left—the possibility that we can be agnostic on the promise of Populism and yet keep the democratic faith, or, what is the same thing, that we can treat the relation between corporate capitalism and social democracy as *reciprocal* rather than antithetical. Their refusal taught me that these possibilities cannot be contemplated, let alone realized, unless we learn to treat the historical fact of corporate capitalism as the source rather than the solvent of a social-democratic promise, that is, until we acknowledge the legitimacy of the third American republic.[2]

I tell this story of the classroom as a way of explaining my purposes in this book. Like Hofstadter and later counter-progressive historians, I assume that the area inhabited by the American Left is larger than Populism, and therefore that the twentieth century represents something more than the non-heroic residue of the tragedy staged in the 1890s, when the Peoples' Party lost its bid for the presidency. Like Hofstadter and later counter-progressive historians, I also assume that to appreciate the reciprocal relation between the emergence of corporate capitalism and the rehabilitation of the body politic is to find a narrative form that allows for local tragedies and unintended consequences, yet refuses the narrative voice of irony. But to make these assumptions, to find this form, is to see in the transition from proprietary to corporate capitalism, circa 1890–1930, the condition of a passage beyond parochial renditions of political obligation, exclusionary principles of social organization, and limited notions of genuine selfhood—a passage navigated by pragmatism and feminism, among other movements (movements such as literary naturalism, marginalist economics, black nationalism, and the "new unionism"). Of course this perspective on the emergence of corporate capitalism must seem strange or scandalous from the standpoint provided by the "anti-monopoly tradition" and the good old cause of Populism, just as the perspectives of W. E. B. Du Bois and Howard Beale on Reconstruction must have seemed strange or scandalous from the standpoint provided by William H. Dunning, Ulrich B. Phillips, and D. W. Griffith. It nevertheless regulates my approach to the history and the historiography of the United States in the twentieth century.[3]

By saying that the transition from proprietary to corporate capitalism was a passage "navigated by pragmatism and feminism," I do not mean to suggest that these intellectual moments were "superstructural" forms that merely *revealed* the more basic content of an inexorably "economic" change. I mean instead to suggest that because these forms *determined* the content of the transition by making it navigable—that is, intelligible and actionable—the transition itself cannot be understood apart from the ideas or idioms through which it was imagined and accomplished. I also mean to suggest that capitalism, whether proprietary or corporate, cannot be reduced to economic phenomena, to "market forces," "material realities," and the like. The advent of capitalism magnified the social significance of commodity production and distribution, to be sure, but only because the modern bourgeoisie had meanwhile transformed the cultural meanings of work by making it the site on which character was built; thus immersion in the realm of socially necessary labor—in the production of commodities—eventually became the condition of freedom rather than the sign of servitude.

Capitalism, in short, is not to be understood as the historical function of the market, the profit motive, or the entrepreneurial persuasion. All three can exist, and have existed, in the absence of capitalism, as both Karl Marx and Max Weber insisted. What distinguishes capitalism from other modes of production is not that the distribution of private property determines the distribution of income, or that the circulation of commodities becomes a means to the accumulation of private fortunes, or that merchants and "middlemen" prey on producers, but that wage labor, or rather "abstract social labor," comes to dominate the social relations of goods production as such. So conceived, capitalism is a complex market *society*, not simply a "market economy," because it permits and requires a market in labor as well as goods—capitalism exists when labor-power, the capacity to produce value through work, becomes a commodity, when its value can therefore be expressed in monetary terms, and when the allocation of labor-power according to market criteria becomes commonplace.[4]

But capitalism cannot emerge from the constraints of a "proto-industrial" or simple market society unless wage laborers and their allies can establish clear limits on the scope of the commodity form—that is, unless they can specify and enforce a meaningful distinction between the value of their labor-time and the worth of their lives. In the absence of this distinction, workers are slaves. That is why the most ferocious, popular, and effective critics of the antebellum South denounced slaveholders for treating human beings as if they were commodities to be bought and sold, "soul by soul," but also welcomed what we call the "market revolution" as evidence of moral progress, and noticed no irony or contradiction or hypocrisy in their position.[5]

Capitalism is, then, a cross-class cultural construction that emerges and evolves only insofar as it *confines* market forces to certain social spaces. "Unlimited greed for gain is not in the least identical with capitalism, and is still less its spirit," as Weber insisted: "Capitalism *may* even be identical with the restraint, or at least a rational tempering, of this irrational impulse." Its adherents, and these typically include the producers as well as the plutocrats, have always dreaded the anarchy of the free market. Thus capitalism does not and cannot exclude socialism any more than feudalism precluded the development of capitalism. In fact, as Daniel Bell, Stuart Hall, Martin Sklar, J. K. Gibson-Graham, and others have suggested, the emergence of a specifically *corporate* capitalism, circa 1890–1930, can be grasped as the origin of a "post-industrial society" in which the two modes of production characteristic of the twentieth century began to function as complementary moments in a new, hybrid social formation—in much the same way that feudalism and capitalism functioned in the early modern period.[6]

So how does corporate capitalism differ from proprietary capitalism, and how does it sponsor a "post-industrial society" that permits, indeed requires, socialism as a component or condition of its development? Let me say at the outset of this exercise in periodization that just as socialism is contained, in both senses, by the corporate stage of capitalism, so proprietary capitalism is contained, in both senses, by the corporate stage—because each is preserved and annulled within the new social formation, we don't have to pretend that it obliterates either the "archaic," proprietary past, or the impending, "socialistic" future. Accordingly, we don't have to claim that periodization in terms of corporate capitalism requires willful ignorance of proprietors and their virtues, or that there are no historical continuities between the nineteenth- and the twentieth-century versions of American civilization. At the risk of being too schematic, then, here is my summary of the ways in which corporate capitalism in the U.S. departs from its predecessor(s):[7]

(1) The most fundamental shift is probably the separation of ownership and control of property which the corporate legal form accomplishes. From this shift follow several significant social-intellectual consequences or possibilities, for example (2) the redefinition of property at the law and in the larger culture and (3) the development of bureaucracy or "bureaucratic rationality," which in turn allow for (4) the regulation and "socialization" of the market through long-range planning as well as the short-run adaptation of supply to demand; (5) the pacification and institutionalization—not the abolition—of class conflict over income shares accruing to labor and capital; (6) the reconstitution of social mobility and the revision of class and gender relations (thus American society) through the incorporation of working-class as well as middle-class men *and* women in clerical, managerial, and/or professional positions; (7) the reconstruction of the labor system to the extent that the formal subjection of labor to capital becomes real, labor-time ceases to function as a universal or reliable measure of value, and the production of surplus value through work no longer determines incomes and corresponding claims on goods; and (8) the articulation of new relations between personality and property, between internal dispositions and external circumstances, between the inner and the outer dimensions of the genuine self—in other words, between subjects and objects as such.

(9) The corporate reorganization of production and distribution, which is essentially complete by 1920, allows for increases of output without proportionate increases of inputs, whether of labor or capital; as Alvin Hansen and other economists noted at midcentury, scientific management, the epitome of "bureaucratic rationality," contributed to "capital-saving" as well as labor-saving techniques in American industry. By the 1920s, therefore, (10) consumer expenditures rather than investment out of savings—that is, out of deferred consumption—had become the fulcrum of eco-

nomic growth and the focus of cultural practices and commentary in the "machine age." (11) The gender trouble produced by the new "tertiary" sector of white-collar work (see 6 above) is compounded by this new consumer culture; for the New Woman is its emblem and agent. (12) Moreover, that culture's promotion of "being through having" seems to reverse the proper relation between active subjects and inert objects by "emptying out" the inner self, by making its private attributes public possessions.

Meanwhile, insofar as social relations of (goods) production are evacuated by the reconstruction of the labor system (see 7 above) and/or complicated by the growth of "tertiary" occupations, (13) the category of class cannot determine social relations as such—thus the categories of gender and race can become more salient in articulating American nationality—and (14) the causative connections between work and character or occupation and identity are attenuated if not dissolved. Finally, (15) as the large corporations take on certain regulatory functions that were hitherto the province of the state, they enable a "dispersal of power" from the state to society; accordingly, (16) the boundary between the private and the public sectors, between the personal and the political, becomes increasingly porous, and (17) *cultural* politics become increasingly pivotal.

The emergence of corporate capitalism sponsors a "post-industrial society," then, because it extricates labor from goods production; because it reconfigures the relation between property and power; and, as Daniel Bell, C. Wright Mills, and Harold Cruse recognized, because it makes the "cultural apparatus"—the "tertiary" sector of service industries, mass communication media, and "information technologies"—the cutting edge of social and political change. By the same token, corporate capitalism enlists socialism as a component or condition of its development because it requires continuous reform, regulation, and manipulation of markets, not adjustment to external and anonymous laws of supply and demand; because it enlarges the public sphere of "self-government"—what the market socialists of Eastern Europe used to call "workers' self-management"—by enabling a "dispersal of power" from the state to society (not merely to corporations and their counterpart in trade unions, but to all manner of organizations and associations); and because it points beyond class society by reducing the scope and significance of the capital-labor relation in determining social relations as such.[8]

The question that remains is how pragmatism and feminism may be said to have navigated the passage to this hybrid social formation in which capitalism and socialism modulate but also invigorate each other. I do not want to claim that the course plotted by these intellectual movements was the only possible way to get from the proprietary past to the corporate future—only that it was, and is, a useful way, because it accommodated both past and future by mediating between previous truths and novel facts. Nor do I want to claim that there are no important differences between these intellectual movements, then and now. I do, however, want to claim that each movement presupposes the other in developing its critique of modern subjectivity—of the unbound individual specified in social contracts—and therefore that the relation between them should be understood as an order of events as well as an order of ideas, that is, in terms of historical connections as well as theoretical affinities. So I will *not* be suggesting that there are interesting parallels between feminist inflections of poststructuralist theory in the late twentieth century and feminist appropriations of pragmatist philosophy in the early twentieth century, as if the latter somehow "anticipates" the former in accordance with some "spirit of the age." I will instead be arguing that these inflections and appropriations comprise an intellectual continuum that begins with pragmatism and ends (for the time being) with feminism—to be more concrete, they comprise an intellectual lineage that begins with William James and ends (for the time being) with Judith Butler. In other words, I will be proposing that feminism incorporates what pragmatism initiates, but also that pragmatism itself is unlikely if not inconceivable in the absence of feminism.

What, then, does pragmatism initiate; how does feminism address, include, and complete the pragmatist project; and, once again, how did they mediate between the disintegrating past and the impending future, between previous truths and novel facts? There are many ways to define pragmatism, of course, but for present purposes I will suppose that its proponents share three premises. First, there can be no cognition without purpose, to paraphrase Charles Peirce. This is a way of saying that values and facts, or reason and desire, are not the terms of an either/or choice because each is ingredient in, *and interchangeable with*, the other— thus "objectivity" is not attained by suppressing or ignoring values and desires, but by recognizing their function in designating the domain of the factual and the reasonable. Second, the meaning or content of any idea cannot be known apart from its consequences or embodiment in the world available to our observation if not our control. "No ideas but in things," as William Carlos Williams, the modernist poet, put it. Taken together, these two premises suggest that pragmatists assume that all knowledge is an effect of *changing the world* in the manner of modern science, by manipulating the objects of our knowledge in light of the provisional conclusions we call hypotheses, and that any *ontological* distinction between thoughts and things, or subjects and objects, or mind and matter, merely obscures the dynamic relations between fluid and porous moments in time. "Matter is effete mind," as Peirce declared, "inveterate habits becoming physical laws." In this sense, it is worth noting, pragmatism demonstrates and develops Marx's first "Thesis on Feuerbach," in which he complained that the "chief defect" of philosophical materialism was its division of the world into separate spheres of "sensuous objects" and "thought objects," so that it could not "comprehend human activity itself as objective."9

Third, the procedures of epistemology, by which we posit the irreducible qualities of a "transcendental" or transhistorical subject as the condition of knowledge, truth, agency, and morality, become useless or irrelevant in light of *historical* change in the character and consequences of subjectivity. This is a way of saying that pragmatists reject the notion of a fixed, "natural" person, or "transcendental" subject, and that in doing so, they historicize the very idea of personality or subjectivity; as a result, they historicize (and relativize) its presumed attributes in knowledge, truth, agency, and morality. But it does not follow that they must then invoke "experience" as the uniform substrate of all knowledge, as if appeals to that foundation would somehow plant us more firmly in the "real world" and afford all of us access to "common ground." Instead, they typically argue along the lines William James proposed almost a hundred years ago, in the essays on radical empiricism, to the effect that the only truths of which we can speak and be aware are those provisional, second-order truths we can represent as they emerge in the *narrative* time of historical consciousness and explanation. We can come to know the practical truth of immediate experience, in short, only by acting on it, by adding to it the second-order truths of retrospection.10

Feminist theory in the twentieth century quite clearly reenacts the deliberate break from epistemology which pragmatism inaugurated—indeed it is convened as a "critique of the subject," as a method for explaining how and why the gender of this "transcendental" subject is so insistently male. As such, it often functions as a radical critique of the same dualisms pragmatists tried to adjourn on their way to a post-metaphysical model of genuine selfhood. Perhaps that is why so many contemporary feminists position themselves in an intellectual lineage that begins with Peirce, the original semiotician, or with George Herbert Mead, the Hegelian pragmatist who profoundly shaped the thinking of Jürgen Habermas. But contemporary feminists have, I think, been more consciously committed than pragmatists to a "double strategy" through which previous truths about the character and consequences of subjectivity—or about the causes and effects of the subjection of women—are both annulled *and* preserved in their new models of genuine selfhood and their pluralist notions of womanhood. I mean that the feminist "critique of the subject" has not, generally speaking, simply refused the legacy of the Enlightenment residing in the "rights of man," but has instead tried to incorporate it in a more inclusive notion of subjectivity which allows for identities that are functions of interdependence and association. This strategy is no more "paradoxical," however, than the "double consciousness" through which black folk have negotiated their specifically American identities; indeed I would say that the "double strategy" of feminism will seem paradoxical to us only insofar as we assume that meaningful change or progress requires not the recuperation but the repudiation of the past.[11]

Feminists have been more willing than pragmatists, for example, to treat modern individualism as an indispensable moment in the development of the "social self"—that is, the socially constituted or culturally constructed self—rather than as an obvious anachronism or the last word on the subject. Feminists have also been more willing than pragmatists to go beyond state-centered, electoral, and policy-oriented politics by treating civil society as the site of significant struggle, by claiming that "the personal is the political," and, consequently, by making the "overthrow of the state" an afterthought. They have been more willing, in other words, to emphasize the kind of *cultural* or *identity* politics that Antonio Gramsci called the "war of position"—the kind of politics made possible and necessary by the "dispersal of power" from state to society which he discerned in the corporate-industrial ("Fordist") world of large-scale production—but they have never agreed that changes in the law, in party programs, or in government policy are irrelevant to the hopes of women and the prospects of democracy. Instead, feminists have developed an attitude toward history which permits both a recuperative reading of the politics of the past and a redemptive reading of the politics of the future. They remain open to the political promise of the twentieth century because they refuse either to repudiate or to reinstate the political vernacular of the nineteenth century.[12]

But it is this refusal to treat the past and the future as the terms of an either/or choice that finally unites pragmatism and feminism, and makes them useful as ways of thinking about the historically variable sources of subjectivity. For pragmatists and feminists, genuine selfhood is an accomplishment that is never quite complete; for it is "a relation that unrolls itself in time," as James put it, and is therefore contingent upon the internal articulation of modern society. "Individuality is not originally given," John Dewey explained, "but is created under the influences of associated life." Or, as Judith Butler would have it, "the constituted character of the subject is the very precondition of its agency." This subject must, therefore, be studied as a historical artifact, as a register of social history, rather than be presupposed as a suprahistorical origin of reason, truth, or knowledge.[13]

Pragmatists and feminists such as Jessie Taft, Jane Addams, and Dewey could, then, suffer the dissolution of modern subjectivity— the form of subjectivity specific to the "era of the ego," circa 1600–1900—because they assumed that the "social self" they saw emerging from the changing circumstances of "associated life" would not simply eradicate what they called the "old individualism." The newer form of subjectivity would instead include *and transform* the cultural function of the old by permitting the "regress of self-sufficiency and the progress of association," as Henry Carter Adams, the University of Michigan economist, put it in 1896. Like Adams, who not incidentally was a close friend and political ally of Dewey, the pragmatists and feminists who came of age around the turn of the last century understood that the "progress of association," and thus the reconstruction of subjectivity, were being driven by the "socialization" of modern industry via corporate devices and by the implication of the family in a new universe of "social organizations." In sum, they understood that what had been private or "individualistic"—even one's "inner self"—was now becoming public or social, and that this process of extroversion or "reification" was animated by the advent of the collective identities residing in the "trust movement," that is, by the creation of corporate bodies. But, again, they saw deviation from the inherited norms of subjectivity as evidence of evolution in the acceptable forms of subjectivity, not the erasure of its content.[14]

So, where most intellectuals and activists saw the tragic demise of the self-sufficient individual—the "natural person" who had typically appeared as the small producer, the male proprietor of himself—these pragmatists and feminists of the last century saw something else altogether. They saw that the increased interdependence and association determined by the corporate "world of large-scale production" would augment the sources and meanings of subjectivity by multiplying the kinds of identifications available to individuals, and by putting the capacities of collective entities or corporate bodies at the disposal of individuals. They saw that individualism would change and develop, not disappear, as the rural idiocy of the pioneer past gave way to the "social claims" of the corporate-industrial future. When the world we still inhabit was just emerging, they apprehended it as an unfinished comedy rather than a completed tragedy.

By saying they apprehended their world in terms of comedy, I don't mean that the pragmatists and feminists of the last century were prone to "indiscriminate hurrahing for the universe," as James characterized Walt Whitman's celebration of American promise. The writers and activists we will encounter hereafter did not recommend the "happy stupidity" and covert sentimentality of *humor* as an antidote to the very real terrors and tragedies of a modern, corporate-industrial society. Nor did they abstain from strong criticism of American institutions. Instead, they conceived a genuinely comic vision of their world which allowed for heroism, and for faith in a future redeemed by their hope, because it acknowledged, indeed emphasized, the gravity, the difficulty, and the enormity of their situation.[15]

So conceived, as a way of "tarrying with the negative," this comic vision demanded the kind of forensic complexity or dialectical sensibility that is foreign to the tragic renditions of the past which now regulate modern American historiography. I mean that the comic vision permitted by pragmatism and perfected by feminism demands serious study of the *conflict* between the world inherited from the immediate past and the world as it would conform to the "social claims" of the foreseeable future; but it does not assume or insist that these worlds merely collide, as if historical circumstances and ethical principles are incommensurable, as if facts and values are antithetical. In this sense, the comedy crafted by the pragmatists and feminists of the last century was neither conservative nor radical because it mediated between the past and the future rather than treating one or the other as the sole repository of the heroic; to put it another way, their comic vision avoided both the conservative urge to ignore novel facts and the radical urge to forget previous truths. They could designate and accommodate what amounted to revolutionary change because they would not sacrifice their hopes for the future on the altar of inherited tradition, established precedent, or "original intent," but could nevertheless treat the past as source of *and* limit on legitimate innovation in the present. Discontinuity and crisis thus appeared to them as opportunities to shape the future rather than reasons to mourn the past. "Change becomes significant of new possibilities and ends to be attained," as Dewey put it; "it becomes prophetic of a better future. Change is associated with progress rather than with lapse and fall."[16]

I believe that we still have a great deal to learn from this attitude toward history. If nothing else, it can teach us that principled abstention from corporate bureaucracy, or simple opposition to corporate capitalism, is neither the equivalent nor the condition of progress toward social democracy. It can also teach us that our political ambiguities—our refusal to define capitalism and socialism as the terms of an either/or choice, for example, or to see "globalization" as the manifestation of merely "market forces"—are sources of strength rather than signs of weakness; for they protect us against the blind and unforgiving faiths of those who have exiled themselves from the present in the name of an illustrious past or a glorious future. To be "divided up in time," as St. Augustine put it, is not such a bad thing, after all. At any rate that is what my study of pragmatism and feminism has taught me, and what I have tried to convey in this book.

In part 1, I examine the political implications of narrative forms by treating historiographical conventions as if they are such forms, and by treating arguments about the sources of genuine selfhood as if they are debates about the political possibilities of our time. In chapter 1, I demonstrate that the extant critique of consumer culture fails as a critique of corporate capitalism because it merely recapitulates the "primal scene" of proletarianization inherited from the Progressive historians; thus it valorizes the simple market society of the early modern epoch and defines alternatives to modern subjectivity as threats to genuine selfhood as such. In chapter 2, I propose that pragmatism is the original American variation on the theme of hegemony, in part because it is a way of positing and practicing cultural politics. Here I enlist Kenneth Burke to argue that pragmatism is a comedic narrative form—a "comic frame of acceptance"— in which the emergence of corporate capitalism begins to look like the condition of new thinking about American history, politics, and culture.

In chapter 3, I argue that the pragmatists and feminists of the early twentieth century collaborated in designing an alternative to modern subjectivity—an alternative, that is, to the unbound bourgeois individual specified in the "social contracts" of the early modern epoch. I also argue that this new design presupposed the "socialization" of property, production, and the market which was determined by large-scale business enterprise and corporate legal forms. As a preface to these arguments, I claim that the feminist "critique of the subject" which apparently derives from French poststructuralism may be better understood as a distant echo of that earlier collaboration with pragmatists. In chapter 4, I use Richard Rorty's recent book, *Achieving Our Country*, as my foil in assessing the politics of the contemporary academic Left. I claim that Marxism and pragmatism are compatible, indeed similar, ways of reconciling Anglo-American empiricism and Continental rationalism; that what Rorty calls "real politics" are made possible and necessary by the cultural politics he dismisses—more specifically, by the cultural politics of black nationalism and feminism; and, finally, that American historians romanticize the "Populist moment" of the 1890s and the "turbulent years" of the 1930s because they cannot recognize the sources of social democracy in their own time.

Part 2 returns to William James. In chapter 5, I suggest that his "Hamletism" was a way of accommodating, or at least addressing, the desublimation of female sexuality which accompanied and enforced the extrication of women from the household in the late nineteenth century. In chapter 6, I explain why he presents pragmatism as a woman who "unstiffens our theories"; how Judith Butler's intellectual lineage can be rewritten to install James as its locus classicus; why Teresa Brennan's reinterpretation of Lacan and Marx won't work as she intends, as a critique of the "world of large-scale production"; and, finally, how corporate capitalism completes the desublimation of female sexuality which began in the late nineteenth century, and so underwrites the reconstruction of subjectivity as such.

Throughout these chapters, I am proposing that pragmatism and feminism are complementary ways of redefining politics to include debates about the origins of agency, the sources of subjectivity, and the scope of the "public sphere." I am also proposing that pragmatism and feminism can teach us to understand corporate capitalism as the necessary but not sufficient condition of progress toward social democracy because both were present at its creation. In the end, therefore, I am insisting that an attitude toward history is perforce a political commitment because it defines what is possible, and thus determines what is actionable, in the present; it is in this sense that I can claim hereafter to be rethinking the politics of American history.

Part 1.
Pragmatism,
Feminism,
and the
Politics
of
Historiography

Modern Subjectivity and Consumer Culture

1

The Revenge of the New Woman

The Terms of Debate

My purpose in this chapter is to explore the relation between modern subjectivity and consumer culture. But I want to emphasize the historiographical dimensions of that relation—I want to demonstrate that the recent critique of consumer culture is an attempt to retrieve the modern subject from the wreckage of nineteenth-century proprietary capitalism, and that the attempt itself continues to command intellectual respect because it reenacts a "primal scene" of American historiography. The point of emphasizing these historiographical dimensions of the relation between modern subjectivity and consumer culture is of course polemical. Ultimately my claim will be that the critique of consumer culture blocks the search for alternatives to the "man of reason" who served as the paradigm of self-determination in the modern epoch, and thus blinds us to the political, intellectual, and cultural possibilities of our own postmodern moment.

Let me begin, then, by defining the terms of my inquiry. By "modern subjectivity" I mean the historically specific compound of assumptions, ideas, and sensibilities that convenes each self as a set of radical discontinuities (e.g., mind vs. body) which are in turn projected, as deferred desires—as work and language—into an "external" world of inanimate objects denominated as elements of nature and/or pieces of property. The sovereignty of this modern self is experienced and expressed as the ontological priority of the unbound individual, that is, the individual whose freedom resides in the release from obligations determined by political communities, or, what amounts to the same thing, in the exercise of "natural rights" that such communities can neither confer nor abrogate.[1] One virtue of this definition is that it permits the connotation of possessive individualism but does not reduce modern subjectivity to ownership of the property in one's capacity to produce value; the emphasis is instead on those discontinuities that finally hardened into dualisms under the sign of Enlightenment.

Another is that it is consistent with Friedrich Nietzsche's claim that the "most distinctive property of this modern man [is] the remarkable opposition of an inside to which no outside and an outside to which no inside corresponds, an opposition unknown to ancient peoples." If we follow his lead a bit further, we can begin to see that the genuine selfhood of the modern subject simply is the oscillation between epistemological extremes in which Ralph Waldo Emerson—one of Nietzsche's heroes—specialized. For all his genius, this modern man was representative because he lived the opposition between *romanticism*, which typically glorifies the "organic" or "subjective" inner self as against the "mechanical" or "objective" circumstances that constitute outward existence, and *positivism*, which typically celebrates the increasing density of that external, thinglike realm of objects as the evidence of progress toward human mastery of nature. By all accounts, the "era of the ego" in which Emersonian self-reliance, that is, modern subjectivity, comes of age is the historical moment, circa 1600–1900, in which the market becomes the organizing principle of European and North American societies, as commodity production comes to reshape and finally to regulate social relations as such.[2]

So conceived, the modern subject has no discernible gender. It discloses an "empty subjectivity" in every sense: its autonomy is formal and its anatomy is irrelevant because the ends or content of its freedom cannot be specified, let alone embodied. But the new history of subjectivity on which various disciplines have recently collaborated clearly shows that the modern subject was the decidedly male proprietor, the *man* of reason—indeed that the "social contract" animating modern bourgeois narratives of citizenship was also a sexual contract allowing men to supervise women's bodies in private, in the household, and to silence women's voices in public, in political discourse.[3] The decline of patriarchal (more or less feudal) states based on kinship and the concurrent return of repressed republican ideology—the "Machiavellian moment" of the early modern age—invariably coincided with the emergence of a bourgeois society in which households became the typical site of commodity production, and the paterfamilias (the male head of the household) became the paradigm of the citizen. This citizen's public identity presupposed his patriarchal standing within the newly private sphere of the conjugal family; in other words, the political capacities of the modern subject presupposed the integrity of the household. Since that integrity was both a material and a moral question, involving the disposition of property and the display of sobriety if not virtue, its maintenance required the containment or sublimation of female sexuality. If we can then say that the confinement of females to the household—for example, through the valorization of "republican motherhood"—becomes the enabling condition of modern subjectivity, we can also say that the extrusion of females from the household signals a crisis of the modern subject. Any devaluation of motherhood or "maternal authority" resulting from a profusion of extra-familial social roles for women would threaten this subject, simply because it would announce the desublimation of female sexuality, and so would force upon male citizens the realization that feminine desire is not synonymous with maternal affection.[4]

By "consumer culture" I mean pretty much what its critics mean, although I see comedy (a narrative form, not humor) where they see tragedy. I would define it as the culture specific to corporate capitalism, which emerges circa 1890–1930 in the U.S.—in Europe, it may be more accurate to speak of "cartelization" rather than corporate consolidation until the 1940s and 1950s—and would suggest that it consists of at least four elements. First, consumer demand becomes the fulcrum of economic growth, in the sense that growth no longer requires net additions either to the capital stock or to the labor force that cannot be producing consumer goods because it is producing and operating capital goods. Second, social relations of production can no longer be said to contain or regulate social relations as such, because the quantity of labor-time required to enlarge the volume or the capacity of goods production ceases to grow and then actually begins to decline; a class-based division of labor is accordingly complicated by the emergence of alternative principles (e.g., gender) of social organization. Third, value as such comes increasingly to be determined not by the quantities of labor time required to produce commodities but by the varieties of subject positions from which goods can be appreciated (marginalist economics, which emerges in the U.S. around the turn of the century, is one way of acknowledging this new fact). Fourth, with the completion of proletarianization under the auspices of corporate management, the commodity form penetrates and reshapes dimensions of social life hitherto exempt from its logic, to the point where subjectivity itself seemingly becomes a commodity to be bought and sold in the market as beauty, cleanliness, sincerity, even autonomy. In short, consumer culture—the "age of surplus" determined by corporate capitalism—is the solvent of modern subjectivity. I am suggesting by this definition that consumer culture is a twentieth-century phenomenon, and that the so-called birth of consumer society in late-eighteenth-century England (or in mid-nineteenth-century North America) should be understood instead as an early stage in the transition from a simple to a complex market society—that is when a market in labor was institutionalized, when artisans became operatives, when resources hitherto appropriated through extra-economic transactions became commodities with monetary equivalents and designations.[5]

Now, what exactly is wrong with consumer culture so conceived? Its critics tend to emphasize the fourth of these elements, although, as we shall see, the third element figures importantly in their worries about the epistemology of excess. They tend, in other words, to see the "bureaucratic rationality" of corporate capitalism or "managerial culture" from the Weberian standpoint first established by Georg Lukács, in an influential essay of 1923 on "reification." As Max Weber understood bureaucracy as the creature of the large corporations, so Lukács, who was Weber's student, understood bureaucracy as the apogee of proletarianization: "Bureaucracy implies the adjustment of one's way of life, mode of work and hence of consciousness, to the general socio-economic premises of the capitalist economy, similar to that which we have observed in the case of the worker in particular business concerns. . . . The split between the worker's labour-power and his personality, its metamorphosis into a thing, an object that he sells on the market is repeated here too." But under the aegis of bureaucracy, "the division of labour which in the case of Taylorism invaded the psyche, here invades the realm of ethics."[6]

Lukács took journalism as the perfect example of that invasion: "This phenomenon can be seen at its most grotesque in journalism. Here it is precisely subjectivity itself, knowledge, temperament and powers of expression that are reduced to an abstract mechanism functioning autonomously and divorced both from the personality of their 'owner' and from the material and concrete nature of the subject matter in hand." At this point of the argument, when it is clear that "bureaucracy" signifies the subjection of mental labor to corporate capital and thus a loss of identity for the man of letters, Lukács summarizes what he means by "reification":

> The transformation of the commodity relation into a thing of "ghostly objectivity" cannot therefore content itself with the reduction of all objects for the gratification of human needs to commodities. It stamps its imprint upon the whole consciousness of man; his qualities and abilities are no longer an organic part of his personality, they are things which he can "own" and "dispose of" like the various objects of the external world. And there is no natural form in which human relations can be cast, no way in which man can bring his physical and psychic "qualities" into play without their being subjected to this reifying process. (98–100)

So the proletarianization of the intellectuals completes the incessant redivision of labor that is the hallmark of capitalism. Even the well-educated man is subject to "the one-sided specialisation which represents such a violation of man's humanity" and, like an uneducated working-class male, he can expect the "prostitution of his experience and beliefs" by the abstract mechanisms of modern-industrial society (99–100). For it is no longer merely manual dexterity that can be bought and sold in the market; now the inner self can be hollowed out as "subjectivity itself" becomes a commodity, as thoughts become things to be owned, as knowledge, temperament, and powers of expression begin to look "like the various objects of the external world."

The critics of consumer culture sound very much like Lukács because they assume what he did—that the generalization of the commodity form (or "relation"), to the point where every personal attribute can circulate as a consumer good, must be the proximate cause of the cultural disease they propose to diagnose. All agree that this "maturation of the marketplace" was invented around the turn of the century by the "bureaucratic organizations"—presumably the large industrial corporations—in which a "new stratum" of more or less scientific managers came of age. They also agree that a "reified" consciousness, a consumer culture, accompanied and enforced these economic and social changes. Richard Fox and Jackson Lears note, for example, that the "late-nineteenth century link between individual hedonism and bureaucratic organizations—a link that has been strengthened in the twentieth century—marks the point of departure for modern American consumer culture." Finally, Lukács and his heirs agree that an "older entrepreneurial economy, formed around a shared sense of contractual obligation and of common moral premises," was displaced, or at any rate mutilated, by the new corporate economy in which a consumer culture thrived. I am quoting William Leach's *Land of Desire* (1993) here, but I might just as well quote Lears—who defines the "commercial vernacular" of the nineteenth century as a usable past, as an appealing alternative to the "managerial culture" and "bureaucratic rationality" brought by the corporations—or again call on Lukács, who could be invoking his intellectual heirs among the critics of consumer culture when he suggests that "traditional craft production preserves in the minds of its individual practitioners the appearance of something flexible, something constantly renewing itself, something produced by the producers" (97).[7]

But if I am right to suggest that the critique of consumer culture simply recapitulates the Weberian logic first proposed by Lukács, I can claim that it is merely a protest against proletarianization *from the standpoint of modern subjectivity*, in the name of possessive individualism. As such, it will typically represent the loss of subjectivity not as the price of entanglement in commerce, but as the loss of control over the property in one's capacity to produce value through work—in short, as the extremity of proletarianization initiated and managed by modern, corporate bureaucracies. From this standpoint, the site of self-discovery is the work of the artisan or small producer who sells the products of his labor, not his labor power; genuine selfhood can no more be derived from the abstract, unskilled social labor of the fully mechanized workplace than it can be derived from the sluggish daily routine of the private household.[8]

Primal Scenes in American Historiography

I want now to go on to claim that the extant critique of consumer culture reenacts a "primal scene" of American history, and does so in a way that permits only one point of entry into, or resolution of, the Oedipus complex. I want to claim, in other words, that this critique ignores or represses the sexual ambiguities and anxieties produced by proletarianization under corporate auspices and unconsciously reinstates the paterfamilias as the paradigm of subjectivity; this is significant cultural work because it reanimates and validates a certain kind or range of (male) subjectivity.

In psychoanalytical terms, a "primal scene" is more construction than recollection; for it is not so much an event experienced by the patient as a story told by the analyst, a story that gives meaning to irretrievable memory traces, mere fragments from the past. The retelling of the story allows the arrangement of past events in an intelligible sequence and accordingly the insertion of the narrative's subjects (these now include the narrator) in a temporal and moral order: it is a "deferred action" that situates, or rather constitutes, its dramatis personae in the present by orienting them toward a past and the future, but also by providing a provisional subject position from which the identifications impending in or deriving from the Oedipus complex can be tested. The strong resemblance between the work of the analyst and the work of the historian, which is registered by their mutual commitment to narrative as all-purpose cure for what ails us—notice that the stories told by both are neither "objective" nor "subjective," neither altogether "factual" nor strictly "fictional"—makes me think that we can profitably export the notion of a "primal scene" from its original domain in psychoanalysis.[9]

Until the twentieth century, the primal scene of American historiography was typically a confrontation between cultures construed broadly as incommensurable "races." For example, the European invasion of America, the "removal" of the Indians, and the tragedies of Reconstruction were staged in historical writing as inevitable consequences of competition between civilized white men and primitive races—that is, as the result of the Other's savagery or backwardness. "Progressive" historiography of the early twentieth century constructed a new primal scene by introducing the figure of industrial or financial capital, and making it the preda-

tor of the small producer and the freeholder. Since then, the hegemonic narratives of American history have habitually been built
around this primal scene of proletarianization. I am not suggesting
that the demise of the small producer and the decline of proprietary
capitalism are the fantasies of twentieth-century historians. But it
is instructive, I believe, that social, labor, and cultural historians—
the cutting edges of American historiography—cannot agree on the
timing or even the etiology of the event in question, and yet can
insist on its synchronic significance. That such a consensus exists in
spite of the obvious chronological confusion indicates that the
"moment" of proletarianization is more historiographical convention than historical event, more construction than recollection.[10]

To see how this primal scene works—how it opens onto the
Oedipus complex, how it inserts us into a temporal and moral
order—we must first consider its "origins." In the Anglo-American
world, it began as the paranoid fantasies of the Commonwealth-
men, who saw encroaching effeminacy everywhere they looked, but
especially in the growth of public credit and the machinations of
the Bank of England. By the late eighteenth century, it became even
more pointed as the parable of corruption, as the story of how the
"hardy virtuous set of men" called Americans might succumb to
"that luxury which effeminates the mind and body": unless they
protected their natural rights of property with the vigilance of the
Gothic freeholder, they would be subject to the whims of Fortune,
the goddess of fantasy, passion, and capricious change. In the nineteenth century, this narrative was complicated by trade unionists
who claimed that the property in one's labor-power could be sold
without alienating one's manhood, and by suffragists who suggested that women could not be forever confined to the household.
But it persisted in the rhetoric of political anti-slavery, and in the
languages of most late-nineteenth-century subaltern social movements. The "Populist moment" of the 1890s was probably its most
poignant expression—or would be, had not the "Progressive" historians constructed a new primal scene out of populist paranoia.[11]

This construction would not matter very much, I admit, if later
historians had become skeptical of the "democratic promise"
offered by Populism. To my knowledge, however, the brief reign of
so-called consensus history, from about 1955 to about 1975, marks
the only departure from the hegemony of Populism in twentieth-
century American historiography. In this interregnum, Richard

Hofstadter and William Appleman Williams, among others, offered "counter-progressive" interpretations of modern American history which treated Populism as something less than the last best hope for democracy in the United States, and which accordingly treated the twentieth century as something more than the non-heroic residue of the tragedy staged in the 1890s. But by the mid-1970s, with the publication of Lawrence Goodwyn's extravagant advertisement for Populism and the concurrent ascendance of the new labor historians, "consensus" was effectively discredited, and the primal scene of proletarianization was reinstated as the pivot on which the plot of American history must turn. The critique of consumer culture which emerged in the 1980s as yet another protest against proletarianization might then be understood as a significant contribution to the recuperation of Populism which began in the 1970s.[12]

In any event, we can now consider the cultural work of this critique—that is, how it constructs a primal scene that permits only one point of entry into the Oedipus complex, how it ignores or represses the sexual ambiguities and anxieties attending proletarianization under corporate auspices. At the turn of the century, these ambiguities and anxieties were clearly expressed in all kinds of publications, from labor journals and popular magazines to scholarly monographs and highbrow novels. That is why Andreas Huyssen, Klaus Theweleit, and Carroll Smith-Rosenberg are so convincing in claiming that the "fear of woman" is a metonymical compression of many other fears, all of which pertained to the dissolution and reconstruction of ego boundaries in an era of profound sexual crisis as well as social conflict. As Huyssen puts it, "fear of the masses in this age of declining liberalism is always also a fear of woman, a fear of nature out of control, a fear of the unconscious, of sexuality, of the loss of identity and stable ego boundaries in the mass."[13]

Not even the masses themselves were immune to such fears. For example, here is how machinists at the New England Bolt Company of Providence, Rhode Island, described their encounter with scientific management in 1913:

> "Cameras to the front of them. Cameras to the rear of them. Cameras to the right of them. Cameras to the left of them." Pictures taken of every move so as to eliminate "false moves" and drive the

worker into a stride that would be as mechanical as the machine he tends. If the "Taylorisers" only had an apparatus that could tell what the mind of the worker was thinking, they would probably develop a greater "efficiency" by making them "cut out" all thoughts of being men.[14]

Now, what troubles the machinists is quite obviously their reduction to items of managerial surveillance. Their trained eye no longer situates them as active subjects in relation to the raw materials and mechanical conditions of their skilled labor; instead they have become specular objects to be monitored by white-collared "Taylorisers." Their "manly bearing" on the job is in question as a result of this visual(ized) inversion. Indeed they use an image that carries the connotation of castration—"'cut out' all thoughts of being men"—to convey their concerns about their identities. From their standpoint, the passage from the formal to the real subjection of labor which is supervised by scientific management looks like the loss of manhood; by their account, proletarianization implies castration, or the "feminization" of identity, because it makes men visible, and thus penetrable.

If this account sounds simply fantastic, we should recall that in the modern epoch, the male subject typically defined himself by dissociation from the visible, by equating woman with what is seen, what is supervised, by man. The logic of the gaze that constituted modern subjectivity was the property of the "man of reason" who could "rise above" the private matters of the household in order to take the long view in political deliberations, and who could get a similarly supervisory distance on the objects of knowledge in order to see them clearly and "objectively."[15] We should also recall that Henry James, who was hardly a working stiff, proposed the same correlation between the "man without means" and a kind of "feminine" identity. Lambert Strether, the narrative compass of *The Ambassadors* (1903), is perhaps the most obvious example of this correlation—he is wholly dependent on Mrs. Newsome for his income as well as his function, he is the object of her close supervision, he is constantly scrutinized by the female characters with speaking roles in the novel, and he is in the "odd position for a man" of being at home in the "society of women." Like his creator, Strether does not so much observe women as identify with female characters.[16]

According to Henry's brother, William James, who thought of pragmatism as a woman ("she unstiffens our theories," he claimed), no one was immune to the identity crisis of the early twentieth century except the "luxurious classes." He correlated the impending demise of the "manly virtues" with "pacific cosmopolitan industrialism," a stage of development in which an older "pain economy" was giving way to a "pleasure economy"—that is, to a world without producers, "a world of clerks and teachers, of co-education and zoophily, of 'consumer's leagues' and 'associated charities,' of industrialism unlimited and feminism unabashed." From the standpoint provided by that correlation, the decline of productive labor and the consequent confusion of male and female spheres became the elements of an identity crisis; for they threatened to dissolve ego boundaries normally determined by the sanctions of scarcity: "The transition to a 'pleasure economy' may be fatal to a being wielding no powers of defence against its disintegrative influences. If we speak of the *fear of emancipation from the fear-regime*, we put the whole situation into a single phrase; fear regarding ourselves now taking place of the ancient fear of the enemy." James worried that this "fear of emancipation" from the older "pain economy" would take a regressively masculine and militaristic form; the "manly virtues" could be reinstated by the violent means of war, he believed, and he designed his moral equivalent with that possibility in mind. He clearly understood that "in the more or less socialistic future towards which mankind seems drifting," a central cultural problem would be how to "continue the manliness" hitherto bred in war and work.[17]

As James paraphrased the social theorist Simon Patten in pondering the effects of a "pleasure economy" on male identity, so Walter Lippmann paraphrased both James and Patten in charting the growth of "consumers' consciousness" and the new importance of "woman's position." In *Drift and Mastery* (1914) Lippmann spoke of a future in which "mankind will have emerged from a fear economy," and, like James, he saw that this was a future over which women would presumably preside as the sanctions of scarcity continued to erode. "The mass of women do not look at the world as workers," he noted: "in America, at least their prime interest is as consumers. . . . We hear a great deal about the class consciousness of labor; my own observation is that in America today consumers' consciousness is growing very much faster." Here, too, the declining salience of productive labor, of the working man's inherited social roles, threatened, or rather promised, to open up identities once fixed by externally imposed imperatives, by the dictates of necessity. And here, too, the identities opened up by political-economic change were male identities.[18]

So the emergence of an "imaginary femininity" was common to very different kinds and levels of discourse at the turn of the century. The insight on which the machinists and the intellectuals converge, for example, is that a male identity or "manly bearing" predicated on a certain political-economic posture was in question as a result of the changes we now summarize under the heading of consumer culture. They suggest that the issue thereby raised was not the eclipse of subjectivity as such but the "feminization" of identity—that is, the real issue was not the erasure but the reconstruction of modern subjectivity in accordance with a confusion of sexual spheres. And this is precisely the issue that the critique of consumer culture elegantly elides. On the assumption that subjectivity itself is dissolved by proletarianization under corporate auspices, the critics of consumer culture can and do ignore the ambiguous sexual identities that turn-of-the-century workers and intellectuals alike recognized as impending realities, as *possibilities* residing in the transformation of the labor process and emerging from the "age of surplus" sponsored by "pacific cosmopolitan industrialism." These critics can therefore construct a "primal scene" around the "event" of proletarianization which permits only one point of entry into the Oedipus complex—in other words, they can produce a narrative that promotes an exclusive identification with the figure of the father, and thus proscribes an "imaginary femininity" that would allow for identification with the figure of the mother, or with an intermediate figure that blurs the binary opposition of male and female. The unintended consequences or cultural effects of their critique would seem, then, to be not only the rehabilitation of the paterfamilias as the paradigm of subjectivity, but the validation of essential sexual difference as the condition of genuine selfhood.

In sum, this critique reinstates modern subjectivity as the ethical principle by which the historical circumstances of the twentieth century are to be evaluated, although it treats the consumer culture specific to that century as the solvent of subjectivity as such. But these are understandable and even persuasive positions to take in a corporate-industrial market society; for in such a society, those who control income-producing assets typically have more opportunities and greater social standing than those who do not. Other things being equal, proletarians have fewer life chances in a corporate-industrial market society than their employers, so that a protest against proletarianization becomes a protest against an unequal distribution of opportunities—that is, against a class-divided society. In this sense, the critique of consumer culture extends an honorable tradition of Anglo-American radicalism.[19]

Epistemology of Excess

And yet it ultimately blinds us to the comic potential, the redeeming value, of proletarianization and reification. I do *not* mean that the twentieth century has been a barrel of laughs. I mean that it was precisely proletarianization and its corollaries that reversed the simple, rigid, transparent relation between active subject and passive object which characterized artisanal forms of work and the household economies they presupposed. By the late nineteenth century, this reversal had gone far enough to allow all manner of intellectuals to treat the reconstruction of the subject-object relation as a pressing, practical problem rather than a metaphysical question; we call the result pragmatism. It was also proletarianization and its corollaries that finally extruded females from the confines of the household, so that, as Ellen DuBois points out, they began to "participate directly in society as individuals, not indirectly through their subordinate positions as wives and mothers"; we call the result feminism. Either way we look at it, a protest against proletarianization is probably the worst way to appreciate the political, intellectual, and cultural possibilities—including pragmatism and feminism—that reside in the demise of simple market society and the decomposition of proprietary capitalism, circa 1850–1940.[20]

Let me take the two most recent contributions to the critique of consumer culture as illustrations of this claim. I mean Leach's *Land of Desire* and Lears's *Fables of Abundance*. We have already seen that Leach celebrates the "older entrepreneurial economy" in which "shared contractual obligations and common moral premises" prevailed. From the standpoint provided by that moral universe, he denounces twentieth-century consumer capitalism as a grotesque "system preoccupied with 'making profits' rather than with 'making goods'" (18), as a "vast system of abstraction" (150: here he is quoting Edmund Wilson approvingly). Indeed it seems that reality itself receded under the new regime of reification. For example, Leach claims that once glass separated shoppers from goods on display, the relation between subjects and objects was obviously attenuated: glass walls "closed off smell and touch, diminishing the consumer's relationship with the goods" (62–63). From here it is a very short step to the conclusion that by the second decade of the twentieth century, "the difference between the real and the unreal" was thoroughly confused if not altogether effaced (189). "The circumstance of material comfort and even of prosperity for most people throughout most of the nineteenth century was being superseded by the idea of possession," according to Leach, "by being through having, by pageantry and show rather than by open confrontation with reality, by desire rather than by fulfillment" (190).

So Leach must believe either that a distinction between "the real and the unreal" is self-evident, or that twentieth-century challenges to this version of metaphysical realism—from pragmatists and feminists, among others—can be safely ignored because they are products of postmodernity.[21] He also must believe that once upon a time, presumably in the nineteenth century, desire did not exceed its normal limits or proper receptacles; meanwhile, I would infer, insubstantial symbols, thoughts, and words corresponded to substantial objects, things, and events "out there" in the "real world." When a "corporate money economy" animated by the "drive for profits" emerged around the turn of the century (190), this equilibrium was broken, and the epistemology of excess was born. An "open confrontation with reality" then became impossible because the difference between (monetary) representations of real things and the things themselves no longer seemed to matter. Now, these beliefs make perfect sense on the assumption that we can apprehend reality without artifice, without *changing* it as well as designating it in and as symbols, thoughts, and words—on the assumption that we can somehow peek over the edges of our own existence as if we are not there. But can we adopt that assumption without evading or ignoring most of the intellectual innovations of the twentieth century? Can we do so, in other words, without reverting to the radical discontinuities of desire and reason, or value and fact, or body and mind, each of which underwrote the idea of modern subjectivity and the ideal of scientific objectivity? I confess that I don't see how we can.

Lears expresses similar concerns in *Fables of Abundance*. He shows us that the nineteenth-century market was a more mysterious mechanism than Leach acknowledges, and wants us to learn from the carnivalesque qualities of an older "commercial vernacular" because he understands that neither markets nor commodities can or should be abolished in the name of democracy. In short, he understands that nostalgia is more symptom of than cure for what alienates us in—and from—the present. Yet Lears is also determined to reclaim the "things themselves" from the weird abstractions of the commodity form as it has been redefined by corporate power and "managerial culture"—that is, from the "bureaucratic rationality" that enforces reification.[22] So he must posit some moment in the past when desire was somehow fixed to its natural or obvious correspondent, when subjects and objects were properly aligned if not perfectly united in what he calls "symbolic consciousness" (19–21). Otherwise his remarks on the "dematerialization of desire" (20, 127, 215) and the related results of a consumer culture animated by advertising lose their critical edge; at any rate they make me want to ask when desire was materialized or grounded, and whether we can think about human desire except in terms of its immaterial excesses.

Lears locates the normative moment he needs in a pre-Oedipal state of bliss which somehow exudes "matriarchal values" (129–33). But, like Teresa Brennan, he understands how difficult it is to find our way back to this moment *before* the acquisition of language and the loss of the Other; for he lets the "carnivalesque commercial vernacular" of the nineteenth century—that is, the vernacular of simple market society—serve the same normative purpose (127–29, 144, 149, 152–53, 159, 161–63, 192, 215).[23] And so that vernacular becomes a kind of substitute for the "symbolic consciousness" specific to a pre-Oedipal moment of transcendent insight. In other words, it is itself a "deferred action," a way of returning us to, or at least reminding us of, the excruciating wonders of that originating moment. It is not so much an event experienced by nineteenth-century Americans as a story told by a historian, a story that gives meaning to irretrievable memory traces, mere fragments of the past. How, then, does it situate or constitute its dramatis personae in the present? Does it reinstate the primal scene of proletarianization or construct another? My answers derive from a reading of those passages in *Fables of Abundance* which assess the status and the symbolism of the female.[24]

In the pivotal chapter 4, "The Disembodiment of Abundance," Lears claims that the icons of abundance, from "mythic emblems" to modern lithographs, have always been female, but that by the turn of the century these images had been "denatured" and disembodied in accordance with the "broad cultural tendencies that accompanied the rise of an urban market economy." As the "source of material wealth became more abstract," and as corporations replaced entrepreneurs, it became easier for Americans "to forget the biological sources of material abundance and to attribute generative powers to male-dominated institutions." When corporations finally "claimed a major share of the mass circulation of images" in the 1890s, "the symbolism of abundance began to be more systematically rationalized"; for the new admen were not only Protestants, they were also "corporate employees rather than artisan-entrepreneurs." As a result, "the images they designed reflected the marginalizing of female generativity in the managerial worldview" (109–11). Meanwhile, "popular notions of abundance were moving away from their origins in the rhythms of agrarian life and bodily existence," because under the regime of reification perfected by corporate managers, "factory and office employees were increasingly cut off from the vernacular artisanal traditions that linked brain and hand in 'local knowledge'" (117).

Lears concludes, in view of these claims, that the "disembodiment of abundance" involved not only the "containment of Carnival"—of the playful and grotesque confusions specific to the "commercial vernacular" and its antecedents—but the "devaluation of female authority" (118). A few pages later, he restates this conclusion in slightly but significantly different language. Now the issue becomes "the devaluation of maternal authority," which flowed, it seems, from two sources—on the one hand, "changes in gender mythology," through which the makers of mass-produced images abandoned "the ancient idea of the maternal origins of abundance," and, on the other, "the strain of masculine protest" in modernist aesthetics, through which artists like Kandinsky hoped to "'free art from its bonds to material reality'" (122).

So there can be little doubt that Lears sees the conversion of artisan-entrepreneurs into corporate employees as the turning point in

the "disembodiment of abundance," or that the primal scene of proletarianization still regulates his narrative. But what are we to make
of the apparent confusion of female and maternal authority? This
confusion is enabled, I think, by Lears's equation of the female as
such with the material, the bodily, and the biological "sources" of
abundance—that is, with the "generativity" that is typically associated with the "nature" of the female body, with the *maternal* functions of women. That essentializing equation blinds him to the
possibility that the *devaluation* of maternal authority was the necessary condition of the *revaluation* of female authority which
reshaped American culture as well as politics after the turn of the
century and led directly toward modern feminism in all its diversity.

But what if we can claim that the extrication of females from the
household in the late nineteenth century opened up a new, discursive space between the "maternal" and the "female"—and for that
matter between men and women—where desublimated female
desire, free at last from its bonds to *maternal* reality, could circulate and so create new sources of subjectivity for men and women
alike? Don't we then need some way of appreciating the comic
potential and redeeming value of the *post*-artisanal market society
that entails proletarianization, corporate bureaucracies, scientific
management, and consumer culture? Don't we then need some way
of telling the story of nineteenth-century artisan-entrepreneurs
which does not treat the decomposition of the market society they
created as a tragedy—in other words, don't we need a way of criticizing the corporate, postindustrial capitalism of the twentieth century which is not merely a protest against proletarianization? We
do, of course, but it is not to be found in the extant critique of consumer culture; for that critique merely reenacts the primal scene of
modern American historiography and functions accordingly as a
kind of defense against the "imaginary femininity" produced in,
and by, an "age of surplus." In the next chapter, therefore, I nomi-
nate pragmatism as a way of appreciating the comic potential and
redeeming value of corporate capitalism which is also a way of criticizing it—that is, a philosophy that proposes to interpret the world
by changing it.

Fighting the "War of Position"

The Politics of Pragmatism

Pragmatism as a Comic "Frame of Acceptance"

Since the 1960s, when "corporate liberalism" entered the lexicon of the American Left, historians and cultural critics have tended to present the rise of corporate capitalism (circa 1890–1930) as a tragedy in two acts. In the first act, subaltern social movements finally succumb to the powers of a specifically corporate plutocracy—here we witness the eclipse of Populism, the "fall of the house of labor," and the "decline of popular politics." In the second act, accordingly, the proletarianization of freeholders, small producers, and skilled craftsmen is completed, and the "reification" of all social relations is effected, under the managerial auspices of the large industrial corporations. In this narrative form, the twentieth century must appear as the non-heroic residue of tragedy, the stuff of satire.[1]

I want to see what happens when we refuse a tragic form in narrating these same events—when we acknowledge the comic potential, the redeeming value, of corporate capitalism, of proletarianization and "reification." Again, I do not want to suggest that the twentieth century has been a barrel of laughs. Instead I want to suggest that by acknowledging the comic potential, the redeeming value, of proletarianization

and "reification," we can sketch a provisional but explicitly pragmatist "frame of acceptance" through which these causes and
effects of corporate capitalism begin to look like the elements of a
usable past.

I begin by addressing the function of cultural *history* in cultural
criticism and cultural politics. I draw on Kenneth Burke to suggest
that pragmatism is both a condition and a kind of cultural history.
Then I claim that, so conceived, as a protocol of cultural politics,
pragmatism improves on the "artisanal critique" of the Left by
accommodating the new forms of subjectivity which appear under
the sign of "reification"; here I am especially interested in demonstrating the affinities of pragmatism and feminism. I conclude by
recasting the debate between John Dewey and Walter Lippmann as
a disagreement on the scope and purposes of politics as such.

Alasdair MacIntyre has repeatedly (and rightly) claimed that a
moral philosophy "characteristically presupposes a sociology"—in
other words, an account of how moral agency is, or can be,
"embodied in the real social world."[2] We are now familiar enough
with the genre of cultural criticism to know that it characteristically
presupposes a history—in other words, an account of how agency
as such has been embodied in historical time, or a narrative of the
past that reveals genuine alternatives to, and perhaps in, the present. Think, for example, of the usable pasts that enabled the cultural criticisms of Christopher Lasch and his predecessors among
the young intellectuals of the 1920s.[3] Can we find such pointed
narratives of the past in pragmatism? To put it another way, is
pragmatism a kind of cultural history as well as criticism?

I would propose two answers. I would claim that pragmatism
permits the emergence of a specifically cultural history. And I
would claim that pragmatism is itself a narrative of the transition
from proprietary to corporate capitalism; which is to say that it is
a historical narrative. Let me take up these claims in order, and then
turn to the larger question of cultural politics.

Over the last twenty-five to thirty years, historians have witnessed a radical reconstruction of their discipline. Whole new fields
have emerged—for example, women's history, labor history, Afro-
American history, family history, southern history, cultural his-
tory—while older fields such as political and economic history have
been recast by their engagement with social theory, social history,
or statistical methods. How do we explain this extraordinary

moment of innovation, and where should we place cultural history within it? Elsewhere I have cited Roberto Unger's treatment of the "principle of analysis" to suggest that, in the 1950s, all manner of influential intellectuals began to claim that if the differences between desire and reason or value and fact were not self-evident, then any claim to scientific, journalistic, or historiographical "objectivity" was compromised, and, more to the point, any privilege hitherto given to the life of the mind—to "ideas with a life of their own"—was unwarranted. Between 1957 and 1962, for example, Thomas Kuhn's studies in scientific revolutions made it clear that there was, and is, no independent body of fact "out there" waiting to be registered by a paradigm with an improved capacity for the available data; instead, he demonstrated, a new paradigm convenes a new domain of fact by redefining what dimensions of reality will qualify as significant data. In short, intellectual revolution presupposes cultural revolution.[4]

So the history of ideas became much more complicated if not altogether impossible in the 1960s; for the significance of ideas could not be known without reference to the social, political, and economic contexts in which they had originally acquired meaning. The desiring body was now ingredient in and inseparable from the history of reason, the life of the mind. Social history, otherwise known as "history from the bottom up," was the immediate consequence of this insight; it has since become the hegemonic element of American historiography. But its promoters and practitioners have generally been unable, or rather unwilling, to address the ideas and the programs of social movements that are not certifiably subaltern movements.

Cultural history appears, in both senses, to fill the breach, to map the high ground abandoned by social history—but not by rejecting the assumptions or aims of social history, not by abandoning the lower extremities of the body politic. Cultural historians typically treat great books, ideas, and individuals with great care because they believe that these "texts" can neither be reduced to nor understood apart from their historical contexts. From the standpoint of cultural history, however, such contexts include the expectations and aspirations of subaltern social strata or movements; contexts so conceived are linguistic and subject to close readings precisely because they are social. The territory mapped by cultural history, in other words, is the borderland between common sense and high theory, the central places where the life of the mind is embodied, where metaphors carry meanings across great idiomatic divides. Cultural historians are geographers who accept the description of their domain offered by Raymond Williams: "The area of a culture, it would seem, is usually proportionate to the area of a language rather than to the area of a class."[5]

You may well agree with this definition of cultural history and still be wondering how pragmatism permits its emergence. It all depends on how we define pragmatism. Let us suppose that William James was not deceiving himself or his audience when he suggested in 1907 that "the term applies itself conveniently to a number of tendencies that hitherto have lacked a collective name, and that it has 'come to stay.'" Let us also suppose that John Dewey was right to claim that "under disguise of dealing with ultimate reality, philosophy has been occupied with the precious values embedded in social traditions, that it has sprung from a clash of social ends and from a conflict of inherited institutions with incompatible contemporary tendencies."[6]

If we grant these suppositions, we can define pragmatism as a protocol of reading and interpreting, a "go-between," as James would have it, "a method only," in and through which new relations among existing schools of thought or rival social traditions are convened. "Pragmatism unstiffens all our theories, limbers them up and sets each one at work," he claimed. "Being nothing essentially new, it harmonizes with many ancient philosophic tendencies." From this standpoint, pragmatism is a posture, an attitude, a sensibility—it is a way of seeing that desire and reason, body and mind, value and fact are not antithetical planes of existence or modes of apprehension. It is a way of seeing that the differences between thoughts and things, or ideas and events, or subjects and objects, are neither natural nor ontological but are rather constructed and contingent—in a word, that they are *historical*. In the twentieth century, this way of seeing takes monographic form in cultural history rather than in philosophy or social history or social theory; for only cultural historians must be "go-betweens," commuters who keep shuttling from ideas to events, from texts to contexts, and back again, without settling in (or for) either neighborhood.[7]

The more difficult claim, to which I now turn, is that pragmatism not only permits, but is itself a kind of cultural history. Here

Kenneth Burke's terminology becomes indispensable. In *Attitudes Toward History*, Burke deployed the notion of "frames of acceptance" to trace the arc of American literature and to assess the modern, liberal "bourgeois interregnum" that seemed, in the 1930s, to be giving way to another stage of cultural development.[8] By "frame of acceptance," he meant what we would probably name as culture or ideology, depending on our discipline and temperament; he defined it as "the more or less organized system of meanings by which a thinking man [or woman] gauges the historical situation and adopts a role with relation to it" (5). But Burke often used the shorthand of "symbolic frames" to emphasize that he was examining shared sensibilities rather than theories. And he insisted that frames of acceptance did not promote passivity: "They draw the lines of battle—and they appear 'passive' only to one whose frame would persuade him to draw the line of battle differently" (20).

Burke's distinction between tragic and comic frames of acceptance is the key to my claim about pragmatism as cultural history. Tragedy, he suggests, "deals in crime"; so it proliferates at moments of sharp and deeply felt social change: "any incipient trend will first be felt as crime," he notes, "by reason of its conflict with established values." The strong resemblance between the nineteenth-century outlaw of the dime novels and the twentieth-century revolutionary of the social science textbooks—each appears as the expression of unwanted and unprecedented change—might be explained in these terms.[9] But Burke also notes that "tragedy deals *sympathetically* with crime. Even though the criminal is finally sentenced to be punished, we are made to feel that his offence is our offence" (37–39). We are made, that is, to feel the disturbing effects of the individualism, the *self*-aggrandizement which becomes possible with the rise of trading empires or commercial republics and necessary with the development of modern market society.

Comedy includes and transcends tragedy, Burke insists, because it too "warns against the dangers of pride, but its emphasis shifts from crime to stupidity." It depicts people as mistaken, not vicious, in the sense Hegel intended when he claimed that "the false is no longer false as a moment of the true."[10] Here is how Burke rendered that dictum: "When you add that people are *necessarily* mistaken, that *all* people are exposed to situations in which they must act as fools, that *every* insight contains its own special kind of blindness, you complete the comic circle, returning again to the lesson of humility that underlies great tragedy." So comedy "requires the maximum of forensic complexity" and declares its independence of the *deus ex machina* that often animates tragedy. In short: "Comedy deals with man in society, tragedy with the cosmic man" (41–42).

The frames of acceptance that derive from these narrative forms have significantly different "vocabularies for the charting of human motives" (92). Tragic frames of acceptance tend toward either a *supernatural* or a *utilitarian* "scheme of motives"—where the supernatural scheme would sublimate the anarchy of profane interests by reference to divine providence, and the utilitarian scheme would debunk every attempt at transcendence by reference to the same interests. A comic frame of acceptance avoids these extremes, *and* the stoic resignation that inevitably accompanies them. "It avoids the dangers of euphemism that go with the more heroic frames of epic and tragedy," Burke points out. "And thereby it avoids the antithetical dangers of cynical debunking, [which] paralyze social relationships by discovering too constantly the purely materialistic ingredients in human effort. The comic frame is charitable, but at the same time it is not gullible" (92–107).

To translate my original claim into the idiom Burke proposes is to say that pragmatism is a comic frame of acceptance through which the transition from proprietary to corporate capitalism, circa 1890–1930, can be apprehended—that is, narrated—as something other than a tragedy to which we must learn to resign ourselves. *Attitudes Toward History* is a precocious example of how this frame of acceptance, which James built from drawings by Emerson and Whitman, can recuperate what Burke called "the most ingenious and suggestive vocabulary of all, the *capitalist* vocabulary of behavior." Burke put that vocabulary to work by claiming that the "synthesizing tendencies" of the human species were expressed "in the growth of holding companies," and that "corporate identity itself was shorn of its unwieldy mysticism when the member of the church, as the 'body of Christ,' became simply the holder of nonvoting stock" (93–94).

Let us see how else this vocabulary was put to work by the original pragmatists. In his brilliant study of American culture, *The Golden Day*, the young Lewis Mumford noted William James's "persistent use of financial metaphors." Mumford treated that

usage as evidence of an "attitude of compromise" with a civilization that honored business enterprise as its highest calling—indeed
he claimed that the core constituents of pragmatism were the docile
"children of industrialism" who merely accepted the fact of
modern capitalism. Mumford's name for that acceptance was "the
pragmatic acquiescence."[11]

Now there can't be much doubt about the persistence of financial metaphors in the vocabularies of the original pragmatists. In
1891, for example, John Dewey claimed that "Every judgment a
man passes on life is perforce, his 'I bet,' his speculation. So much
of his saved capital of truth he invests in the judgment: 'The state
of things is thus and so.'" James was equally playful in 1904 and
1905, in the essays on radical empiricism, and again in the lectures
of 1906 and 1907 which became *Pragmatism*. Here the metaphors
of money, banking, and credit do carry the weight of philosophical
argument. In "A World of Pure Experience," for example, he suggested that verification was an unusual moment in the development
of knowledge: "Mainly, however, we live on speculative investments, or on our prospects only. But living on things *in posse* is as
good as living in the actual, so long as our credit remains good."[12]

In *Pragmatism*, truths become the provisional representations of
moments that do not yet exist "out there" in the "real world," in
which speculation therefore becomes the normal procedure of
thought, and in which crisis is signaled by a generalized demand for
immediate verification—or redemption in cash—of the symbolic
tokens of truth: "Truth lives, in fact, for the most part on a credit
system. Our thoughts and beliefs 'pass,' so long as nothing challenges them, just as bank-notes pass so long as nobody refuses
them. But this all points to direct face-to-face verification somewhere, without which the fabric of truth collapses like a financial
system with no cash-basis whatever. You accept my verification of
one thing, I yours of another. We trade on each other's truth."[13]

James refers repeatedly to the *cash value* of words and ideas in
Pragmatism, as if there is a bottom line—a foundation of truth, a
point of rest—in the ledger that records our intellectual transactions; in a similar vein he also cites "our general obligation to do
what pays." Yet he emphatically rejects the notion that the function
of mind or consciousness is to copy or represent a fixed, external
reality and, by implication, the notion that money is only a means
of exchange, that is, a set of symbols that necessarily corresponds

to objects "out there" in the "real world" constituted by the products of labor. In effect James is simply claiming that money, as redefined by modern business enterprise, is an appropriate metaphor for mind, language, and thought. For example: "You must bring out of each word its practical cash-value, set it at work within the stream of your experience. It appears less as a solution, then, than as a program for more work, and more particularly as an indication of ways in which existing realities may be *changed*."[14]

We may well notice that the "cash value" of language resides in the surplus—not the equivalence or the equilibrium—it produces. And we may also notice that this surplus must be reinvested if it is to make a difference, that is, if it is to bear more interest in the future by changing existing realities. But Mumford is clearly right to draw our attention to the ubiquity and centrality of financial metaphors in the vocabulary James uses to explain the meaning of truth under the sign of pragmatism. The only question is what we should make of this pragmatic acquiescence to the language of credit, the future tense of money.

Edward Bellamy may help us recall the significance of credit in the late nineteenth century. In *Looking Backward*, the utopian novel that reached a circulation of over one million by the mid-1890s, Bellamy summarized the crisis of representation that followed from the development of a credit *economy*—an economy in which the value of substitutes for currency, such as checks, drafts, bills, deposits, clearinghouse certificates, stock exchange securities, and the mysterious "futures," exceeded even the value of banknotes, which seemed themselves to lack any necessary or objective correlates: "Already accustomed to accept money for commodities, the people next accepted promises for money, and ceased to look at all behind the representative for the thing represented. Money was a sign of real commodities, but credit was but the sign of a sign."[15]

In populist perspective, this credit economy was the product of collaboration between the bankers and "the trusts" and their paid agents among politicians. It created a situation in which there was no discernible or reasonable relation between legal claims on income and tangible assets—that is, between the symbols of wealth which were the sources of income and the real wealth of the nation which was produced by the "toiling millions." The solutions to the problem of a credit economy so conceived were to abolish "the trusts"—this is how the political vernacular named the large corporations—which were inconceivable without speculation in the stock market, and to reinstate an equivalence between signifiers and signified, between the money supply and the things it was supposed to represent, not displace.

So to speak of a credit economy or a credit system in or after the 1890s was to situate one's utterance in the popular, political discourse of the money question, and to assume that its metonymy made sense of nineteenth-century history. In doing so, however, one had to take a stance on the consequences of that history. In populist perspective, for example, approval of a credit economy was something like sympathy for the devil, because the trusts were cause and effect of speculation in the stock market; to be for the people and against the plutocrats was to be scandalized by the credit economy in which all manner of altogether artificial accretions accumulated. The phenomenology of the market determined by this perspective, let us note, could acknowledge a future for neither the social nor the symbolic surplus generated by the emergence of the trusts—that is, by the emergence of corporate capitalism. To acknowledge these surpluses, and to suggest that they could be productively invested, was, then, to see genuine possibilities where the Populists could see only distressing problems: it was to narrate the impending consequences of nineteenth-century history with a kind of comic ambivalence—with a certain sympathy for the devil—rather than with a tragic sense of loss.

And that is pretty much what the original pragmatists did when they mobilized the metaphors of money to make their philosophical claims. By insisting that the habitat of truth was a "credit system," they suggested that the "trust question" of their time—what is to be done with these large corporations that can manipulate the market?—had become the warrant for intellectual innovation, the cause of intellectual progress. They suggested that there was something to be gained from the contingency or fluidity introduced into the market by the credit economy specific to "the trusts," and by the social purpose embodied in the administrative capacities of the corporations.[16]

Their pragmatism qualifies, therefore, as a narrative form, a frame of acceptance that treats the rise of corporate capitalism as the first act of an unfinished comedy, not the last act of a bitter tragedy. Accordingly it can serve as an alternative to the narrative form that now dominates the historiography of the Progressive

Era—the form through which the "democratic promise" of the "Populist moment" was betrayed and the house of labor was demolished by corporate capital, the "popular politics" of the nineteenth century declined with the rise of professional expertise and the bureaucratization of the bourgeoisie, and the self-mastering citizens characteristic of proprietary capitalism gave way to the rootless, hedonistic, apolitical, and artificial personalities—the "other-directed" individuals—sanctioned by consumer culture.[17] Pragmatism can serve, in other words, as an example of the new narrative, the new cultural history we need to appreciate the evidence of progress in the Progressive Era, and to comprehend the remainder of the twentieth century—our own time—as something more than the non-heroic and unintelligible residue of tragedy. Pragmatism is the comic form we need to appreciate the real *but local* tragedies of this era; for it will let us narrate without closure, without removing ourselves from the scene of events. It won't let us read for the ending because it makes us both narrators of and characters in the story it tells.

Cultural Criticism and Corporate Capitalism

If pragmatism is a narrative form that permits a new cultural history of the Progressive Era by putting the "capitalist vocabulary of behavior" to work, it should enable a political sensibility, a kind of cultural politics that makes sense in, and of, the late twentieth century. This is the possibility I can now consider. I will do so by proposing that we should evacuate the terrain on which arguments about the politics of pragmatism have been routinely situated—that is, the debates of the late 1920s between Dewey and Mumford on the one hand, and between Dewey and Walter Lippmann on the other.

The debate between Dewey and Mumford began with the publication of *The Golden Day* in 1926. In two long chapters, Mumford broadened the attack on pragmatism first mounted by Van Wyck Brooks, Harold Stearns, and Randolph Bourne during debate on American entry into the First World War. Mumford argued that because James was no less guilty than Dewey of simpleminded respect for results—indeed "James was only warming over again in philosophy the hash of everyday experience in the Gilded Age"—he was no more innocent than Dewey of promoting

technical efficiency, instrumental logic, and bureaucratic rationality at the expense of significant cultural values and worthy social
goals. By making pragmatism as such the issue, Mumford let later
generations of young intellectuals (from C. Wright Mills, Christopher Lasch, and John Diggins to Casey Blake, Robert Westbrook,
and Jackson Lears) assume that American implication in world war
and support for European reaction were effects of a specifically
pragmatic inversion of ends and means.[18]

Rebellion against the brute facts of modern industrialism
required another attitude toward American history—an attitude
that, in keeping with the young intellectuals' flight from the "cult of
politics," would discover a usable past in the domain of cultural
and literary history. "The weakness of Mr. Dewey's instrumentalism is a weakness of practical emphasis," as Mumford put it. "He
recognizes the place of the humane arts, but his preoccupation has
been with science and technology, with instrumentalism in the
narrow sense." His politics were not cultural enough, in short; for
pragmatism was sunk too deep in the realm of practical affairs, in
what George Santayana once called "the subsoil of American life."
Here is how Mumford made the point: "Mr. Dewey has . . .
confirm[ed] by philosophic statement tendencies which are already
strong and well-established in American life, whereas he has been
apathetic or diffident about things which must still be introduced
into our scheme . . . if it is to become thoroughly humane and
significant."[19]

Dewey replied to Mumford in the pages of the *New Republic*, a
journal that often featured the contributions of both thinkers. But
it was not much of a reply. And in subsequent accounts of the
debate, even in those sympathetic to Dewey, Mumford is the clear
winner. In two recent versions, for example, by Robert Westbrook
and Casey Blake, Mumford's "cultural" criticism of pragmatism is
accredited without explanation; both authors assume that until
Dewey's linguistic turn of the late 1920s, pragmatists were quite as
uncivilized, as uninterested in literature and the fine arts, as *The
Golden Day* would have it. Accordingly Westbrook and Blake
defend Dewey by stressing the bad timing of the debate, by suggesting that in the late 1920s he was beginning to study cultural
matters, and to engage in cultural politics, along lines sketched by
Mumford and the other young intellectuals. A defense of James on
the same grounds is presumably impossible; indeed Westbrook sug-

gests that "Mumford's treatment of James [is] less misleading than his criticism of Dewey" because Mumford was criticizing precisely "those features of James's pragmatism to which Dewey most objected."[20]

I want to suggest that these accounts are ideologically overdetermined by their affiliation with Mumford's "artisanal critique" of corporate capitalism, and, more important, that this form of critique points us toward a political dead end. I also want to suggest that pragmatism was a different form of cultural critique, and the premise of a cultural politics, long before Dewey's linguistic turn. Then I can take up the problem of the so-called phantom public, to see how a pragmatist politics might solve it.

The affiliation with an artisanal critique is most obvious and explicit in Casey Blake's book on the young intellectuals, *Beloved Community* (1990); but it is no less significant and normative in the cognate works of Lasch, Westbrook, Diggins, and Lears (including his new book, *Fables of Abundance* [1994]), as well as the recent work of William Leach, *Land of Desire* (1993). In fact, I would insist that the critical stance toward corporate capitalism and consumer culture which characterizes the counter-progressive historiography of the postwar period—especially its New Left variant—is a function of the same artisanal affiliation.[21]

I have already noted that from the standpoint of social and labor historians such as Lawrence Goodwyn, Steven Hahn, Herbert Gutman, and David Montgomery, the consolidation of corporate capitalism in the twentieth century is the effect of the tragedy residing in the eclipse of Populism, the fall of the house of labor, the decline of popular politics. By this account, subaltern social movements and "cultures of resistance" held out a democratic promise to the future only so long as they remained outside the global markets and mechanized labor processes determined by corporate capital—only so long as their constituents retained control of their capacity to produce value through work, by owning the property in their labor. That promise was betrayed when the market power of corporate capital became a simple fact, a premise of normal political discourse, rather than an obvious incentive to grassroots mobilization in opposition to "the trusts" and their scientific managers.[22]

From the standpoint of cultural critics such as Lasch, Leach, and Lears (but also social theorists such as Roberto Unger, Teresa Brennan, and Juliet Schor) consumer culture or society is the effect of the same tragedy; for under the aegis of corporate capital, they witness the completion of proletarianization (the end of the "craftsmen's empire") and the corresponding commodification of every sphere of social life. In other words, they witness the highest stage of what Georg Lukacs called "reification." So conceived, consumer culture is the frontier of commodity fetishism mapped by the trusts, the railroads, and the industrial corporations that integrated the national market in the 1880s and 1890s. It can be defined as a consumer culture because everything, even subjectivity as such, is finally implicated in the price system—because the self-determining personality now becomes a consumer good, the elements of which can be advertised and are for sale in the market, as beauty, cleanliness, sincerity, independence, and so forth.[23]

Note that from either standpoint (social-labor history or cultural critique), the rise of corporate capitalism represents a political problem because it commodifies personality or selfhood—that is, because it creates a *moral* problem. Note also that the ethical principle animating the historical narrative and authorizing the critique of the circumstances in question is the autonomy or integrity of what Marx called, with no little sarcasm, the "natural individual" who suddenly appeared in the seventeenth century. Now, if we recall MacIntyre's claim that a moral philosophy characteristically presupposes a sociology, an imagined community in which an intelligible relation between intentions and actions can be plausibly embodied, then we can see that the imagined community from which the critique of corporate capitalism and consumer culture plainly derives is a simple market society composed of those "natural individuals" we usually designate freeholders, small producers, skilled craftsmen, or artisans—these are independent men, rugged individuals, because they retain control over their own labor-time, their capacity to produce value through work. They inhabit a modern market society, to be sure, but it is a market society in which labor is not a commodity; it is a market society in which commerce pertains to the occasional transactions between patriarchal households, not to the constant interactions of individuals who sell (and buy) their capacity to produce values; it is a market society in which a fixed, transparent relation between active subjects and inert objects is routinely realized in the work of the skilled artisan—work, I would emphasize, that is not the abstract social labor specific to the fully mechanized factory but is rather creative *composition* in the sense conveyed by the Greek word for "making," *poiesis*, which is also, and not coincidentally, the root of the word "poetry."[24]

It follows, I think, that the contemporary critique of corporate capitalism and consumer culture should be understood as a protest against the proletarianization of freeholders, small producers, skilled craftsmen, or artisans. In other words, it is a protest against the bureaucratization of simple market society, of bourgeois society, by the large corporations. This critique, this protest, therefore remains perfectly consistent with possessive individualism; with the patriarchy specific to simple market societies or household economies; and with the ontological distinction between subject and object—the dualism—that became a regulative principle of knowledge as such in the modern cultures of the West. So I am claiming that the standpoint of contemporary cultural criticism and counter-progressive historiography is the paterfamilias, the male proprietor as head of household. I am also claiming that this artisanal figure, this male proprietor, covertly reinstates the epistemological and other dualisms that the pragmatists moved to adjourn in the early twentieth century.

To take Mumford's "artisanal critique" for granted is then to assume that there is a necessary contradiction between the development of *capitalism* and the development of *character* because proletarianization destroys the human personality's foundation or fixed location in space and time, in *property*, and thus threatens its moral substance or stability. Taken at face value, this assumption inspires cultural critique on *ethical* grounds: to discover the genuine self is to reject capitalism. But it also undermines political critique (or action) on *historical* grounds: to discover the genuine self is to recover the transparency of the social conditions specific to simple market society, or, failing that, to find an Archimedean point, a "clearing," outside of existing social relations—perhaps in the "cultures of resistance" afforded by radical movements or in the austerity of the artist's garret, but more likely in the "free social space" of academe. In view of this assumption, future and past appear as fundamentally incommensurable because the ethical principle—the integrity of the self—does not seem to reside in or flow from the historical development of capitalism.[25]

Long before Mumford appointed himself the curator of intellectual alternatives to pragmatism, James and Dewey had turned the assumption into a question, by entertaining the possibility that character is a consequence of capitalism—by putting "the capitalist vocabulary of behavior" to work on the redesign of subjectivity. In doing so, they had suggested that the ethical and the historical are not antithetical but commensurable and indeed indissoluble forms of narrative or planes of existence. To follow their lead would be to accept proletarianization as an irreversible historical fact that multiplied the possibilities of subjectivity *precisely because* it destroyed the human personality's fixed location in space and time (in property), *precisely because* it disrupted the fixed, transparent relation between subjects and objects realized in artisanal forms of work. To follow the pragmatist lead would then be to accept the loss of *modern* subjectivity—better known as the death of the subject—without protest or mourning. Within this comic "frame of acceptance," the central question becomes how to *change* the subject of modern political theory and practice by rethinking the sources of subjectivity and self-determination.[26]

Let me try another approach to the same point. Consider the political implications of proletarianization. Perhaps the most obvious consequence of nineteenth-century industrialization was to remove commodity production from the household; hereafter the market in labor ("the economy") mediated between the state and the family, by creating social roles that were neither bound by familial functions nor contained by conventional party politics. In the late nineteenth century, both men and women could therefore become "individuals" whose identities and political capacities were not necessarily derived from their standing within the household, as paterfamilias or dutifully republican mother. Significantly different gender roles were of course inscribed in the new division of labor between the family, the market economy, and the public sphere of state-centered electoral politics.[27] But once the political economy was no longer constituted or dominated by households, and the public, political sphere was no longer limited to male heads of *propertied* households, the exclusion of women from this sphere required a new rationale—a rationale, I would emphasize, that could not treat female sexuality, or the proliferation of extra-familial female roles, as a self-evident threat to the integrity of the household and thus to the virtue of citizens. By the late nineteenth century, interested observers had then to demonstrate that the exclusion of females from the ranks of citizens made good political sense: they could no longer assume that this exclusion was self-justifying.[28]

Now we know that the proliferation of extra-familial roles in the nineteenth century was the consequence of industrialization and proletarianization—of the movement beyond a household economy, toward a post-artisanal market society or a post-proprietary capitalism. We also know that proletarianization was completed under the auspices of the large industrial corporations, which were able to muster the economic, social, and intellectual resources needed to transfer control of machine production from skilled workers to scientific managers. In fact, the corporations created a new labor system by fully mechanizing the labor process, by making science a force of production in its own right. "This comprehensive industrial process draws into its scope and turns to account all branches of knowledge that have to do with the material sciences," as Thorstein Veblen explained in *The Theory of Business Enterprise* (1904): "The adjustment and adaptation of part to part and process to process has passed out of the category of craftsmanlike skill into the category of mechanical standardization." And we know, finally, that the rise of modern, anti-essentialist feminism presupposes the proliferation of extra-familial social roles residing in the proletarianization of the American majority—in the mid-nineteenth-century passage beyond a household economy to begin with, but more clearly and completely in the late-nineteenth-century passage from proprietary to corporate capitalism.[29]

It follows, I think, that modern, anti-essentialist feminism presupposes a passage beyond simple market society in theory as well as practice—that is, it presupposes an acceptance, in Burke's sense, of the complex market society created under corporate auspices. If we are to treat the cultural politics of twentieth-century feminism with the seriously comic ambivalence it deserves, we must then dispense with the artisanal critique of corporate capitalism and consumer culture which still regulates historical narratives of the Progressive Era and its aftermath. In other words, if we are to accredit feminist alternatives to the possessive individualism of the "man of reason," the male proprietor, and his brethren, we must then accept proletarianization as pragmatism teaches us to, as an irreversible historical fact that multiplies the possibilities of sub-jectivity. We must also accept corporate capitalism in the same spirit, as the stage of development in which those possibilities were realized in new forms of "tertiary" labor and in a larger re-definition of work as such. For just as we cannot commence any cultural criticism that is consistent with the loss of modern subjec-tivity by following Lewis Mumford's example—by repudiating pragmatism—so we cannot convene a cultural politics that is con-sistent with the rise of modern feminism by repudiating the conse-quences of corporate capitalism.[30]

Corporate Capitalism and Cultural Politics

I want to conclude by emphasizing that pragmatism is, or enables, a very different cultural politics than Mumford and his followers have created. I will do so by briefly rehearsing the debate between John Dewey and Walter Lippmann on the intellectual problem of the "phantom public." Again, I will be proposing to evacuate the terrain on which these contestants met, as a way of allowing for another, more interesting debate.

Perhaps the best way to recall the meaning and significance of Lippmann's *Phantom Public*, which appeared in 1925, is to hear its distant echoes in the 1950s, when historians, political scientists, and social theorists noticed that "other-directed individuals" and "authoritarian personalities" were unlikely bearers of liberal prin-ciples. Like Lippmann, they wondered about the durability of a political philosophy that could not be plausibly embodied in the real social world, by ascribing ideological consistency, or "rational belief systems," or even rudimentary knowledge of salient issues, to American voters.[31] But Lippmann was a great deal more candid than his heirs among the postwar thinkers. For example, here is how he summons the ghost his book is meant to exorcise:

> These various remedies, eugenic, educational, ethical, populist and socialist, all assume that either the voters are inherently competent to direct the course of affairs or that they are making progress toward such an ideal. I think it is a false ideal. . . . An ideal should express the true possibilities of its subject. When it does not it per-verts the true possibilities. The ideal of the omnicompetent, sover-eign citizen is, in my opinion, such a false ideal. (38–39; cf. 146–51)

Even so, Lippmann provided a more redemptive reading of political disenchantment than his postwar heirs. In concluding his chapter on the principles of public opinion, he insisted that democratic and aristocratic theorists alike "miss the essence of the matter, which is, that competence exists only in relation to function; that men are not good, but good for something; that men cannot be educated, but only educated for something" (150). I would interpret this as a modern version of Gerrard Winstanley's dictum of 1650: "A man knowes no more of righteousness than he hath power to act." And so I would claim that, in ridiculing the self-mastering, "inner-directed," proprietary citizen of nineteenth-century political lore, Lippmann was merely completing the critique of modern-liberal individualism which began in the 1890s, when the "social self" emerged as a practical alternative to the unbound self specified in social contracts. He was suggesting accordingly that public opinion was neither an organic whole to be treated as the "will of the people" nor the sum of its functional parts. In this sense, he was mapping a middle ground between republicanism as Jean-Jacques Rousseau interpreted it and syndicalism as G. D. H. Cole interpreted it—between the people construed as a homogenous unity and the people disaggregated according to their economic functions. Lippmann was trying to let us see a plurality of publics rather than an indivisible people or an aggregation of occupations.[32]

This attempt was consistent with a more explicitly pragmatic endorsement of the "social self" and its political implications. That is probably why Dewey was not as disturbed by Lippmann's analysis as later critics and theorists have been. His "reply" to *The Phantom Public* concluded, for example, by demonstrating that no progress could be made in forming a public worthy of the name so long as everyone assumed the ontological priority of unbound individuals:[33]

And as the activity of each cell is conditioned and directed by those with which it interacts, so the human being whom we fasten upon as individual *par excellence* is moved and regulated by his associations with others; what he does and what the consequences of his behavior are, what his experience consists of, cannot even be described, much less accounted for, in isolation. (188; cf. 147–59, esp. 157–58, also 95–101)

Like Lippmann, Dewey acknowledged that the public specific to "the political affairs of prior ages" was scattered by the *corporate* consequences of industrial revolution: "Its outcome was the development of those extensive and invisible bonds, those 'great impersonal concerns, organizations,' which now pervasively affect the thinking, willing and doing of everybody, and which have ushered in the 'new era of human relationships'" (126, 107; Dewey is quoting Woodrow Wilson: see 96). As he saw it, his task was to think through the conditions under which the "enlarged, complicated and multiplied public interests" created by this new corporate era could be convened as a Public (131–42, esp. 137–38, also 157ff.).

But here, too, later critics and theorists treat Dewey as the obvious loser in a debate that is supposed to have forecast the future of democracy.[34] I cannot concur. I would insist that both contestants were in essential agreement as to the central problem of political representation in "the new age of human relationships" determined by corporate capitalism—both contestants clearly defined this problem as the eclipse of possessive individualism, of modern subjectivity—and that their agreement is more important than their differences. I would also suggest that for all his homage to local community as the condition of rational political deliberation (homage that should in any event be diagnosed as the return of the repressed), Dewey understood the new scope and significance of cultural politics better than Lippmann.

Let me leave aside further proof of essential agreement for now, and proceed directly to the issue of cultural politics. Dewey was interested, I think, in the kind of public that Lippmann ignored—a public that is not immediately or even necessarily "political" by virtue of its orientation to government policy-making or to electoral campaigns and party programs. Dewey was interested, that is, in the kind of public sphere created by the *erosion* of the boundary between the domains of state and society. His good friend and former colleague George Herbert Mead—another pragmatist—had described this tendency of corporate-industrial society in an essay of 1899: "The functions of government, as an institution, are merging with equal rapidity into the industrial world which it is supposed to control.... [Everything] point[s] to the passing of functions which are supposed to inhere in the government into activities that belong to the community simply through its organization apart from government." Jessie Taft, Mead's student at the

University of Chicago, took a different approach to the same confusion of spheres; like many social scientists at the turn of the century, she stressed the encroachment of "social organizations" on
the ostensibly private domain of the family: "As a matter of fact,
the family has undergone a complete revolution of all its activities,
and its center of gravity has been shifted to the factory, the brewery,
the bakery, the delicatessen shop, the school, the kindergarten, the
department store, the municipal department of health and sanitation, the hospital, the library, the social centers and playgrounds,
and dozens of other similar institutions."[35]

Notice that from either approach, the tendency in question is not
to be grasped as the expansion of the public sector at the expense
of the private sector, in the kind of zero-sum game depicted by both
proponents and opponents of the regulatory state. Instead, the
public sector "goes private" as investment planning and market
regulation, for example, become the normal functions of private
associations such as corporations and (to a lesser extent) trade
unions. Meanwhile, retail trade and commercial amusement
expand their domain as the economic functions of the family—presumably the seat of privacy—contract. I am not suggesting that the
public sector shrinks in the Progressive Era; far from it. I am suggesting that the more significant change is the expansion of large-
scale enterprise, association, and organization that blurs the line
between state and society because its results are neither public nor
private. As Dewey put it in *The Public and Its Problems*, "modes of
private business become 'affected with a public interest' because of
quantitative expansion" (48).

I am suggesting that the corporations presided over the dispersal
of power that was the original promise of civil society—that is, they
allowed and enforced the diffusion of power from the state to a
larger society that was now so internally articulated and variegated
that the organization of "private" interests, even of gender and
sexual identities, acquired public, political connotations. In this
sense, the corporations made the "private" sector the site of conflict on political questions that once required a state-centered, electoral approach; to borrow the terms proposed by Antonio
Gramsci, the rise of corporate capitalism made the "war of maneuver" obsolete by broadening the terrain of political struggle—by
opening up the middle ground between the domains of public

policy and familial privacy, the middle ground on which a pro-tracted "war of position" must be waged.[36]

This middle ground is the terrain of cultural politics—in fact, Gramsci's "war of position" simply is what we have come to know as cultural politics. Its conduct requires a *political* posture, but it doesn't anticipate the overthrow of the state, as if all power resides there, and it is only sporadically interested in government policy-making, or in electoral campaigns and party programs. Instead, it is a political posture that takes for granted the dispersal of power from the state to society and positions itself accordingly (indeed it would not be a *cultural* politics if it looked to the state apparatus rather than civil society as the scene of all significant struggle). The publics that compose the constituencies of cultural politics so con-ceived have opinions and "interests," to be sure, but they are not easily translated into the languages of electoral politics or govern-ment policies because their immediate aim is the expression and legitimation of subject positions that neither derive from nor con-form to inherited norms of subjectivity.[37]

These are the publics we see emerging in Dewey's reply to Lipp-mann (who ignored them precisely because their opinions and interests were inexplicable from the standpoint of policy-makers). Note that Dewey distinguishes between states, governments, and publics—the latter are the "lasting, extensive and serious conse-quences of associated activity"—as a way of explaining the differ-ences between political and more fundamental forms of democracy (67–71, 141–52). Note also that he emphasizes the appearance of "enlarged, complicated and multiplied public interests" specific to the new corporate era, but admits that "existing political and legal forms and arrangements are incompetent to deal with the situa-tion" (138, 128). From Dewey's standpoint, a state-centered approach to the problem of inchoate publics is nevertheless unwarranted; for the state itself is a "secondary form of associa-tion" (70–71). Moreover, "the questions of most concern at pre-sent" (sanitation, public health, housing, transportation, city planning, etc.) are not so much political as administrative: "They ignore forces which have to be composed and resolved before tech-nical and specialized action can come into play" (124–25). Ques-tions of greater significance will therefore be addressed "out of doors," out of the hearing of experts and policy-makers, out of the sight of the state.

My reading of *The Public and Its Problems* as a call for a cultural politics has the advantage of making the book more interesting as well as more intelligible. Consider, for example, the penultimate chapter, which is entitled "Search for the Great Community." It begins, as the author sees it, where Graham Wallas, Walter Lippmann's mentor, ended his influential book of 1914, *The Great Society*. Here Dewey summarizes his preceding arguments, and then asks, "What are the conditions under which it is possible for the Great Society to approach more closely and vitally the status of a Great Community, and thus take form in genuinely democratic societies and state?" (157) But he proceeds directly to a long-winded discussion of *habit* as "the mainspring of human action" (158–71). This excursion sounds like so much evasion of the real issue—until we realize that by "habit" Dewey means what we would call *culture*, and that his notion of habit presupposes the insights of William James, who is quoted at length, but also recalls the dictum of Charles Peirce: "Matter is effete mind, inveterate habits becoming physical laws."[38]

"Habit does not preclude the use of thought," Dewey notes, "but it determines the channels within which it operates. Thinking is secreted in the interstices of habits" (160). Indeed "habits of opinion are the toughest of all habits" (162). These inherited habits of opinion are the proper objects and the pivots of *political* struggle, according to Dewey—that is why the remainder of the book focuses on the "control of opinion" or the "management of publicity" or the "means of communication," and why artists figure so prominently in the corresponding discussion of presentation. "Poetry, the drama, the novel, are proofs that the problem of presentation is not insoluble," Dewey claims: "Artists have always been the real purveyors of news, for it is not the outward happening in itself which is new, but the kindling by it of emotion, perception and appreciation" (182, 184, 208–10).

We might then say that the culture wars commenced when the publics Dewey saw forming in the 1920s finally came of age, in our own postwar epoch. We might also say, in view of the end of the American century, that Dewey's cultural politics had greater staying power and predictive value than the policy-oriented politics of Lippmann or his heirs. So we might even say that pragmatism is the philosophy of the "war of position"—that is, the American variation on the theme of hegemony.

The Strange Career of the "Social Self"

From Royce to Wahl to Kojève

In "The Priority of Democracy to Philosophy" (1988), Richard Rorty claimed that the tendency or the effect of twentieth-century intellectual innovation "is to erase the picture of the self common to Greek metaphysics, Christian theology, and Enlightenment rationalism." He meant that since the 1890s, intellectuals have learned how to abandon "the idea that the human self has a center (a divine spark, or a truth-tracking faculty called 'reason') and that argumentation will, given time and patience, penetrate to this center." Aside from quibbles about those changes in Christian theology that eventually produced a specifically Protestant notion of reason as a human frailty incapable of tracking truth, I don't see how to argue with Rorty's claim except to note that the return of the repressed is always already under way: every report of the death of the subject is greatly exaggerated, even this late in the millennium.[1]

I mean that it is probably more accurate to say that twentieth-century intellectuals have been redrawing rather than erasing the picture of the self they inherited; for they have tried, more often than not, to retain what is still recognizable in this picture. I do not want to suggest that their attempts have been motivated by a Hegelian urge to recuperate every available moment in Western civilization. But I do want to suggest that we should follow their example of reconciling previous truth and novel fact by searching for models of the self that annul *and* preserve modern subjectivity (or, if you like, possessive individualism) rather than repudiate it.

In my view, there is no better place to begin this search than among the pragmatists and feminists who came of intellectual age around the turn of the last century—among those who discovered, or designed, the "social self" as a plausible alternative to the modern (bourgeois) individual specified in social contracts. But it is more difficult to make our way back to these theorists, activists, and writers than my assertion of their importance might suggest. For in this case the hermeneutical imperative is complicated, perhaps even countermanded, by our inability to see pragmatism as a fertile source of contemporary theorizing along poststructuralist lines, or as a crucial moment in the "decline of the paternal metaphor," as a leading feminist characterizes the intellectual crisis of the late nineteenth and early twentieth centuries.[2] Let me cite two examples of that persistent inability and then try to explain why we cannot seem to acknowledge the pragmatist origins of our own post-liberal thinking; at that point, we can hope to find our way back to the turn of the century.

My first example is Anthony Giddens, the celebrated social theorist from Cambridge University. In the introduction to what is probably his most-cited book, *Central Problems in Social Theory* (1979), he notes that he has been "strongly influenced by Heidegger's treatment of being and time," and goes on to illustrate what he means by reference to the author of *Pragmatism*: "William James echoes aspects of Heidegger's view when he says of time: 'The literally present moment is a purely verbal supposition, not a position; the only present concretely realised concretely being the "passing moment" in which the dying rearward of time and its dawning future forever mix their lights.'"[3] The chronological perversity of this passage could be explained, I suppose, by the citation Giddens provides—he quotes from the 1943 Longman edition of *A Pluralistic Universe*, which we, as citizens or students of the United States, know was first published in 1909. But is it plausible that one of the most sophisticated and broad-gauged social theorists of our time does not know that James was dead long before Heidegger took up his duties at Freiburg? We could also explain such perversity by saying that Giddens was just trying to illustrate a point in language more accessible than Heidegger's. But why not then just go to the source that clarifies the original claim? Wouldn't this be the obvious and proper procedure for someone whose project is the recuperation of classical social theory?

Perhaps not. If we are trying to bring classical social theory, and therefore Continental philosophy, to bear on the Anglo-American empiricist tradition, as Giddens obviously is, we are not likely to be admirers of that tradition. Indeed our ignorance of it, even contempt for it, could very well serve as an intellectual credential in the court of high theory, where everyone knows that the Anglo-American tradition has always emphasized the particular as against the universal, and has typically resisted the appeal as well as the idiom of metaphysics. If this conjecture seems too cynical, or too global, let us consider my second example. In *Gynesis: Configurations of Woman and Modernity* (1986), a strange, ambitious, and brilliant book, Alice Jardine (my "leading feminist" from above) ponders what the "refutation of the humanist self" means in historical as well as theoretical terms—that is, she explores the social conditions and intellectual spaces in which the figure of "woman" could begin to represent if not resolve cultural problems. In Jardine's account, these conditions and spaces are highly specific to postwar France, where writers were presumably in a unique position to retrieve Husserl, Freud, and Heidegger, or Levinas, Bataille, and Blanchot, from obscurity, mutilation, or vulgarization. That is why she introduces part 2, "Interfacings," of the book as follows:

> while Americans were busy reading Sartre, intellectuals in France were rereading Heidegger and Nietzsche, becoming obsessed with Mallarmé and the texts of such writers as Georges Bataille and Maurice Blanchot, and requestioning Hegel's master/slave dialectic as elaborated in Kojève's reading. . . . In its structuralist version, at least in terms of literary theory, [their] refutation of the humanist self (that is, Man) often took on the same forms as American "new criticism": pointing to the illusions of intentionality, psychology, expressivity, and to the fallacy of communication. But, in France, this voiding of the person was more expansive. . . . The object here is not to review the rich and varied work toward new conceptions of the speaking subject as it has been and still is being pursued in lin-

guistics, semiotics, psychoanalysis, and philosophy. But it is important to remember, and wonder at, the fact that this complex and far-
reaching theoretical dismantling of the knowing and finally
imperialistic speaking subject did not reproduce itself in Anglo-
American theory, and most especially not in the United States.4

In social theory, it seems, the U.S. still counts as an exception to
every rule. Somehow even its intellectuals have escaped the vicissitudes of historical time and avoided the sophistication that
inevitably comes with ideological complexity and conflict. That a
social theorist as accomplished as Jardine could unconsciously
recapitulate the themes of American exceptionalism—on this side
of the Atlantic, she insists, the avant-garde embarks on an errand
into an arid wilderness—is almost unnerving. But it does let me
convert my earlier conjecture into a plausible claim about the oddly
amnesic effect of fluency in classical social theory and Continental
philosophy.

Now, the relation between American and European intellectuals
which Jardine treats as self-evident—it is something like the relation of jolly country bumpkin to serious city slicker—would have
been unrecognizable on both sides of the Atlantic before 1940.
Until then, many influential European intellectuals would have
cited their encounter with American philosophers, particularly
those affiliated with pragmatism (e.g., Charles Peirce, William
James, Josiah Royce, George Herbert Mead, John Dewey), as the
formative moment in their development. But regardless of what
their footnotes and prefaces and diaries divulge, the discourse
through which these intellectuals began to redraw the inherited
"picture of the self" in the early twentieth century was clearly a
transatlantic dialogue in which pragmatism was a central issue. For
example, in 1937, Karl Mannheim called recent books by Dewey
and Mead "of epoch-making significance." "The American
philosophers," he claimed, "have tried to interpret man [sic] above
all as an acting being and have thus made available to our time of
activism a new access to the understanding of man." Ludwig
Wittgenstein apparently agreed. His lengthy preoccupation with
James's *Principles of Psychology* was reflected in his teaching,
according to John Passmore's account in *A Hundred Years of Philosophy*: "One of his former pupils, Mr. A. C. Jackson, tells me that
Wittgenstein very frequently referred to James in his lectures, even

making on one occasion—to everybody's astonishment—a precise reference to a page number!" Edmund Husserl was similarly drawn to, and profoundly affected by, *The Principles*: he read it within a year of its original publication in 1890 and cited it repeatedly thereafter, often noting that James had led him beyond "psychologism" and toward a new science of phenomenology.[5]

But in view of Jardine's remarks, the most interesting instances of European engagement with questions originally raised by pragmatism come from the new citadel of high theory, France itself. We know by now that Henri Bergson borrowed freely from James in rehabilitating a romantic version of modern subjectivity and that Georges Sorel published a huge study of pragmatism. We also know that Emile Durkheim was virtually obsessed with meeting the challenge to epistemology which James issued in the essays on radical empiricism of 1904–5. The great work of 1912, *The Elementary Forms of the Religious Life*, was not so much a reply to *The Varieties of Religious Experience* as it was an answer to "Does Consciousness Exist?"—that is, a rejoinder to radical empiricism. The lecture course that Durkheim designed for 1913–14 was less oblique in addressing James—it was eventually published as *Pragmatisme et sociologie*—but it was no more concerned with philosophical questions, with the "problem of knowledge" as such, than *The Elementary Forms*.[6]

My final French example is evident yet unknown, I would guess, except to those who still study phenomenology and/or existentialism. It involves tracing the genealogy of Alexandre Kojève's Paris lectures of the 1930s, which determined intellectual agendas in France even after the "poststructuralist moment" of the late 1960s and 1970s (e.g., in the feminist appropriation of Jacques Lacan's Hegelian psychoanalysis). Kojève's focus, on Hegel's first systematic statement of a post-Kantian yet extra-romantic philosophical trajectory in *The Phenomenology of Spirit*, was something of an innovation in Western Europe; for the earlier "rediscovery" of Hegel by Croce and Dilthey had featured the youthful theological writings and the mature philosophy of history. In fact, until the late 1920s, the *Phenomenology* was everywhere eclipsed by the *Logic* and the *Encyclopedia*—except in Russia, where V. S. Soloviev's articles of the 1890s and Gustav Shpet's translation of 1913 kept it visible if not central, and in the U.S., where, as we shall see, Royce promoted it as Hegel's finest work and as the turning point in modern philosophy. As a Russian émigré (né Kozhevnikov), Kojève was uniquely able to appreciate Shpet's translation, and as the author of a dissertation on Soloviev, he had long since been alerted to the significance of the *Phenomenology*.7 But he was also able to draw on the American appropriation of Hegel, although his intellectual indebtedness is less obvious on this side of the ledger.

Kojève began his Paris lectures in 1933, two years after the *Revue de métaphysique et de morale* published a special issue on Hegel, and four years after the appearance of Jean Wahl's book *Le Malheur de la conscience dans la philosophie de Hegel*, which according to George L. Kline was "the first serious twentieth-century European study devoted mainly to Hegel's *Phenomenology*." In an essay translated from the German for the *Revue de métaphysique*, Nicolai Hartmann called the master-slave dialectic "the universal foundation for a philosophy of work," and so anticipated Kojève's reading. But the other essay in the special issue which dealt with the *Phenomenology,* by Charles Andler, ignored this moment and the attendant issues of alienation, "the unhappy consciousness," etc. We should of course acknowledge Alexandre Koyré's important essays on Hegelian terminology (1931) and the youthful works of the Jena period (1935), not to mention the new "phenomenological" orientation of his compatriots among the young intellectuals of Paris (e.g., Emmanuel Levinas, Georges Bataille, Maurice Merleau-Ponty) who were reading if not studying with Husserl and Heidegger. But we should also acknowledge that in 1933, when Kojève began his lectures, the only revisionist sources in French that directly addressed the *Phenomenology* were Hartmann's essay and Wahl's recent book. Let Jean Hyppolite's recollection of this moment stand as a summary of that book's impact: "I should say that the first real shock came from Jean Wahl, and that reading *La conscience malheureuse [sic] dans la philosophie de Hegel* was a sort of revelation."8

Le Malheur de la conscience was Wahl's third book. His second book, published in 1920, was *Les Philosophies pluralistes d'Angleterre et d'Amérique*, in which Royce and James appear as the pivotal figures. Royce reappears, moreover, as an eminent authority in the 1929 study of Hegel, that is, as a scholar who is not only cited but respectfully quoted in the text. Wahl had good reasons to treat Royce as such an authority, perhaps even as his inspiration. For the American philosopher had been trying since the late 1880s to displace what he called the "traditional description of [Hegel's] system"—the dominant interpretation of the British neo-idealists Edward Caird and T. H. Green, among others—by rehabilitating the *Phenomenology*. In *The Spirit of Modern Philosophy* (1892), Royce claimed that Hegel's self-appointed task was to demonstrate the social dimensions of the "absolute self," and accordingly that the *Logic* and the *Encyclopedia* were of secondary importance in understanding his thought: "Of the systematic fashion in which he attacked this task in his 'Logic,' in his 'Encyclopedia,' and in his various courses of lectures, I can give no very satisfying notion. To my mind, however, he did his work best of all in his deepest and most difficult book, the 'Phenomenology of Spirit.'" Royce emphasized, moreover, that the setting in which these social dimensions of genuine selfhood were realized was a recurrent but increasingly sublimated "struggle for recognition," the "*Kampf des Anerkennens* of the *Phänomenologie.*'"[9]

Wahl made greater use of Royce's later book, *Lectures on Modern Idealism* (1919), which was originally a series of lectures presented at Johns Hopkins in 1906. But I don't mean that he cited this book more often than *The Spirit of Modern Philosophy*. I mean that *Le Malheur de la conscience* can be understood as a variation on themes introduced in *Modern Idealism*. In a discussion of the "unduly neglected" *Phenomenology* that takes up more than a third of the book, Royce suggested that "it has very close and important relations to the literary movement of the time," and showed, by reference to Goethe and Novalis, how it can be read as a "romance whose hero is interesting to us principally as a type," that is, allegorically, as what we would now call a bildungsroman. He also devoted a long section of this discussion to an analysis of the "unhappy consciousness," the metahistorical moment in the *Phenomenology* that had recently become one of his intellectual preoccupations (to the point where he had translated it for the first edition of Benjamin Rand's anthology *Modern Classical Philosophers*, in a selection which appeared *before* J. B. Baillie's 1910 translation of the entire work). Wahl followed Royce's lead, I think, by placing the notion of the "unhappy consciousness" in the context of romantic poetics and religious rhetorics (Novalis again appears as a key figure)—that is, by fleshing out the category with modern historical allusion and illustration, so that it begins to function as the concept of alienation would in later social theory. Wahl's central concern was the estrangement of the human species from itself and its environments which is expressed in modern individualism. He therefore claimed, in a passage reminiscent of Royce, that to study Hegel is to understand Nietzsche: "on peut dire que le problème de Nietzsche et le problème de Hegel sont un seul et même problème."[10]

I would conclude that the American appropriation of Hegel in the 1890s and after determined the French reception of the *Phenomenology* in the 1930s and after—that we cannot understand the postwar "voiding of the person" in France without understanding its American antecedents. But surely it is safe to say that Wahl was led to Hegel's *Phenomenology* by Royce, and that, in choosing to be influenced by Wahl, Kojève was assimilating the American appropriation of Hegel. Our question should then be, what happened after 1940? How did Jardine's account of the relation between American and French intellectuals become plausible? Giddens offers an important clue in his *New Rules of Sociological Method* (1993), when he tries to explain why symbolic interactionism, a trend in social theory often associated with George Herbert Mead, is not a real alternative to functionalism or structuralism:

> Symbolic interactionism is the only one of these three schools of thought to accord primacy to the subject as a skilled and creative actor; in American social theory in particular it was for many decades the only major rival to functionalism. Mead's social philosophy, in an important sense, was built around reflexivity: the reciprocity of the "I" and the "me." But even in Mead's own writings, the constituting activity of the "I" is not stressed. Rather, it is the "social self" with which Mead was preoccupied; and this emphasis has become even more pronounced in the writings of most of his followers. Hence much of the possible impact of this theoretical style has been lost, since the "social self" can easily be reinterpreted as the "socially determined self," and from then on the differences between symbolic interactionism and functionalism become much less marked.[11]

Now our questions can become more historically specific: how and why, and by whom, was the "social self" reinterpreted as the "socially determined self," so that the pragmatist sources of the original

notion could be discredited as conformist if not crypto-fascist cele-
brants of the "authoritarian personality," the "other-directed individual," the "managed self"?

Eight years ago, when I was writing a book in which the reception of pragmatism formed a crucial chapter, I suggested that "the
repression of the social self is completed when the American critics
of consumer culture—whose intellectual lineage includes the critics
of 'mass culture'—announce their affiliation with the Frankfurt
school." At the time it was no more than a conjecture, although I
was aware that some day I might have to prove it. Meanwhile, Wilfred McClay was writing an extraordinary book in which he
demonstrated, without benefit of any suggestion from me, that
anxieties about the "social self" antedate the 1940s but do reach a
certain crescendo in the 1950s, with the rapid acceptance and pop-
ularization of David Riesman's Frankfurt-inflected notion of
"other-directed" individuals. He notes, for example, that long
before Riesman met Erich Fromm, Walter Lippmann was portray-
ing the electorate as a manipulable mass, a "phantom public," and
Reinhold Niebuhr was worrying about the dangers of "group
egoism," indeed insisting that the behavior of "all human
collectives" was simply "brutal." Even so, McClay shows that the
decisive moment in the equation of the "social self" and the
"authoritarian personality" came in the 1940s—when the diaspora
of Central European intellectuals who, like Franz Neumann, felt
"nothing but 'contempt for empiricism and pragmatism,'" was
complete. Here is a summary of the argument: "The evolving
perspectives of Niebuhr and Lippmann . . . clearly betokened a . . .
fear of social tyranny. It took the emigré voices from the maelstrom
of Europe, however, to give impetus and intellectual focus to such
[perspectives], particularly in the years after the Second World War,
when emigré insights seemed increasingly germane to the concerns
of postwar American intellectuals."[12]

From the standpoint provided by McClay, we can see the intellectual continuum that links the works of Erich Fromm, Hannah
Arendt, Theodor Adorno, David Riesman, Dwight Macdonald, C.
Wright Mills, Richard Hofstadter, Lionel Trilling, Betty Friedan,
Stanley Elkins, and, yes, even Norman Mailer. For each of them,
the "challenge was the recovery of the autonomous self" from the
clutches of mass society, bureaucratic rationality, white-collar conformity, and consumer culture, that is, from the habitat of the

"social self."[13] The great irony of meeting this challenge was of course that by ignoring or repudiating the *modern* rendition of the "social self" once sponsored by the original pragmatists, these postwar writers had in effect proposed that the *ancient* rendition of that self—the strenuous citizen of classical republicanism—was the only viable alternative to both the unbound individual specified in social contracts and the "lonely crowd" in which white-collar automatons congregated. Little wonder that subsequent critics of modern liberalism have so often invoked the participatory virtue(s) of the polis.

By McClay's account, the centrifugal 1960s look like the inevitable result of the intellectual project that dominated the 1950s. We might say accordingly that it was only when the project of recovering the "autonomous self" began to seem pointless, destructive, and perhaps even "sexist"—no later than 1970 by my reckoning—that the return of the repressed "social self" became likely. But this is a way of saying that the rebirth of feminism permitted the rediscovery of pragmatism. Certainly feminist theory since 1970 has illuminated and interrogated the gendered connotations and consequences of the masterless, humanist self called "Man," yet has not, generally speaking, denied the possibility of genuine selfhood; in other words, feminist theory has developed a "double strategy" that might annul *and* preserve modern individualism within a new model of subjectivity. As Jane Flax puts it: "Gender can be used as a lever against essentialist or ahistoric notions of the self. A feminist deconstruction of the self, however, would point toward locating self and its experiences in concrete social relations, not only in fictive or purely textual conventions. A social self would come to be partially in and through powerful, affective relationships with other persons."[14] The question that follows from this formulation, I think, is whether pragmatism and feminism are different but related moments in the *re*construction of subjectivity which has preoccupied theorists, activists, and writers of every political persuasion since the turn of the century.

Jane Addams, Jessie Taft, and the "Social Claim"

At any rate, that is the question I want to address hereafter, by studying three exemplary texts from what William James designated the "Chicago School." These are "A Modern Lear" by Jane

Addams, which was written and presented as a lecture in 1894 but not published until 1912 (although Addams did interpolate this reading of Shakespeare's tragedy into her *Democracy and Social Ethics* [1902], pp. 94–101, 139–54); *The Woman Movement from the Point of View of Social Consciousness* by Jessie Taft, a student of George Herbert Mead, which was submitted to the philosophy department at the University of Chicago as a Ph.D. dissertation in 1913, then published by the university's press in 1915; and *Individualism Old and New* by John Dewey, which was written as a kind of coda to *The Public and Its Problems* (1927), and published in 1929.[15]

Addams's two texts were Shakespeare's *King Lear* and the apparent apogee of class conflict in the summer of 1894, when the fledgling American Railway Union expressed its solidarity with striking workers from the Pullman Car Company by establishing a boycott of freight traffic through Chicago, the hub of the nation's railway system. The strike and the boycott quickly succumbed to the firepower of federal troops imported over the objections of John Peter Altgeld, the governor of Illinois, but the spectacle of armed struggle in Chicago's streets only eight years after Haymarket left Addams appalled.[16] She wanted, therefore, "to consider this great social disaster, not alone in its legal aspect nor in its sociological bearings, but from those deep human motives, which, after all, determine events," and found that a comparison of the "family relationship" explored in *King Lear* to the "industrial relationship" expressed in the Pullman strike modified (without canceling) her initial, reflexive identification with the strikers. Lear's modern counterpart, by this reading, was George Pullman, known as one of the great philanthropists of his day because he had built a "model town" for his employees, complete with company housing and store, wide streets and flower beds, a church, and even a theater (107–8). Like Lear, "the magnitude of his indulgence and failure corresponded," mainly because he could not acknowledge the new moral universe, the broader range of human sympathies, emerging from the experience of those whom he had tried to indulge: "Were not both so absorbed in carrying out a personal plan of improvement that they failed to catch the great moral lesson which their times offered them?" (109, 113). Cordelia's modern counterpart was the labor movement that challenged Pullman's suffocating paternalism, but there was more than a hint of an autobiographical identification with Lear's youngest daughter: "[She] had caught the notion of an existence so vast that her relationship as a daughter was but a part of it. . . . She felt the tug upon her emotions and faculties of the larger life, the life which surrounds and completes the family life" (113–14).

By Addams's account, the strikers represented the "social consciousness," the "social ethics" that had perhaps superseded the older "individual virtues" to which Pullman appealed: "He felt himself right from the commercial standpoint, and could not see the situation from the social standpoint," whereas "their watchwords were brotherhood, sacrifice, the subordination of individual and trade interests to the good of the working class" (117, 115). Lear could not imagine how his daughter "should be moved by a principle outside of himself," outside, that is, of the familial, dynastic domain that contained the centrifugal tendencies of every individualism. Pullman could not imagine that the "divergence between the social form and the individual aim" (110)—the impending conflict between the "social standpoint" from which property appeared to be increasingly socialized by corporate enterprise and the "commercial standpoint" from which profits still looked like legitimate private gain—would be decided in favor of the labor movement. Pullman's tragedy recapitulated Lear's, then, but at a later and higher stage of human development, when women who aspired to the "larger life" beyond the "family claim" no longer threatened either the continuity of dynastic authority or the integrity of patriarchal households, and when workers who asserted "managerial" prerogatives in the factories no longer violated the "natural right" of property.

Addams was aware, I think, that the relation of Cordelia to Lear as she depicted it had reversed the relation of Antigone to Creon; at any rate she suggested that the daughter and the sister, not the patriarch, now represented an emerging new world in which most significant social relations and obligations were extra-familial: "Certain it is that someone had shaken her from the quiet measure of her insular existence and that she had at last felt the thrill of the world's life. She was transformed by a dignity which recast her speech and made it self-contained, as is becoming a citizen of the world" (113). This same citizen turns up in *Democracy and Social Ethics*, just before Addams reintroduces *King Lear* as a parable of contemporary moral dilemmas: "The modern woman finds herself educated to recognize a stress of social obligation which her family did not in the least anticipate when they sent her to college. She finds herself, in addition, under an impulse to act her part as a citizen of the world. She accepts her family inheritance with loyalty and affection, but she has entered into a wider inheritance as well, which, for lack of a better phrase, we call the social claim" (84–85). So we can say that, for Addams, the figure of Cordelia represented the promise of a social ethic through which both the modern woman and the modern labor movement could voice their objections to an archaic individualism and articulate a new moral universe predicated on solidarity.

This doubled identification makes her criticism of Cordelia all the more interesting and important. The "narrow conception" of a "higher duty" to the infinite world beyond the "family claim" allowed the youngest daughter to "assume that her father had no part in her new life," according to Addams, and to "break thus abruptly with the past." So Cordelia's sisters simply put into practice what she had put into words. Her abrupt break from the past announces the advent of the moral universe in which Goneril and Regan can demand that all evidence of Lear's kingly retinue be erased as a relic of barbarism—the moral universe in which anything is possible because inherited principles and practices cannot function as a tradition that limits innovation. Here is how Addams makes the point:

> As the vision of the life of Europe caught the sight and quickened the pulses of Cordelia, so a vision of the wider life has caught the sight of workingmen. . . . But just as Cordelia failed to include her father in the scope of her salvation and selfishly took it for herself alone, so workingmen in the dawn of the[ir] vision are inclined to claim it for themselves, putting out of their thoughts the old relationships; and just as surely as Cordelia's conscience developed in the new life and later drove her back to her father, where she perished, drawn into the cruelty and wrath which had now become objective and tragic, so the emancipation of working people will have to be inclusive of the employer from the first or it will encounter many failures, cruelties, and reactions. It will result not in the repentant position of Cordelia but in that of King Lear's two older daughters. (120)

In short, Addams insisted that the older, "individual virtues" had to be preserved within the new moral universe already animated by social ethics, that the "social self" discovered in the solidarities of the labor movement and the woman movement should *contain* but not replace its predecessors: "Of the virtues received from our fathers we can afford to lose none" (116).

I want to emphasize that her argument cannot be summarized or characterized as liberal Protestant faith in gradual amelioration, in reform rather than revolution. I want in fact to claim that this argument permits reform, and even revolution, by precluding mere radicalism, by reminding us that if the political legitimacy of governments determined by majority rule ultimately derives from the *consent* of the governed, then the legitimacy of innovation as such similarly derives from the sanction of public opinion, the active embodiment of consent. "It is so easy for the good and powerful to think that they can rise by following the dictates of conscience[,] by pursuing their own ideals," Addams noted, "leaving those ideals unconnected with the consent of their fellow-men." But to do so is to violate the postulate of equality which makes consent—not to mention democracy—possible and necessary; thus to make the exercise of power, no matter how lofty its goals, illegitimate; and finally to treat historical circumstances in the form of inherited customs, traditions, and social norms as if they were only obstructions on the path to enlightened ethical principles.[17]

By this account, the "failure of the model town of Pullman" was the consequence of power exercised without regard to the historically determined capacities, needs, desires, and opinions of those directly affected by it: "[Pullman] had the power to build [his] town, but he did not appeal to nor obtain the consent of the men who were living in it" (122). The "cruelties and reactions" that followed were inevitable. The conclusion I would draw from Addams's account is quite simple: the contempt for public opinion and the wish to repudiate the past express the same *radical* urge to ignore the postulate of equality and its entailment in consent, the urge, that is, to let "the good and powerful" impose their higher ideals on those who are not as enlightened or endowed; if left unmodulated by a larger vision of the relation between past and future, this radical urge must become the condition of reaction, not revolution.[18] A different approach to the same issues would suggest that the preservation of the older, "individual virtues" within a broader scheme of "social ethics" was not an unprincipled concession to the "respectable society" from which Addams herself had come; it was instead a way of seeing the past as both source of and limit on legitimate innovation in the present, a way of understanding that the modern individual and the "social self" are not the terms of an either/or choice.

Throughout my reading of Addams, I have assumed, on the evidence given by Mary Jo Deegan, Charlene Haddock-Seigfried, Katherine Kish Sklar, Allen F. Davis, Robyn Muncy, and Regina Leffers, that she was both a pragmatist and a feminist. But this assumption may be anachronistic; for if we confine our search to figures from around the turn of the century, it is impossible to find an avowed pragmatist who was not also sympathetic to the emerging feminist agenda. I am not suggesting that the "woman question" was an obsession or even a central concern of the pragmatists, or that we can supply them with feminist credentials by proving that it was. I *am* suggesting that they tended to follow Addams's lead on social questions, and that their challenge to existing epistemological models was in effect a challenge to male supremacy. I will have more to say in chapter 6 about the relation between epistemology and sexual politics. For now I want to claim merely that pragmatism and feminism converged in the early twentieth century, as social movements and as intellectual tendencies.[19]

To illustrate this claim, I turn to the life and work of Jessie Taft. In 1908, when she left Des Moines to attend the new summer school at the University of Chicago, she was already twenty-six years old and a seasoned schoolteacher. In Hyde Park, she stayed at the home of James Tufts (who had just coauthored a huge treatise on ethics with his erstwhile colleague, John Dewey), took courses on social psychology with W. I. Thomas and James Angell, and met Virginia Robinson, another schoolteacher, who became her lifelong friend and companion. "Pragmatism is in the air," Robinson exclaimed in a letter to a former classmate from Bryn Mawr, "and everybody starts with it as a basis." By the time the two women returned to their teaching posts at the end of the summer session, they knew they wanted somehow to recreate the intellectual excitement and community they had experienced in Chicago. Taft was able to return to the university in 1910 with a graduate fellowship, but in 1912 she and Robinson moved to New York City to work for Katherine Bement Davis, a Chicago alumna who, as superintendent of the Bedford Hills Reformatory, was trying to categorize criminal women through psychological testing and interviews (in doing so, Davis was drawing on the theories of yet another Chicago alumna, Frances Kellor, who had published a strong critique of Cesare Lambroso's physiological taxonomy of female criminals). Taft finished her dissertation under Mead's direction in 1913 and, lacking offers of a university position, resumed her duties at Bedford Hills. Soon thereafter she began lecturing on social psychology and social work at the University of Pennsylvania—here she enlisted Otto Rank to complicate what she had learned from Tufts, Mead, and her own thinking—but it was not until 1934 that she obtained a regular, full-time academic position in Penn's School of Social Work.[20]

Taft's dissertation was athwart, not "ahead of," its time: it was both an elaboration of current though novel ideas and an expression of evident yet unknown intellectual possibilities. She cited Walter Lippmann's *Drift and Mastery* (1914) in support of her contention that the woman movement and the labor movement were different versions of the same impulse to *socialize* institutions that seemed exempt from historical change because they were fundamentally "private" or "natural" or both (as in the *natural* right of *private* property, or in the nuclear family). But by 1914, this comparison was almost a commonplace—as we have seen, it animated Addams's analysis of the Pullman strike and informed her reading of the New Woman's claim on citizenship in the modern-industrial world.[21] The originality and importance of Taft's approach lie elsewhere, I think, in her explicit periodization of subjectivity and her application of this periodization to contemporary social questions and political problems. She wanted to historicize the very idea of selfhood, to treat it as something that was still evolving: "If we conceive of the self as something which is given, static, present from the beginning both in the individual and the race, or, what is practically the same thing, as something which develops absolutely, reaching its full growth regardless of any known conditions, then we have put the self outside of our own world, have made it mysterious and unknowable, and by so doing have given up the hope of social reconstruction, for there is no reconstruction of society without a reconstruction of selves" (36).

Change in the *form* of selfhood did not mean that the moral *content* of the self would erode, Taft therefore insisted, although it was likely that most people, the deep thinkers included, would interpret such change as a threat to genuine selfhood: "the natural tendency of the human mind to identify form with value and to attribute to the unchanged form the very possibility of the continued existence of value would show itself peculiarly stubborn with regard to woman[,] bound up as she is with the sex life" (32). But Taft was just as critical of the apparent teleology residing in existing models of the social self, particularly, as she saw it, in Royce's notion of an "absolute self" that developed "first of its own accord . . . and then [by] projecting itself into others who thereupon are perceived as selves likewise." She argued accordingly that an "escape from the absolute self" could be effected by following Mead, by "conceiving of the self to appear and develop as the *result* of its relations to other selves" (37). Even so, we should read her argument not as a rejection of Royce—and thus of Hegel—but as a different inflection of the Hegelian idiom; for in mapping a departure from his mentor, Mead had drawn just as heavily as Royce on the authority of the *Phenomenology*.[22]

Taft claimed, in fact, that convincing evidence for "the birth of a new type of consciousness" was to be found in "the very general tendency of modern thought to conceive of the self as social in character" (42, 37). She identified "three fairly distinct and characteristic stages in the development of consciousness of self in the historical period":

> There is first the type of consciousness we shall designate by the term *objective consciousness of self*, which colors Greek life and thought, although with the Greeks and through the Middle Ages it is already in the process of evolving into the second stage, which may be labeled *subjective consciousness of self*, and [which] reaches its climax in Kant and the personalities of the French Revolution. Lastly comes what we have termed the period of reflective or social consciousness of self[,] which is just now making its appearance. (42)

We should note that this periodization is perfectly consistent with both the Nietzschean and the Aristotelian version of recent cultural criticism. For example, what Taft calls "subjective consciousness of self" corresponds to what Alice Jardine calls the "speaking subject" or the "humanist self," to what Alasdair MacIntyre calls the

"Enlightenment Project," to what Charles Taylor as well as Anthony Giddens call "modern identity," and to what I call "modern subjectivity" in chapter 1.[23] But we should also note that Taft does not force us to choose between an "objective" and a "subjective" consciousness—that is, between the ancient and the modern world—as MacIntyre does by claiming that Aristotle is the only alternative to Nietzsche. Instead she suggests that the "new type" of synthetic, social consciousness mediates, indeed incorporates, the rival claims of its predecessors.

Taft was in certain respects more radical than Addams; but, like Addams, she refused to choose between past principles that confined women to domestic roles and present purposes that projected women into the larger society. As inherited from the artisanal past rather than as integrated into the emerging "industrial system," the home reminded her of a zoo: "He ['Man'] cannot live in the world his new economic organization has created and maintain actively the attitudes of the medieval [guild] system, but he likes to think these are still kept alive in woman and the home just as he likes to preserve different species of animals which are becoming extinct under civilization" (30). Yet she was not willing to promote its demise or pronounce it dead:

> People are afraid to let their values be tampered with, and, in this case, having identified women from the beginning of time with sex and family, they dread, in any alteration in the family or the woman's activities within it, the possible injury to contents which are of supreme worth to humanity. This is only right and wise as a measure of protection against sudden changes that tend to let drop values too precious to be lost, and any theories which the woman movement advances will have to meet that test, will have to make clear that what they propose will either increase human values or at least not sacrifice any of them. (31)

But Taft had previously shown that the family had recently "undergone a complete revolution of all its activities," so that, "far from being an independent unit," it was already implicated in the social complex created by modern industry and government. "The continued existence of the values centering in women and the family" depended, therefore, on a renegotiation of the relation between the family and the larger society—"an adjustment of the external conditions"—which would permit further "change in the form of the home and in the methods of the industrial world" (27, 35). The "social self" would then come of age when men and women recognized that the older, "individualistic" family was, practically speaking, an empty shell: "its center of gravity has been shifted to the factory, the brewery, the bakery, the delicatessen shop, the school, the kindergarten, the department store, the municipal department of health and sanitation, the hospital, the library, the social centers and playgrounds, and dozens of similar institutions." The ostensibly private realm of the nuclear family was actually a province of the public sector, Taft insisted: "it exists by virtue of its relations to these social organizations, it is formed by them and in turn reacts upon them" (27).

So there was no point in pretending that the ethics or personalities impending in an increasingly socialized market economy were foreign to the family or to feminism—for they were the causes, in both senses, of the woman movement. The task of social science, as Taft understood it, was to comprehend this process through which social ethics and social selfhood were already remaking the family and redefining the relation between the sexes by reconstructing womanhood (36–37, 56–57). She turned, accordingly, to the philosophers and theorists who *initiated* the "tendency in modern thought to conceive of the self as social"—that is, to James, Dewey, Mead, Tufts, and Royce, pragmatists all, and, at another remove, to Charles M. Cooley and James Baldwin (25, 37, 41, 48, 51).[24] The woman movement, in her view, was inexplicable, and perhaps indefensible, in their absence. From the standpoint she provides, we can see that modern feminism presupposed the reconstruction of subjectivity which the pragmatists apprehended as the salient feature of their historical moment; but we can also see that the reconstruction of subjectivity was a salient feature of this moment because domestic or familial functions no longer described the limits of female desires and ambitions, because the woman movement had acknowledged and acted on the "social claim" specific to modern-industrial civilization.

In her last chapter, Taft summarizes the three historic stages of self-consciousness by reference to a corresponding mode of "social control" (by which she means what we would term cultural consensus, social cohesion, or national identity). During the first and second stages, she contends, such control is *external* if not arbitrary, for even "when society flies apart into hostile individuals [and] thought recognizes its own power in handling the physical world"—when the "subjective consciousness of self" dominates Western culture—any association or solidarity or obligation that is not part of a contractual agreement will seem an externally imposed constraint on one's "abstract freedom." The "social control" made possible by the emergent "social self" was, by contrast, an *internally* generated commitment to the "common life":

> Our age is witnessing the disappearance of the isolated individual and the growth of an internal control based on the recognition of the dependence of the individual on social relations and his actual interest in social goods and in the discovery that thought is social in origin and can be used to the advantage in the social as well as the physical world. The freedom that was supposed to reside in the individual is seen to be realizd only through society. The individual is not economically or morally free except when he is able to express himself, to realize his ends through the common life. (51)

This is a far cry indeed from the "other-directed" individual who eventually evolved into the "managed self" of contemporary cultural criticism. We should therefore ask why Taft and her pragmatist antecedents didn't notice what now seems obvious, that a "social self" could be *more* susceptible than its predecessors to external manipulation if not complete control. A different way of posing the same question is to ask how, and how well, they explained the moral agency and the political capacity of the "social self." John Dewey, whom Taft cites as her authority at the passage I just quoted, will serve as the source of my answers.

Dewey and the Self's Determination

Long before the publication of *Individualism Old and New*, Dewey was insisting on the ineluctably social character of the self, and claiming that a coherent ethical system could be built on this foundation. For example, the premise of his second book, *Outlines of a Critical Theory of Ethics* (1891), was the post-Kantian, avowedly Hegelian notion that "self, or individuality, is essentially social, being constituted not by isolated capacity, but by capacity acting in response to the needs of an environment—an environment which, when taken in its fullness, is a community of persons." He tried accordingly to explicate the meanings of moral community by reference to unity of purposes, and found an example of such unity on the unlikely site of the modern-industrial workplace. "The term 'moral community' can mean only a unity of action," he noted, "made what it is by the cooperating activities of diverse individuals"; it followed that "there is unity in the work of a factory, not in spite of, but because of the division of labor."[25]

Over the next three decades, Dewey developed a social ethics in the terms he derived from James's *Principles of Psychology* (1890)—that is, by acknowledging "the entire uselessness of an ego outside and behind" the scene of action. To do so, he understood, was "to substitute a working conception of the self for a metaphysical definition of it" and to treat agency or capacity not as a natural property or innate propensity of "a fixed and presupposed self" but as an *effect* of a larger situation. In this sense, Dewey was treating the moral capacity of an individual as if it were something like a linguistic capacity: it was realized and refined—in a word, created—in specific transactions through which individuals adapted themselves to social conventions they did not invent and could not circumvent without making themselves unintelligible; and yet there was plenty of room for innovation, variation, and deviation in any individual's development of the capacity in question. As he put it in his *Lectures on Ethics* of 1900–1901, "all morality is social in its content."[26]

In these same lectures, Dewey claimed that "Individualism, stated in its really logical, coherent, thoroughgoing character, has a comparatively small number of supporters today." But he also admitted that it was "much easier to criticize and condemn it . . . than it is to state a substitute theory." His subsequent statements demonstrated the point. Dewey noted that by 1900 there were four "typical conceptions" of the relation between the individual and society. The first gave ontological priority to unbound individuals as the "original data" of society; it underwrote all versions of "contract theory," found ethical expression in utilitarianism, and treated every institution, including the state, as "a device for multiplying and intensifying the satisfactions of the individual." The second was "philosophical socialism," which simply inverted the relation specified in the first conception by bringing "all individuality as such into subordination to the welfare and ends of society as such";

for obvious reasons, it had "not found many representatives" in the Anglo-American intellectual tradition, although we should note in passing that from the standpoint of the Frankfurt School, it was only the mirror image of what Dewey, Taft, Addams, and many others called the "social self." The third was the "dualistic" outlook of the "everyday practical man," which enabled an inarticulate ethical federalism by designating a separate and inviolable, but local, sphere for the individual as against the society. The fourth was the "organic conception," which preserved the relations posited in the other three conceptions and yet was greater than the sum of these parts. "In the movement of thought," Dewey suggested, "the reaction against individualism has undoubtedly been in the direction of this organic conception." Even so, it was not a movement that was easily characterized: "But the difficulty is in giving it a clear and definite statement, telling after all what is meant by [the] organic relationship: what is meant by it in detail, theoretically, and what is meant by it practically."[27] The difficulty is on display in these lectures—hereafter they become an erudite evasion of the questions Dewey himself has raised.

But they do serve to remind us that, like both Addams and Taft, he tried to locate the "social self" in the space between the family and the state, to discover those forms of subjectivity that were neither functions of citizenship nor realized by political action. "Historically, it seems to me there has been in social philosophy a hypnotic influence exercised by the political factor," Dewey complained: "But there is no particular sacredness or exclusive importance attaching to the political occupation." So his purpose was not to reinstate the virtuous citizen of antiquity, who had no appreciable identity apart from his membership and participation in a political community, apart from his relation to the state. It was instead to sketch a selfhood derived from voluntary as well as inherited *associations*, and from the "reconstruction" of subjectivity (of habits, of consciousness, of personalities) that becomes normal in modern, "progressive society." In such a society, departures from custom and tradition no longer signify the onset of crisis, or rather "crisis becomes the rule" because nothing, not even habit, is exempt from scientific scrutiny and method. But if the "psychical or subjective type of individual shows himself in a changing society or in a disintegrating society"—that is, when crisis becomes the rule—a plausible account of the emergent "social self" would have to acknowledge the *legitimacy* as well as the resilience of its predecessor. Dewey clearly understood the problem in just this way. "The organic theory says that the individual in his individuality is still social," he claimed, "and his individuality is one mode of social expression and not a limit." Thus continuous and open-ended social "reconstruction" became the condition of moral progress, the guarantee of a creative tension between, not a simple identity of, self and social forces: "I do not see how the organic conception can be made to include the obvious and important facts of the individual on any static conception of society and social welfare. When there is such a static conception, this fourth view, to my mind, always practically reduces itself to the second, that is to say, to [philosophical] socialism, to a subordination of the individual to society."[28]

By the time he wrote the lectures that became *Reconstruction in Philosophy* (1920), Dewey had given up on this "organic conception." He restated the alternatives as he had presented them in the lectures of 1900–1901 (leaving out the "dualistic" view of the "practical everyday man") and pronounced them all inadequate. To be sure, he did suggest that "the 'organic' conception meets all the objections to the extreme individualistic and extreme socialistic theories."[29] But he went on to claim that by "transferring the issue from concrete situations to definitions and conceptual deductions," this more or less Hegelian theory had become "the apparatus for intellectual justification of the established order": it tended "to minimize the significance of specific conflicts" by abstraction from everything except the "organized community as a whole" (191). And yet Dewey had not changed his mind about the profoundly social and contingent character of the self; nor had he decided that self-consciousness and moral agency were functions of political community or commitment. If anything, he had enlarged the scope of his earlier arguments. For example, he still insisted that individuals are the effects, not the causes, of "social arrangements" or institutions, and that since they are so constituted, as moments in an "active process" rather than as natural facts or given data, "social modifications are the only means [to] changed personalities" (196). Here is how Dewey summarized his argument: "Now it is true that social arrangements, laws, institutions are made for man, [not that] man is made for them; that they are means and agencies of human welfare and progress. But they are not means for obtaining something for individuals, not even happiness. They are means of *creating* individuals. Only in the physical sense of physical bodies that to the senses are separate is individuality an original datum" (194). Or again: "individuality is not originally given but is created under the influences of associated life" (198).

Dewey also insisted that, so conceived, a "social self" was not by definition a virtuous citizen: "We repeat over and over that man is a social animal, and then we confine the significance of this statement to the sphere in which sociality usually seems least evident, politics" (185). He was quite emphatic on this point, for he saw, even in view of the recent "struggle to complete the nationalistic movement," that the cultural importance of state-centered political organization and activity was already declining. On the one hand, "trans-national interests" were challenging the "traditional doctrine of exclusive national sovereignty" (205). On the other hand, civil society was being reshaped and complicated by new forms of association and identification:

> Along with the development of the larger, more inclusive and more unified organization of the state has gone the emancipation of individuals from restrictions and servitudes previously imposed by custom and class status. But the individuals freed from external and coercive bonds have not remained isolated. Social molecules have at once recombined in new associations and organizations. Compulsory associations have been replaced by voluntary ones; rigid organizations by those more amenable to human choice and purposes—more directly changeable at will. What upon one side looks like a movement toward individualism, turns out to be really a movement toward multiplying all kinds and varieties of associations: Political parties, industrial corporations, scientific and artistic organizations, trade unions, churches, schools, clubs and societies without number, for the cultivation of every conceivable interest. . . . As they develop in number and importance, the state tends to become more and more a regulator and adjuster among them; defining the limits of their actions, preventing and settling conflicts (203).

For Dewey, this dispersal of power from the state to society made "traditional theory," whether individualistic or "socialistic," practically useless: "Groupings for promoting the diversity of goods that [we] share have become the real social units. They occupy the place which traditional theory has claimed either for mere isolated individuals or for the supreme and single political organization [i.e., the state]" (204).

As I have already suggested (in chapter 2), Dewey elaborated on this conclusion in *The Public and Its Problems* (1927). *Individualism Old and New* would seem, then, to be merely a recapitulation of familiar themes—except that it is much more explicit in explaining the "new age of human relationships" by reference to the universally "socializing" effects of the modern corporation. In a chapter entitled "The United States, Incorporated," for example, Dewey outlines his argument:

> There is no word which adequately expresses what is taking place. "Socialism" has too specific political and economic associations to be appropriate. "Collectivism" is more neutral, but it, too, is a party-word rather than a descriptive term. Perhaps the constantly increasing role of corporations in our economic life gives a clue to a fitting name. The word may be used in a wider sense than is conveyed by its technical meaning. We may then say that the United States has steadily moved from an earlier pioneer individualism to a condition of dominant corporateness. The influence business corporations exercise in determining present industrial and economic activities is both a cause and a symbol of the tendency to combination in all phases of life. Associations tightly or loosely organized more and more define the opportunities, the choices and actions of individuals. (36)

The pressing intellectual problem was then to posit a form of subjectivity consistent with the "change of social life from an individual to a corporate affair" (39); for "the absence of mentality that is congruent with the new social corporateness that is coming into being" would only deepen and prolong the "crisis in culture" whose characteristic gesture was the young intellectuals' embrace of "romantic individualism" (83, 138–42, 64).

Dewey understood that the first step toward the necessary reconstruction of subjectivity was an "acceptance" of the new corporate realities. "Individuals will refind themselves," he insisted, "only as their ideas and ideals are brought into harmony with the realities of the age in which they act" (70). But as Kenneth Burke understood, he was not preaching conformity or promoting acquiescence.[30] Dewey was instead proposing "an acceptance that is of the intellect," which meant "facing facts for what they are" (72). The central fact, as he saw it, was of course the profoundly corporate quality of American civilization, yet facing it meant *neither* sacrificing individualism *nor* celebrating capitalism. It meant grasping the corporation, or rather "corporateness," as the terrain on which socialism would be defined. "We are in for some kind of socialism," Dewey announced, "call it by whatever name we please, and no matter what it will be called when it is realized." For the socializing imperatives of the new corporate order were too powerful to be contained by the advocates of the older, pioneer individualism— even the Republican Party favored the "extension of political control in the social interest" (109–19). But since there was nothing inevitable about the form socialism would take in the U.S., its citizens faced "a choice between a blind, chaotic and unplanned determinism, issuing from business conducted for pecuniary profit, and the determination of a socially planned and ordered development." For Dewey, this was "the choice between a socialism that is public and one that is capitalistic" (119–20).

In effect the choice was between the old individualism and the new, between a pecuniary measure of subjectivity and a "social self." "Individualism has been identified with ideas of initiative and invention that are bound up with private and exclusive economic gain," Dewey explained, so that *any* defense of its correlative virtues would sound like praise of the uncivilized entrepreneur, of the unrepentant philistine (71, 90). The way to rediscover and redeem it, to permit each person to become more than an unbound, empty, and ever restless calculus of utilities, was then to move toward a new social complex in which something other than "private and exclusive gain" could be the gauge of achievement; for "social arrangements" and institutions were still the means of creating individuals: "A stable recovery of individuality waits upon an elimination of the older economic and political individualism, an elimination which will liberate imagination and endeavor for the task of making corporate society contribute to the free culture of its members. Only by economic revision can the sound element of the older individuality—equality of opportunity—be made a reality" (72).

So the "social self" that emerges from these texts of the "Chicago School" is not the middle manager who betrays the artisanal past, the faceless bureaucrat who violates the aesthetic imagination, the "other-directed" and probably "authoritarian" personality who identifies with the violently anti-modern forces of order. It is instead Cordelia, the new citizen of the world who enters a "social claim" on behalf of both women and workers; it is the "*result* of its relations to other selves," and so cannot thrive, let alone exist, in the absence of equality between individuals, regardless of their class or gender; it is the effect of social arrangements and institutions—of *association*—but in a "progressive society," where departure from custom is the rule, and where associations are plural, it is not the creature of any monolithic organization or state or ideology; it is the form of subjectivity specific to a "corporate age." This "social self" exhibits or enacts moral agency *because* it lacks the political capacity attributed to the virtuous citizen of antiquity, or rather its agency, moral and otherwise, is not derived from its political capacity, its orientation to the state. And although it questions the "individual virtues" of the "new man," the American who invented himself in the Machiavellian moment, it is neither inversion nor rejection of modern subjectivity. No wonder it looks like the New Woman.

Narrative Politics

Richard Rorty
at the "End of Reform"

Derek Nystrom and Kent Puckett introduce their recent interview of Richard Rorty with a warning to readers who expect professional philosophers to discount or deny the political import of their scholarship: "Rorty's work is well known for its geniality and measured tone, . . . [but] there appears in these pages a combative Richard Rorty familiar, perhaps, to those who have seen him in debate, but new to those who know him only from his published work."[1] This combative Rorty has of course been in print since 1991, when he treated Andrew Ross of *Social Text* as the representative of a cultural Left that deserved debunking, even dismissal, by those who understand that "cynical greed" still regulates party politics and public policy. Nystrom and Puckett are nevertheless right, I think, to draw our attention to the split between the genial, academic Dr. Jekyll, who wants to "keep the conversation going" because there are no transcendental principles that can justify any one voice, and the combative, indeed combustible Mr. Hyde, who wants to silence certain voices because there are good practical reasons to do so. In what follows, I ponder this split by examining the either/or choices that seem to proliferate in Rorty's approach to both political and philosophical questions. In concluding, I suggest that such choices can be avoided or postponed by revising the historical narratives they presuppose—that is, by rewriting American history. Throughout, my point of departure is Rorty's new book, *Achieving Our Country: Leftist Thought in 20th Century America.*[2]

Marxism or Pragmatism?

Recent scholarship in American intellectual history suggests that the relation between Marxism and pragmatism is much more complicated, and perhaps less antagonistic, than we have assumed since the 1950s. At any rate, it demonstrates that their estrangement is specific to the Cold War era.[3] For those with a vested political interest in either camp, or with a personal, professional stake in American intellectual history, two questions follow. As pragmatists, can we reclaim the "legal Marxisms" that flourished here as elsewhere before 1940—for example, in the works of William English Walling, E. R. A. Seligman, and Sidney Hook? As Marxists, do we have a legitimate claim on the pragmatist tradition? Our leading pragmatist, Richard Rorty, says no, and no again in thunder. There is no pluralism in Marxism, he insists in *Achieving Our Country.* He argues accordingly that if the American Left wants to have an effect on this world—the profane world in which the day-to-day compromise of principle is a requirement of sanity as well as success—it must choose between John Dewey and Karl Marx (36–37, 41–46, 53, 65, 102–4). So he sounds like the post-presidential John Quincy Adams, who kept urging his abolitionist comrades to put off holiness and take on intelligence, that is, to stop worrying about the state of their souls and start worrying how to win elections on anti-slavery grounds. We can only hope that Rorty has a similar political effect.

Not that we should accredit his invidious distinction between "real" and "cultural" politics (on which see below), as if the ideological work done by the moral absolutes of the abolitionists did not prepare the electorate for subsequent anti-slavery appeals—as if political progress does not require intellectual innovation. To do so would be to hollow out his refreshingly broad definition of "leftist thought," which includes the ideas of Cold War liberals (even the dreaded Arthur Schlesinger Jr.), and to forget what Abraham Lincoln taught us, that "he who molds public sentiment, goes deeper than he who enacts statutes or pronounces decisions."[4] But we can and should learn a great deal, I think, from Rorty's polemical periodization of the American Left, and from his attempted reconciliation of its Old and New and contemporary incarnations.

As Rorty tells the story, once upon a time there was a "reformist Left" animated by an alliance of workers and intellectuals, dedicated to income redistribution in the name of equality, and certain of "the thesis that the state must make itself responsible for such redistribution" (48). By his reckoning, it included "all those Americans who, between 1900 and 1964, struggled within the framework of constitutional democracy to protect the weak from the strong." After 1964—as we shall see, Rorty here adopts the influential historical perspective fashioned by Todd Gitlin, Nelson Lichtenstein, and Alan Brinkley, among others—a New Left emerged to question the political credentials of its reformist predecessor; the constituents of this more radical Left were those Americans ("mostly students") who had decided that the weak needed much better protection, indeed "that it was no longer possible to work for social justice within the system" (43).[5] These Americans, the "heirs of the New Left of the Sixties," went on to graduate school, and eventually took over the pilot disciplines of the liberal arts curriculum. So they were present at the creation of the contemporary "cultural Left," which "thinks more about stigma than about money, more about deep and hidden psychosexual motivations than about shallow and evident greed," apparently because it is confined to the pampered precincts of higher education (76–77).

Rorty is critical of all three Lefts, although his own roots are deeply and plainly sunk in the anti-Stalinist social democracy of the New York Intellectuals—in the "reformist Left" that enabled the New Deal, the CIO, and, yes, the Cold War as well ("I am still unable to see much difference between fighting Hitler and fighting Stalin," he declares [63]). The New Left abandoned "American national pride," he claims, and therefore made itself irrelevant to the electoral campaigns and legislative processes that can make a real difference in the real world.[6] Yet he also suggests that the New Left redeemed the Old: "It would be pointless to debate whether the New Leftists were justified in breaking with the reformist Left. . . . But if their patience had not run out at some point, if they had never taken to the streets, if civil disobedience had never replaced working within the system, America might no longer be a constitutional democracy" (68–69). And he suggests as well that the "cultural Left" might be an improvement on its predecessors because it is not satisfied to explain everything by reference to "economic injustice" (76). Rorty treats these three Lefts as episodes in a chronological sequence, but he understands that we can see them as pieces of a larger contemporary puzzle—as estranged but indispensable elements of an actually existing and still growing social movement originally convened in the early twentieth century. Otherwise his proposed reconciliation of the cultural and reformist Lefts would make no sense (see 91–92).

But that reconciliation cannot be negotiated if the Left gathered under Rorty's banner insists that we must choose between Dewey and Marx—in effect, between reform and revolution. We must therefore avoid or postpone the choice Rorty offers us. But how? We can do so, I think, if we can demonstrate that, in theory, Marxism and pragmatism are commensurable or continuous moments in the Western intellectual tradition, and that, in practice, Marxism and pragmatism were interwoven threads in the fabric of American thought until the 1940s, when left-wing intellectuals in the United States began to unravel them in the belief that they now represented the terms of an either/or choice. If we can see, as a result, that the profuse and revisionist Marxisms of Walling, Seligman, Hook, and others were replaced in the 1950s by a more univocal Marxism that took its cue from Leninist sources, we will understand that to choose between Dewey and Marx is to repress and mutilate much of the American Left's own history.

Let me explain how Marxism and pragmatism can and should be treated as commensurable or continuous theoretical moments in the Western intellectual tradition, and then turn briefly to the history of their imbrication in modern American thought. It is a commonplace to say that the origins of Marxism lie in the intersection of German idealism and British empiricism. Marx himself was of course the young Hegelian who tried to make sense of modernity by drawing on political economy, the new science of society that emerged most systematically and programmatically from the Scottish Enlightenment. But in doing so, he was recapitulating the intellectual itinerary that Hegel, the so-called idealist, sketched in *The Phenomenology of Mind* (1807) and finally fleshed out in *The Philosophy of Right* (1821). It was Hegel who first tried to bring modern political economy to bear on the questions raised by Kant; it was Hegel who first understood not only that "labour is the essence of Man"—this is Marx's insight of 1844—but that the bourgeois invention he called "civil society" was the site on which the future of freedom would be built; and it was Hegel who first claimed that the "discipline of culture" was composed of two similarly and profoundly social activities, language and work.7

Marx followed this lead, not without reservations and not altogether successfully; but so did other late-nineteenth century thinkers such as Charles Peirce, who believed that "pragmaticism" was closely related to Hegel's "objective idealism."8 And so did William James, the philosopher who, like Marx, vowed to "fight Hegel" but eventually understood how and why there was no escaping him. James's essays on radical empiricism of 1904–5 inhabit exactly the same space—between German idealism and British empiricism—that Marx defined as his intellectual domain, and they propose a radical revision of the relation between Kant and Hume— between German idealism and British empiricism—that is quite similar to what Marx proposed in the "Theses on Feuerbach." As Marx insisted, in addressing Feuerbach, that "thought objects" and "sensuous objects" were not separated by an ontological divide, so James insisted, in addressing Kant, that thoughts and things were made of the same "stuff," and would take on the characteristics of one or the other only in social-historical contexts determined by different purposes. As Marx demonstrated that Adam Smith's theories of value were no less metaphysical than "the German ideology" of post-Kantian philosophy, so James demonstrated that David Hume's dogged empiricism was predicated on "higher principles of disunion," that is, on a metaphysics of temporal discontinuity. No wonder the young Sidney Hook claimed in 1928 that the "Theses on Feuerbach" were a "striking anticipation of the instrumentalist theory of knowledge"; he saw that both Marxism and pragmatism were results of an intellectual struggle "against two opposed tendencies—sensationalistic empiricism and absolute idealism."9

Hook was not the first Marxist to argue that pragmatism and Marxism had similar origins in and effects on the Western intellectual tradition. But he was probably the only avowed Leninist to make that argument. Hook's many predecessors among those who attempted a synthesis of Marx, James, and/or Dewey were typically suspicious of Bolshevism, or at least more sympathetic than Lenin to the revisionist Marxism of Eduard Bernstein. They were the intellectuals, such as Ernest Untermann, Louis Boudin, John Spargo,

Max Eastman, and William English Walling, who congregated around the old Socialist Party USA before the Great War, and who concluded, in 1918 if not before, that the October Revolution aimed to subordinate Russian society—thus the working class—to the revolutionary party and its state apparatus. But the fact remains that regardless of their posture toward the revolution, all of them, from Walling to Hook, drew on both Marxism and pragmatism in trying to understand the development of corporate (a.k.a. "monopoly") capitalism and the conditions of democratic socialism.[10]

In this sense, Hook stands at the end of a long line of American intellectuals who were pragmatic Marxists, or Marxist pragmatists—a Plantagenet lineage, it seems, whose descendants still skulk about the palace but have no standing at court and no claim on the future. Yet that line(age) was clearly not a deviation from the mainstream of the American Left until the 1950s; for no matter how the old Sidney Hook or the young Daniel Bell defined their usable pasts, the Left of the half century between the Progressive Era and the Cold War was *neither* Marxist *nor* pragmatist: it was both. Aside from a few strange tantrums in the late 1960s, when "democracy is in the streets" became a battle cry, the Left of the next half century was, and is, equally ambivalent. To insist, as Rorty does, that we must choose between Dewey and Marx is then to deny the historical significance of this ambivalence, and to reinstate the impossible choice between reform and revolution that has fueled so many sectarian dreams since 1917.

Of course Rorty believes that the choice he offers us is the same choice Sidney Hook had to make in the 1930s. But Hook himself was far more ambiguous. After 1937, at any rate, he kept trying to complicate the mutually exclusive choice between capitalism and socialism—between reform and revolution—which he had previously posited. As Christopher Phelps has shown, he did so by bringing his Deweyan sensibilities to bear on political and historical questions, by treating "social systems and political ideologies in the same way that pragmatists treat[ed] philosophical dualisms." This procedure apparently drove him to the conclusion that even though capitalism and socialism had typically appeared as the terms of an either/or ideological choice, they had developed in history and in theory, as events and as ideas, in reciprocal relation to each other. "Because he follows the lead of scientific method, Dewey refuses to be bound in his thinking by easy oppositions like capitalism *or* socialism, socialism *or* fascism, totalitarianism *or* democracy," Hook wrote: "Once these terms are given empirical content, we can see that their presence or absence is a matter of degree."[11]

To be sure, Hook would someday see more than an "easy opposition" between totalitarianism and constitutional democracy. I cite him here, at the moment of truth for the New Deal coalition, because his refusal of these either/or choices strikes me as more consistent with the original pragmatists' attempt to mediate between seemingly irreconcilable positions—for example, between British empiricism and German idealism—than Rorty's outright rejection of Marxism, and because the refusal may help us decipher the rejection. Hook never did repudiate Marx, but he did repudiate the perversions of Marxism (and socialism) undertaken in the name of Soviet Communism. Rorty, the heir apparent to Hook's intellectual legacy, will not make this distinction between theory and practice, even though he compares his rejection of Marxism to the early Protestants' rejection of the Papacy (that is, a rejection not of Christian doctrine but of the institutional forms it had taken under Catholic auspices: see 41). Why not? He clearly values Marx as a theorist of immiseration and as a thinker who took the hierarchies of social class very seriously (see, e.g., 42). But he cannot detach Marx's ideas from the Soviet experiment with statist socialism, with an "elsewhere" that is not "American." So "Marxism" finally signifies just that—a botched experiment conducted somewhere else, in a foreign place or state of mind. "For us Americans, it is important not to let Marxism influence the story we tell about our own Left," Rorty declares, as if we could somehow immunize historians and their narratives against the contaminant from the other shore (41). "We Americans did not need Marx to show us the need for redistribution," he goes on to say, "or to tell us that the state was often little more than the executive committee of the rich and powerful" (48). The choice between Dewey and Marx boils down, therefore, to the Cold War's choice between the United States, its allies, and its enemies, between the "free world" and the rest of the world. So conceived, the choice for Dewey becomes an instance of "American national pride," a way of honoring the intellectual tradition that came of age when pragmatism emerged around the turn of the century.

Now this is not such a bad idea. If American intellectuals were more aware of their own antecedents—that is, more cognizant of how influential the original pragmatists were in reshaping European (especially French) philosophy after 1920—they would be less eager to don the latest theoretical fashion imported from Paris. But it is not that simple. In Rorty's Manichean conspectus, "Marxism" also signifies what Frank Lentricchia calls "theory desire," and thus turns the contemporary Left from its appointed redistributive tasks.[12] Indeed this urge to "theorize" is not merely superfluous, it is insidious and ultimately disabling: it allows leftists "to give cultural politics preference over real politics," to insist on a "preference for knowledge over hope," and finally "to step back from their country" and become spectators on their own historical moment (36–37). For example:

> The Foucauldian Left represents an unfortunate regression to the Marxist obsession with scientific rigor. This Left still wants to put historical events in a theoretical context. It exaggerates the importance of philosophy for politics, and wastes its energy on sophisticated theoretical analyses of the significance of current events. But Foucauldian theoretical sophistication is even more useless to leftist politics than was Engels' dialectical materialism. Engels at least had an eschatology. Foucauldians do not even have that. Because they regard liberal reformist initiatives as symptoms of a discredited liberal "humanism," they have little interest in designing new social experiments. (37)

So the choice between Marxism and pragmatism is in effect a choice between theory and practice, between a spectatorial and an activist Left, between cosmopolitan sophistication and "national pride," between cultural and "real" politics—between the Old World and the New. Søren Kierkegaard's intellectual agenda seems positively Hegelian by comparison to this one. But how can that be if Rorty designates Hegel as the source of Whitman's secularism and Dewey's historicism? (see 19–25, 37)

Real or Cultural Politics?

This is not a question we can adequately address until we understand why and how Rorty can dismiss cultural (a.k.a. identity) politics as a red herring—as more than a distraction from and less than a supplement to the real thing. Here the interview with Nystrom

and Puckett becomes quite useful, for in that venue Rorty clarifies
the premises of his argument in *Achieving Our Country*. But let us
first go back to the book. How does the author define cultural politics, and what exactly is wrong with it? To begin with, the "principal enemy" of the cultural Left is "a mind set rather than a set of
economic arrangements" (79). Whereas the residual reformist Left
"thinks more about laws that need to be passed than about a
culture that needs to be changed," the academic leftists who spe-
cialize in stigmata believe their mission is to "teach Americans to
recognize otherness" or difference (78–79). So the great irony of a
cultural Left that eschews "totalization"—that is, any "meta-
narrative" purporting to explain every historical circumstance by
reference to an evolutionary model—is that it "thinks that the
system, and not just the laws, must be changed" (78). In this sense,
it indulges an apocalyptic absolutism that paralyzes any piecemeal
reforms and precludes any sympathy for people who are victims of
"economic selfishness" rather than "socially accepted sadism." The
turning point in the creation of a cultural Left so defined, Rorty
suggests, was the "shift of attention" from money to stigma which
occurred when "intellectuals began to lose interest in the labor
unions" (80, 77). So, where the reformist Left focused its energies
on class struggle and politics, that is, on changing "economic
arrangements," its successor builds theoretical models to explain
how group identities and social differences are constructed and
reproduced from the raw materials of race, gender, ethnicity, and
sexual orientation (76–84, 88–90); that is why this newer Left has
nothing whatsoever to say about the invidious domestic effects of
"globalization"—the spread of market economies since 1989—
which Rorty rightly sees as the social and political equivalent of
nineteenth-century industrialization (84).[13]

As bona fide members of the cultural Left, Nystrom and Puckett
are eager to press its claims against Rorty's residually reformist
position. In this setting, therefore, his objections to "group identity" as the pivot of contemporary political theory and practice can
become more specific than in a series of lectures covering the entire
twentieth century.[14] On the one hand, he objects to the "politics of
difference" because he wants us to think about " individual difference instead of group difference," because he sees self-conscious
adherence to an *inherited* affiliation or association as a betrayal of
the American dream: "I don't care whether anybody thinks of

themselves as Vietnamese-American, Italian-American, or Baptist. I would just like them to be free to make up their own lives, in a good Nietzschean manner" (22). Once upon a time, Rorty insists, "we used individual models to create a self for ourselves." So his question is, "Why *group* identities?" (28) On the other hand, he objects to an exclusively cultural Left that spends "all its time thinking about matters of group identity, rather than about wages and hours" (32). So his abiding concern is not the centrality of group identity in politics—the group identities represented by trade unions, expressed as working-class solidarity, and articulated in collective bargaining agreements constitute his ideal of "real politics"—but the political significance of the categories invented by the so-called new social movements, that is, the political significance of *ascribed* rather than *achieved* collective identities.

Rorty is no doubt correct to worry about the complacency and inertia produced by unthinking loyalty or self-conscious adherence to inherited affiliations and associations. To put his case in this way, so that we can see how the labor movement becomes the bearer of "real politics" is, however, to realize that his argument against cultural politics reinstates the priority of class as the irreplaceable principle of social organization, intellectual inquiry, and political struggle. And so that argument also validates the vulgar Marxism Rorty wants us to forget.

If we are to prevent this return of the repressed, we must then learn to avoid or postpone the either/or choice he offers us between cultural and real politics. But to do so is to defend the promise of cultural politics on historical grounds, where, as Rorty himself points out, the "moral justification" of all institutions and practices is accomplished in retrospect, in historical narratives.

As we will see, this defense ultimately requires criticism and revision of the narratives on which Rorty relies; for now I want merely to explain in historical terms why he should follow the lead of John Dewey, and thereby realize that cultural politics are necessary as well as possible in the hybrid social formation we call corporate capitalism.

As we have seen, in the 1920s Dewey recognized that the emergence and consolidation of a specifically corporate political economy made the classical liberal distinction between the public and the private sector problematic if not unintelligible. Because he understood that the public sphere specific to "the political affairs of prior ages" was distended by the *corporate* consequences of industrial revolution, he was interested in the "enlarged, complicated and multiplied public interests" that Walter Lippmann ignored—in publics that are not immediately or even necessarily "political" by virtue of their orientation to government policymaking or to electoral campaigns and party programs. Dewey was interested, that is, in the new kind of public sphere created by the *erosion* of the boundary between the domains of the state and civil society: "modes of private business become 'affected with a public interest,'" as he put it in *The Public and Its Problems* (1927), "because of quantitative expansion."[15]

I have already suggested in chapters 2 and 3 that the new corporations presided over this "dispersal of power," which, as Hegel first understood, was the original promise of civil society—that is, they allowed and enforced the diffusion of power from the state to a larger society. As a result, even gender and sexual identities acquired public, political connotations. So the rise of corporate capitalism, circa 1890–1930, made the "private" sector the site of conflict on "political" questions that once required a state-centered, electoral approach—in Gramscian terms, it made the "war of maneuver" obsolete by opening up the middle ground between the domains of public policy and familial privacy, the middle ground on which a protracted "war of position" must be waged, the middle ground that is the terrain of cultural politics.[16] The publics that compose the constituencies of cultural politics so conceived have opinions and "interests," but since their immediate aim is the expression and legitimation of subject positions that neither derive from nor conform to inherited norms of subjectivity, they tend to sound as if they are abstaining from politics as such.

Again, these are the publics we see emerging in Dewey's replies to Lippmann in the late 1920s. But as I noted in chapter 3, his most pointed attempt at a redefinition of politics in terms of intermediate "private" associations or "groupings" is probably *Reconstruction in Philosophy* (1920), where he insisted that the "social selves" created by institutional means were multiplying rapidly:

Compulsory associations have been replaced by voluntary ones; rigid organizations by those more amenable to human choice and purposes—more directly changeable at will. What upon one side looks like a movement toward individualism, turns out to be really

> a movement toward mutliplying all kinds and varieties of associa-
> tions: Political parties, industrial corporations, scientific and artistic
> organizations, trade unions, churches, schools, clubs and societies
> without number, for the cultivation of every conceivable interest. . . .
> As they develop in number and importance, the state tends to
> become more and more a regulator and adjuster among them, defin-
> ing the limits of their actions, preventing and settling conflicts.

For Dewey, this dispersal of power from the state to society made
"traditional theory" practically useless: "Groupings for promoting
the diversity of goods that [we] share have become the real social
units. They occupy the place which traditional theory has claimed
either for mere isolated individuals or for the supreme and single
political organization [i.e., the state]."[17]

This retort to "traditional theory" can be read as an answer to
Rorty's question—"Why *group* identities?"—and an explanation
for the recent shortage of "individual models" of identity. Even so,
we should not misconstrue Rorty's dismissal of group identity and
its consequences in cultural politics. His fundamental objection to
the "politics of difference" is that by his definition it entails an
embrace of the stigmata that mark certain groups as oppressed:
"You can't write your autobiography without mentioning the
stigma you inherited, but the stigmas were somebody else's idea,
not yours. . . . I guess what bothers me about the politics of difference is the suggestion that you have some duty to embrace it [the
culture that constitutes your group identity] rather than forget
about it" (27). In other words, the acceptance of an ascribed identity precludes the achievement of a genuine individuality through
what Dewey would call voluntary association.

There are two ways to address this objection to the theory and
practice of cultural politics. The first is to note that the salience of
"economic arrangements" and its attendant, the priority of class
politics, cannot be taken for granted in a post-industrial society—
a society, as Daniel Bell has suggested, in which "culture has
replaced technology as a source of change." As the quantity of
"socially necessary labor" declines, due to the instrumentation and
automation of goods production under corporate auspices, circa
1900–1930, the capital-labor relation describes, includes, or determines a diminishing proportion of social relations as such; the possibility of choosing or achieving an association that is not derived

from a position within the social complex of goods production increases accordingly. Thus a "group identity" deduced from something other than one's class position—or rather *in addition to* this position—becomes a matter of choice as the realm of necessity, the scope of socially necessary labor, recedes. That is why alternatives to the principle of class, for example the principles of race and gender, begin to multiply when the problem of production is solved by the mechanization of the labor process under corporate auspices. In short, the development of corporate capitalism makes the "double consciousness" of cultural politics necessary as well as possible.[18]

The second way to address Rorty's objection is a great deal more complicated because it requires an examination of the relation between race, gender, culture, and the politics of "American national pride." "Before we knew that there was an African-American culture, or a gay culture, or a female identity," he complains, "we talked about blacks, gays, and women getting an unnecessarily hard time because people were prejudiced against them. I guess I'm not sure that discovering they've all got cultures, or encouraging them to have cultures, has added anything" (27–28). We could of course read this complaint as a form of resistance to the "essentialization" of gender and race, through which the differences between males and females or black and white folkways are rendered natural, thus more or less immutable. But when read in view of Rorty's valorization of working-class solidarity against "the bosses" and their allies, "the oligarchs" of the Republican Party, it raises an interesting question: why is working-class solidarity exempt from his criticisms of "group identities"? To put it another way, what exactly is wrong with the solidarities convened by feminism or by black nationalism? Rorty would respond, I think, by saying that working-class solidarity is uniquely legitimate because it is an artificial and contingent phenonemon that is neither celebrated nor perpetuated by its bearers. But is this distinction so obvious? Is working-class identity something inherited or something achieved? Or is it both? Do feminists and black nationalists always or even typically essentialize "womanhood" and "negritude" when promoting their respective solidarities? Or do they, too, understand that what binds them, in *both* senses, is the artificial and contingent phenomena of culture? If so, are the "group identities" they sponsor commensurable with working-class solidarity, and thus admissable evidence in the court of "real politics"?

To answer such questions, we need to begin by revisiting the arguments of Harold Cruse's seminal work on black nationalism, *The Crisis of the Negro Intellectual* (1967); for in this book, Cruse outlined an indispensable rationale for a cultural pluralism that would acknowledge the crucial role of "race" in shaping—*but not merely disfiguring*—the American nation and thus the national identifications of Americans. We should note at the outset of our visitation that he was recapitulating the arguments on race and culture which Alain Locke proposed in the 1920s and 30s, in assessing the Harlem Renaissance, and was doing so as a way of both enlarging and revising them in light of new historical circumstances.[19] As I understand him, Cruse argued that the cultural landscape of the United States was a space in which different ethnic groups vied for supremacy, or, as we would now say, for hegemony; these groups, not individuals (and not social classes), were the main characters in the drama of American politics. Without a "Negro ethnic consciousness"—that is, without a cross-class alternative to integration and assimilation—black Americans could never hope, therefore, to contribute *on their own terms* to a pluralist redefinition of the American nation that would recognize ethnic difference as the source of "cultural democracy" rather than the solvent of American nationalism. From this standpoint, the key to creating that cross-class alternative, which in practical terms meant forging new ties between Negro intellectuals and the "black masses," was a new historical consciousness or narrative that would acknowledge the plausibility, or at least allow the discussion, of two controversial claims.[20] One is that the "cultural apparatus," a phrase borrowed from C. Wright Mills, had become the central site of political struggle:

> Nineteenth-century capitalism was an industrial system without the twentieth-century trappings of the new industry—mass cultural communications, a new and unprecedented capitalistic refinement of unheard-of social ramifications. Marx never had to deal with this monster of capitalist accumulation. Mass cultural communications is a basic industry, as basic as oil, steel, and transportation, in its own way. Developing along with it, supporting it, and subservient

to it, is an organized network of functions that are creative, administrative, propagandistic, educational, recreational, political, artistic, economic and cultural. Taken as a whole this enterprise involves what Mills called the cultural apparatus.

The other and probably more controversial claim is that the "leftward turn" of Negro intellectuals in the 1930s—that is, their adoption of postures sanctioned by the Communist Party, which gave priority to the principle of class in every instance—was both a diversion from the pressing cultural questions posed by the writers of the Renaissance and an evasion of the new political questions raised by the advent of mass cultural communications: "Unable to arrive at any philosophical conclusions of their own as a *black intelligentsia*, the leading literary lights of the 1920s substituted the Communist left-wing philosophy of the 1930s, and thus were intellectually sidetracked for the remainder of their productive years." The "great default of the Negro intellectuals" in the interwar period, and perhaps of intellectuals as such since then, was their inability to grasp the significance of the *cultural* revolution residing in and flowing from the development of mass communications media after 1910—the revolution "they instinctively started out to make" but could not complete, "the revolution that imported Russian politics confounded."[21]

This confounded cultural revolution, through which black Americans could finally speak for themselves *and* for the nation, serves in Cruse's argument as the necessary condition of a new birth of freedom. But we should note the ambiguities of that argument. In keeping with his skeptical stance toward the vulgar Marxism authorized by the Communist Party in the 1930s and 1940s, he refuses to posit the priority of class, and thus allows for the articulation of the principle or category of race: "The Negro question, contrary to Marxist dogma, is more a group problem than a class one." And yet he also refuses to propose a strictly racial solution to that problem: "In America, the Negro group is more an ethnic than a racial group—meaning a group of mixed African, Indian, and white strains." So its solidarity is something to be achieved in cultural forms, in aesthetic terms, not something already determined by natural causes. Indeed, at the point where the various strands of his argument come together in a summary statement, Cruse suggests that the United States, an unfinished "nation of minorities," will come of age when American national pride is founded on a cultural pluralism that acknowledges the originality and autonomy of a "black aesthetic":

> The path to the ethnic democratization of American society is through its culture, that is to say through its cultural apparatus, which comprises the eyes, the ears, and the "mind" of capitalism and its twentieth-century voice to the world. Thus to democratize the cultural apparatus is tantamount to revolutionizing American society itself into the living realization of its professed ideas. Seeing the problem in another way, to revolutionize the cultural apparatus is to deal fundamentally with the unsolved question of American nationality—Which group speaks for America and for the glorification of which ethnic image? . . . But this kind of revolution would have to be predicated on the recognition that the cultural and artistic originality of the American nation is founded, historically, on the ingredients of a black aesthetic and artistic base.[22]

Cruse's argument reminds us that if the "moral justification" of inherited institutions and practices is "mostly a matter of historical narratives," as Rorty has insisted, it is also true that the "principal backup for historiography is not philosophy but the arts, which serve to develop and modify a group's self-image by, for example, apotheosizing its heroes, diabolizing its enemies, mounting dialogue among its members, and refocusing its attention."[23] I mean that his argument addresses Rorty's concerns about cultural politics because it asserts not the existence of an African-American culture but the historical and thus *national* significance of a "black aesthetic." By Cruse's account, to acquire American national pride is to understand that American culture is convened in the relation, or by the tension, between black and white folkways; effacing their differences—"melting ethnicities together into shared citizenship," as Rorty puts it (25)—is therefore a way of ignoring the originary "black aesthetic" and forgetting that the color line is the shifting boundary on which American identities have always been imagined. To put it another way, "American national pride," which Rorty stipulates as the presupposition of "real politics," requires that we appreciate ragtime, blues, and jazz, the inventions of black artists in the United States, as musics that express the promise of

American life rather than the stigmata borne by members of an oppressed race; so the "black aesthetic" that constitutes the collective identity of the "Negro group" represents a bulwark, not a rejection, of American nationality.

But can the politics of gender difference be understood in similar terms? Has gender been as salient as race or ethnicity in the development of an American national identity? If not, how can we defend the cultural politics implicit in the claim that "the personal is political"? We can, I think, if we realize that the intent of the slogan and the aim of feminism is to change the subjects of political discourse—at the very least, to redefine the agents of political power and to enlarge the scope of political theory. These goals emerged before 1920, of course, and they were given new urgency thereafter because male supremacy was apparently unaffected by women's suffrage; but it was not until the 1950s and 1960s, when the priority of class was no longer a self-evident means of mass political mobilization, and when the liberal definition of power (as the province of the state) lost explanatory adequacy, that they could again become the goals of a cross-class social movement dedicated to equality between the sexes.[24] From the standpoint of liberals, these are not genuinely political goals—they are not the purposes of "real politics"—for they represent only the preliminaries to passing laws. From the standpoint of feminists, however, they are the substance of politics. Anne Phillips explains why:

> The language through which we think our needs, interests, and rights continually subverts the impulse to liberation, drawing us back into the either/or dichotomies of being like men, or else "naturally" different. . . . Women themselves are as much at the mercy of these dichotomies as men; it is not just that we "know" what we want but have been unable to make ourselves heard. Voting *per se* cannot deal with this, for it is changing our perceptions and agendas that is the most urgent and difficult task.[25]

Notice that Phillips does not rule out electoral and state-centered politics. Instead she suggests that they have not, and cannot, effect the broader cultural or ideological changes that would allow for new concepts, and new forms, of political agency and power. In this sense, the cultural politics of feminism has an ideological function comparable to that of nineteenth-century socialism, Marxism, and trade unionism. All three movements demonstrated in their own way that the exchange of equivalents between capital and labor produced a working class with nothing to lose but its chains; so they could plausibly claim that what classical liberalism had designated the "private" sector of non-coercive, strictly contractual social relations was now a public sphere permeated by power and characterized by inequality. In short, they demonstrated that since civil society was not a refuge from the corruptions of state power, it was subject to the categories of political analysis and the consequences of political organization. Twentieth-century feminists have similarly demonstrated that what modern liberalism still designates the "private" realm of familial intimacy has become a political problem—a pressing issue of public policy and social theory—because the identities of women can no longer be routinely derived from familial roles or reproductive functions and because inequality between men and women can no longer be explained or justified by reference to differences, natural or not, in political capacity. In short, they have demonstrated that since the family is not a refuge from the corruptions of public life, but is instead the *social* source of the gender norms through which the separation of public and private gets reproduced, it is subject to the categories of political analysis and the consequences of political organization.[26]

From its inception in the early twentieth century, modern feminism has also posited alternatives to the modern (bourgeois) individual specified in social contract theory—that is, to the "man of reason" who acquired character and political standing insofar as he could effectively repress or modulate his desires and, what amounts to the same thing, insofar as he could critically detach himself from any inherited traditions, communities, or commitments. Modern feminism has done so by sponsoring the notion of a "social self," an intermediate bearer of moral agency and political capacity which was neither the unbound individual who emerged from the wreckage of the patriarchal household in the mid-nineteenth century nor the paterfamilias who preceded him in the seventeenth and eighteenth centuries as the representative of the family as such.[27] So conceived, the "social self" is the contribution of modern feminism to what Rorty has characterized as the general tendency of twentieth-century intellectual innovation, viz., "to erase the picture of the self common to Greek metaphysics, Christian theology, and Enlightenment rationalism." It is a crucial contribution because it carries the connotation of collective agency or "group identity," and thus allows for gender solidarity as well as many other contingent, voluntary associations, yet never forgets that the modern individual, the "humanist self," will remain as an indispensable moment of the newer "social self." This "double strategy" of annulling *and* preserving the older model of selfhood produces a "double consciousness" through which group identities do not exclude individual identity, but rather presuppose it—*and vice versa.*[28]

It follows, I think, that the cultural work or ideological function of twentieth-century feminist theory is to provide a crucible of citizenship and national pride for American women who know that *as individuals* they bear the same rights as men but who also know that they are not the equals of men unless they organize *as women*; in other words, the cultural politics they practice—the "politics of difference"enabled by gender solidarity—becomes the condition of what Rorty calls "real politics." And so, once again, we are left wondering why he insists that these are the terms of an either/or choice.

Tragedy or Comedy?

The easy way to answer this question, and my previous question about the Kierkegaardian quality of Rorty's Hegelianism, is to cite his roots in the "reformist Left" of the 1930s and 1940s, when, as he tells the story, the New Deal coalition was launched and "real politics"—issues of "economic arrangements"—were meanwhile engaged as the immediate results of an alliance between left-wing intellectuals and the reawakened labor movement. An answer along these biographical lines would suggest that he cannot seem to forget the culture that produced him; either/or choices ("Which side are you on?") did, after all, seem to proliferate back then. But the easy answer would make Rorty an uninteresting prisoner of the Popular Front: when he insists on "real politics" as against cultural politics, for example, we would hear only echoes of Mike Gold denouncing V. F. Calverton or Kenneth Burke, and when he insists on pragmatism as against Marxism, we would hear only echoes of the Party hacks who tried to peddle communism as "twentieth-century Americanism."[29]

A better answer can be found, I think, in the valorization of the New Deal coalition, especially the cross-class alliance between intellectuals and organized workers, which American historians have recently offered as the left-liberal antidote to the "Reagan Revolution" of the 1980s and the Republican resurgence of the 1990s; for this historiographical movement has both reanimated and validated the political choices of Rorty's intellectual infancy. As always, the return of the repressed requires a new stage of development as a condition of its enunciation and elaboration. In this case, the new stage of development is the passage beyond the New Deal coalition registered by the party realignments and social-cultural changes of the 1960s—or rather the passage that now appears in historical narratives not as a normal phase in the maturation of the body politic but as a degenerative disease from which there is no promise of recovery without a return to the more vigorous habits of its youth. The diagnostic consensus produced by these narratives is starkly summarized by Nelson Lichtenstein, one of Rorty's colleagues (and crucial sources), in an interview with a *New York Times* reporter: "The whole anti-capitalist, anti-racist impulse in American life, which reached its apogee in the 1930s and 40s, is on the line."[30]

In view of the civil rights movement, the women's movement, and the broader cultural revolution of the 1960s, Lichtenstein's periodization of leftist impulses should sound truly bizarre. It has nonetheless become the predominant periodization among professional historians—we might even say that Rorty is merely following their lead. Let us see how and why this is so, and then see what happens when we recast the *form* of their narratives, that is, when we rewrite twentieth-century American history as comedy rather than tragedy.

Generally speaking, modern American historians maintain their critical stance toward the powers that be (whatever they may be) by positing a moment in the past when there was an opportunity to slow or to stop the juggernaut of capitalist accumulation, and thus to democratize American society; this moment functions, then, as the historical origin of ethical-cum-political alternatives to the oligarchic present, that is, as the empirical evidence of such alternatives, and thus as a good reason to keep hoping for deliverance from evil. Since the Progressive Era and the advent of so-called progressive historiography, the two moments that have most consistently served these purposes are the populist revolt of the 1890s and the labor-led reforms of the 1930s. In the first, a biracial alliance of farmers and workers aimed to abort the emergence of corporate capitalism by abolishing "the trusts"; when this alliance was defeated by the creatures of corporate capital, the segregation and commodification rather than the democratization of American society inevitably followed. The twentieth century appears in such perspective as the non-heroic residue of tragedy. In the second moment, the promise of the first was almost redeemed by workers who organized new industrial unions that did not exclude black workers, by their supporters among radical, left-wing intellectuals, and by the "trust-busting" trajectory of the New Deal; but when workers gave up on their demands for control of the workplace, when intellectuals turned away from the unions (or the masses), and when the New Deal's anti-corporate animus expired, American society reached another "end of reform." Consumer culture and political passivity inevitably followed, at least for the masses. For the remainder of the century—except for one brief, shining moment in the *early* 1960s, when the New Left had not yet taken to the streets and the cultural Left had not yet taken up "identity politics"—the "anti-capitalist, anti-racist impulse in American life" seems to have disappeared.

In this view of the twentieth century, which is drawn from the influential narratives on which Rorty relies, and which is corroborated in recent books by Alan Brinkley, Gary Gerstle, Steve Fraser, and Michael Kazin, the "Populist moment" and the New Deal era function as comic relief in an epic tragedy.[31] A happy ending can be arranged, moreover, only if the militantly anti-capitalist spirit of the 1930s is conjured by a new alliance of organized labor and left-wing intellectuals, that is, by the kind of class-based politics which can change existing "economic arrangements." The regulative assumption of this approach is of course that there is no socialism in the United States and for that matter in the rest of the world. It follows that the only recourse for the American Left is to adopt a more or less populist political idiom, through which an anti-corporate sensibility can be cultivated and a strong welfare state can be reinstated. Kazin is more explicit than the others in promoting Populism as the last best hope of the Left, but all of them are deeply skeptical of the "rights-based liberalism" that emerged in the aftermath of the New Deal because, while it "sought to extend civil rights to minorities, women, and others previously excluded from the mainstream," as Brinkley points out, it also departed from an earlier "reform liberalism" that concentrated on "broad efforts to reshape the capitalist economy." To be more precise, they are deeply skeptical of the new, postwar liberalism because it betrayed the "essentially democratic aspirations" embedded in the "anti-monopoly" reform tradition shared by Populism and Progressivism—the tradition animated by "a belief that the public interest would best be served by ensuring that the institutions of the economy remained accountable and responsive to popular needs and desires."[32]

Among the ironies produced by this diagnostic consensus is the rehabilitation of the Progressive historiographical paradigm, the intellectual device by which historians long ago learned to define "big business" as a cancerous growth on the body politic, to treat the large corporations that emerged at the turn of the century as the obvious enemy of reform, and thus to naturalize class formation and struggle. In Progressive historiography, class superseded race as the central category in narratives of the American past. But the price of such intellectual progress was, and is, a certain blindness to the crucial role of business *in* reform. The corrective to this blindness was supplied by the counter-progressive (or "consensus") historiography of the late 1950s and 1960s, which proposed that by the end of the nineteenth century, *all* social classes and strata, including businessmen large and small, understood that the central social question of their time was not whether but how to reconstruct and regulate the market, that is, how to reform the market society inherited from the past rather than let it disintegrate. In most counter-progressive accounts of the 1970s and 1980s, however, the relation between business enterprise and reform was construed as ironic, as a transaction to be grasped as "co-optation," for their authors—all of them alumni of the New Left—continued to assume that neither small businessmen nor corporate leaders could have a vested interest in market regulation supervised by "positive government." In counter-progresssive perspective, therefore, the emergence and consolidation of corporate capitalism, circa 1890–1930, still looked pretty much the way it had in Progressive historiography, like the first act of the bitter tragedy called the twentieth century.[33]

Since the 1980s, we have been forced to get beyond this irony and to rethink the relation between business enterprise and reform, perhaps because we can finally see, in the aftermath of the events of

1989–90, that markets are the necessary (not the sufficient) condition of pluralist democracy in any and every sense. We can accordingly acknowledge what remained invisible to the Progressive historians and what remains unthinkable to Richard Rorty and the historians on whom he relies—that the relation between the large corporations and social-political progress ("essentially democratic aspirations") cannot be construed as self-evidently antithetical, as it was, and is, in the "anti-monopoly" tradition most poignantly expressed in American Populism (or rather in neo-progressive historiography). We can, for example, acknowledge that the socialization of markets, which Joseph Schumpeter defined as the entering wedge of socialism as such, is an imperative issued from the private sector as well as the public sector; for the anarchy of completely competitive markets is anathema to private corporations as well as public officials. Everyone except Jeffrey Sachs—the Harvard economist who has almost single-handedly ruined the Russian economy—wants and needs to modulate the unruly forces of the market in the name of a more broadly social or political purpose. We can also follow Karl Marx, of all people, in acknowledging that the rise of the large corporations (what he called modern "joint-stock companies") announced a "phase of transition to a new form of production" organized around "social property." He meant that the separation of ownership and control specific to the management of corporate assets signified "the abolition of capital as private property within the boundaries of capitalist production itself," because when "the mere manager, who has no title whatever to the capital, whether by borrowing or otherwise, performs all real functions pertaining to the investing capitalist as such, only the functionary remains and the capitalist disappears from the production process as a superfluous person." In short, he meant that the modern corporations were the conditions, not the negation, of socialism.[34]

To follow the lead of Schumpeter and Marx would not require that we declare the United States a soviet republic, or that we become Marxists, or that we dismiss the "Populist moment" and its distant echoes as rest stops on the long march toward scientific socialism. It would, however, require that we acknowledge actually existing *left-wing* alternatives to the "anti-monopoly" tradition— among them the cultural or identity politics sponsored by the so-called new social movements—and realize that these alternatives are not diversions from the "real politics" invented by the New Deal coalition but are rather harbingers of a civilization that derives its ethical principles and political programs from something other than "economic arrangements." It would accordingly require that we narrate twentieth-century American history as something more than the non-heroic residue of tragedy, that is, as if there is still socialism in the United States.

To narrate the American century in the pragmatic, comedic terms I am proposing would be to argue that since the militant, class-bound postures of the past are not the only sources of political progress in the present, the Old Left cannot be granted a monopoly on reform in the future. But since our choice is not class *or* gender, class *or* race, the newer Lefts should not aspire to an oligopolistic control of ideological supply. Instead, their adherents should try to keep the conversation going between Richard Rorty and Andrew Ross, between Sidney Hook and Anne Phillips, between Harold Cruse and Mike Gold, between John Dewey and Karl Marx, between Progressive and counter-progressive historiography, between liberals, populists, feminists, black nationalists, and socialists. They should try to keep their "double consciousness" intact by avoiding or postponing the either/or choices Rorty wants them to make. By doing so, they will maintain the party of hope's majority.

Appendix: Memo to the Cultural Left, or, How to Be "Critical of 'the System' and Crazy about the Country"

An American Left that ignores Richard Rorty's arguments will someday be able to congratulate itself on its exceptional purity, but it will by then be confined to the higher circles of higher education. And yet I can't imagine that my colleagues—the left-wing academics and intellectuals who compose his most influential audience— will be persuaded by these arguments. What is the difference, they will ask, between "American national pride" and missionary faith in a "city upon a hill" that stands not only as example to the world but as savior of the world? Didn't the erasure of this difference fuel the Cold War, and thus cause the Vietnam War, and so create a New Left that was incapable of pride in the American political tradition? As critics of the national myths that have inspired imperial adventures from Luzon to Managua, how can we stop speaking "truth to power"? To his credit, Rorty not only welcomes such questions, he asks them: "Granted that the Vietnam War was an atrocity of which America must always be ashamed, does this mean that the Cold War should not have been fought?" (57) He wants to engage the Left that can't yet understand how Alfred Kazin could claim to be "both critical of 'the system' and crazy about the country."[35]

Rorty designates Whitman and Dewey as the left-Hegelian prophets of a secularized "national pride." He thinks they can teach us how to measure the moral progress that is still possible by means of "piecemeal reform within the framework of a market economy" (15–33, 105–7). These two are inspired choices, in my view, for they did take the commodity form as their point of departure, and they did assume, correctly I think, that markets were the necessary condition—not the sufficient condition, and not the solvent—of democracy.[36] But it is not enough to say that Whitman and Dewey cast off all religious and transcendental criteria in defining their hopes for an American nation, as for example: "For both Whitman and Dewey, the terms 'America' and 'democracy' are shorthand for a new conception of what it means to be human—a conception which has no room for obedience to non-human authority, and in which nothing save freely achieved consensus among human beings has any authority at all" (18). It is not enough because we know that reason and revelation are not antithetical modes of apprehending, or changing, the world, and because we know that people don't try to reach consensus unless they have purposes beyond reaching consensus. So we need to think about the continuum that conjoins these different ways of seeing, or rather being in, the world—as James Kloppenberg insists, we need to "acknowledge that the American political and cultural tradition has been shaped by the constant interaction of religious and secular passions and ideals." Otherwise we have excluded too many people from our conception of America, and, for that matter, of humanity. We also need to think about our purposes for reaching consensus, to ask whether they are consistent with justice. Otherwise we have reduced the meaning of democracy to majority rule. Since Rorty invokes the notion of "social justice" as the exclusive property, in every sense, of the Left, he understands this latter concern (18). But he is so determined to avoid a fixed or metaphysical standard by which to assess American achievement that his argument in favor of "national pride" begins to sound like an argument in favor of the methods or principles specific to pragmatism—in effect, the argument becomes theoretical, even philosophical, and thus unconvincing (e.g., 27–31).[37]

If Rorty still wants to engage those who can't yet understand Alfred Kazin's comic ambivalence, he will, I believe, have to develop a different idiom. In my view, a less abstract, more historical idiom is the most promising of those available, mainly because it is the medium in which the New Left and its successors have typically pressed their complaints against nationalism as such. An argument for "American national pride" presented in the idiom I recommend—or, as I would prefer, a historically grounded argument for faith in the American political tradition—would pivot on the claim that the Left, here as elsewhere, has a great deal to learn from the varieties of nationalism in the United States. Understood historically, they appear as commitments regulated by a constitutional tradition (that is, as assumptions and practices that require but cannot be reduced to constitutional procedure or jurisprudence), as commitments that typically include the ethical principle of equality enunciated in the Declaration of Independence, and that honor the central principle of American politics: the sovereignty of the people "out of doors," not the state or its agents.

We can scrutinize this claim from two angles. One way to look at it is to see that since the rise of the abolitionists in the 1830s, the social movements that matter in the U.S. have been animated by what Arjun Appadurai, an eminent anthropologist and a savage critic of nationalism, associates exclusively with a "queer nation," that is, by a "patriotism totally divorced from party, government, or state." The civil rights movement that comes of age in the postwar period is probably the best example of what I mean here, but the labor movements of the nineteenth and twentieth centuries can also demonstrate the claim. Insofar as we acknowledge that modern women's movements appeal to constitutional principle or precedent in defending the rights of females, they, too, might serve the same purpose; for such appeals more often than not seek to protect rights of privacy or individual autonomy as against the powers of husbands, fathers, and governments, and in doing so they broaden both the meaning of individualism and the composition of the body politic. All of these movements began by imagining a community that lives up to the principles on which the American nation was explicitly founded—by expanding the social boundaries of that nation, by dismantling its silent but effective exclusions, by complicating its internal articulation. And all of them have remained firmly committed to the supremacy of society over the state, that is, to the sovereignty of the people.[38]

Another way to look at my claim is more removed from contemporary events, but it can return us to the present with a usable political past. I will restate it by saying that the promise of American nationalisms resides in the constitutionally determined capacity of American politics to preclude a racialized *national* identity. That capacity derives, in my view, from the anti-majoritarian purposes and democratic consequences of the original constitutional design, particularly the division of labor *within* the legislative branch, and the equation of "person" and "citizen" posited—not realized, but posited—in the Fourteenth Amendment. Let us work backward from 1868, when this amendment was ratified, toward "original intent." The Fourteenth Amendment repudiated the infamous *Dred Scott* decision of 1857, in which a five-to-four majority of the Supreme Court had held that slaves and their descendants, emancipated or not, could never become citizens of any state. By doing so, that is, by restricting the scope of states' rights in defining citizenship, by expanding the compass of due process of law, by drawing every *person* into the ambit of federal jurisdiction, and in these ways proscribing a racialized notion of citizenship, the Fourteenth Amendment created a modern, unitary nation-state out of what had been a loose confederation, a "union" of states. And this is the *nation*—the imagined community in which no person could be denied the equal protection of the laws—to which the civil rights movement always appealed, even, or especially, while engaging in acts of civil disobedience. It is also, and not incidentally, the inchoate, impending, immanent nation to which Abraham Lincoln refers four times in the 271 words of the Gettysburg Address, the nation once conceived in liberty and dedicated to the proposition that "all men are created equal," the nation now and always hereafter in need of a new birth of freedom.[39]

As Lincoln understood, the original constitutional design sanctioned slavery. How then can anyone claim (following Lincoln) that the capacity of American politics to preclude a racialized national identity derives from that design (quite apart from the fact that the

Constitution makes no mention of race in defining the rules of apportionment)? Let us look at it from the standpoint of the designer, James Madison, a slaveholder from Virginia. As he saw it, his task was to construct a framework for popular government that did not rest on the social foundation stipulated by the theorists of earlier republics and city-states, from Aristotle to Machiavelli to Montesquieu—that is, on the foundation of a homogenous or relatively undifferentiated population. Madison knew that a modern republic could not escape the social divisions and conflict brought by historical time (the time rendered intelligible by the metaphor of "commerce"), so he tried to incorporate such division and conflict into the very structure of the body politic. To "extend the sphere" of the American republic, he claimed, would be to multiply the interests, factions, and classes contending for the allegiances of the electorate and the larger public. Thus the formation of majorities would become more difficult as the population became more diverse, more divided.[40]

Madison believed that to make majority formation more difficult in this manner was not to thwart but to preserve popular government—*and he was right.* For the exercise of state power in the name of the people cannot be justified by reference to the power of numbers any more than it can be justified by reference to the power of money or intellect or weaponry.[41] To put it in modern parlance, the cause of democracy cannot be served when a majority uses its power of greater numbers to oppress a minority. When white majorities disenfranchised and terrorized the black minority in the American South long after the Civil War and Reconstruction, for example, the cause of democracy was betrayed. It was finally redeemed by that minority's insistence on simple justice—on the consent of those governed by law—as the condition of legitimate state power.

The postponement of majorities in the increasingly diverse and extensive republic meant that debate over rival goods, and dialogue between different interests, factions, and classes, could be sustained over the very long run. What Rorty's "cultural Left" calls the omnipresent Other was "domesticated," if you will, in Madison's design; unless it continued to generate internal differences, he surmised, the nation in which the people were supposed to be sovereign could not survive. So his use of historical time or change as the device by which the United States would avoid either/or choices between rival goods, interests, factions, or classes was not an accident. According to Madison, there were "two cardinal objects of government, the rights of persons and the rights of property." At the outset of the American Revolution, he told Jefferson, there was no reason to distinguish between these "two classes of rights," and most observers of the 1780s continued to believe that they would be "more and more identified." But "experience and investigation" had proved them wrong, he declared in 1787: "in all populous countries, the smaller part only can be interested in preserving the rights of property." So the conflict between "the Class with property and the Class without property" was inevitable, and the class without property—the working class—would someday become the majority.[42]

Madison therefore proposed not only to separate the powers of the three branches of government, but to divide the legislative branch against itself, so that each forum would become the effective (not necessarily the exclusive) representative of one class of rights, either the rights of persons (the House) or the rights of property (the Senate). In this way, he made the impending conflict of classes irresolvable at the national level of government; which is to say that his constitutional design precluded a nation defined in terms of class, however much it might be divided by class. Political accomplishment or innovation at the national level of government would require cross-class coalitions; by the same token, the nation itself could not evolve or develop except as a cross-class construction, as an increasingly inclusive representation of the sovereign people in all their variety.[43]

I belabor Madison's design because doing so lets us appreciate the argument Benedict Anderson proposes in *Imagined Communities*, that "dreams of racism actually have their origins in ideologies of class" rather than in ideologies of nationalism. If we suppose that he is correct, it follows that by postponing majorities, by promoting class formation but preventing any conclusion to class conflict at the national level of government, Madison's original constitutional design made a racialized national identity unlikely if not impossible. Of course that design could not and did not preclude persistent "dreams of racism," or for that matter the proliferation of ideologies of class. But the new nation predicted in 1863 and announced in 1868 did ultimately allow John Dewey to suggest—correctly, I think—that, *as amended and enforced by social movements stridently claiming, "out of doors," to speak for a nation still in the making*, the constitutional tradition of the U.S. had enabled a "separation of nationality from citizenship." Here is how he elaborated on this suggestion: "Not only have we separated the church from the state, but we have separated language, cultural traditions, all that is called race, from the state—that is, from the problems of political organization and power. To us, language, literature, creed, group ways, national culture, are social rather than political, human rather than national interests."[44]

To translate Dewey's suggestion into an idiom accessible to the contemporary American Left would, I think, be to say that because the U.S. has developed as, or into, a nation of nations, we can read its history as a tattered but still legible map of a transnational, post-imperialist future. The study of American nationalisms would then serve as a guide to the larger Left, here and elsewhere, as it tries to follow Slovoj Žižek's advice and learns "to invent forms of political practice that contain a dimension of universality beyond Capital."[45] But this is a way of saying that what the American Left needs for now is not a greater pride in the nation's many pasts but a more rigorous and inclusive historical consciousness of them. What it needs is the capacity to learn from—not just about—those pasts.

Part 2.

Escaping the

"Economy

of Heaven":

William James

at the Edges

of Our Differences

Hamlet, James, and the Woman Question

Reinstating the Vague

When I first started lecturing on pragmatism in undergraduate courses—this was in 1990—I had the good
fortune to be hounded by an extremely intelligent and
able student named Andrew Schroeder. He was a
junior political science major who had been reading
Horkheimer and Adorno and Benjamin for three years
by the time he landed in my intellectual history class,
"American Thought Since 1850." In fact, we knew
each other because he had already taken a European
intellectual history course that I ended up teaching for
a colleague who had fallen ill. But by the time he
enrolled in "American Thought," each of us was
trying to convert the other to his cause. He wanted to
show me—and the undergraduates who might, in
their ignorance of the Frankfurt School, be seduced by
William James—that pragmatism was the most insidious kind of "instrumental reason." I wanted to show
him that he was merely recapitulating the logic of the
frontier by repudiating the intellectual tradition that
comes of age, for better or worse, in the work of
James, Jane Addams, and John Dewey.

Luckily, neither of us quite convinced the other, or
converted the ready-made audience of undergraduates

to his way of thinking. But we did unconsciously collaborate on an after-class epiphany that changed us both by illuminating our disagreements. Andrew approached me after a particularly spirited class discussion of radical empiricism, the philosophical edifice James intended to build on the cornerstone of pragmatism. Andrew said, "So, pragmatism is not really a philosophy in its own right, it's just a way of reading other philosophies. Like it stands between them or something—it has nothing to say unless philosophers have already disagreed." And without thinking, I said, "Yes, that's exactly right." I suppose I was remembering what James said in Lecture 2 of *Pragmatism*: "It has no dogmas, and no doctrines save its method. As the young Italian pragmatist Papini has well said, it lies in the midst of our theories, like a corridor in a hotel."[1]

Well, Andrew thought he had finally won the argument, and I thought I had finally gotten through to him. He thought, "Now we can start talking about reification," and I thought, "Now he'll stop talking about reification." We were both right, as it turned out. We found that to treat pragmatism as a protocol of reading and reconciling discordant traditions—to treat it as James did, as a "mediating way of thinking"—was to make it *useful*. For both of us, it became a way of postponing either/or choices, of prolonging debate, of preserving the other's point of view in reaching our conclusions. Pragmatism, so conceived, was not erudite expedience: it was not a cynical compromise between rationalism and empiricism, not a practical program for splitting the difference between Kant and Hume. It was instead the relation between them convened by a narrative voice in which rationalism and empiricism could appear as commensurable moments in the same story—the story in which the verifiable experience of temporal discontinuity served as self-evident proof of *both the existence and the absence* of transcendent or universal truths. Pragmatism was not the *product* of the relation between these positions, it was the *relation itself*. I mean that pragmatism now looked like discourse rather than doctrine—it was not so much a new event in the story of Western philosophy as a new way of relating, of narrating, previous events.[2]

I begin with this scene from the classroom because it demonstrates that pragmatism can help us to postpone either/or choices. By revisiting it, I mean, of course, to praise pragmatism. But the critics of pragmatism have always cited the same spirit of hesitation to prove that it fails as both moral philosophy and critical theory—

to prove that it is instrumental or technocratic or scientistic in the worst sense because it can specify effective means to almost any imaginable end, but cannot discriminate between ends. By their account, pragmatism conforms and contributes to what the film historian Robert B. Ray has called "the general pattern of American mythology: the denial of the necessity for choice." Ray is worth quoting at length because when he defines this general pattern of mythology as a species of "frontier ideology," as a variation on the theme of exceptionalism, he echoes both the early critics of pragmatism—especially Lewis Mumford, who treated James's pluralism as the "animus of the pioneer, translated into dialectic"—and their intellectual heirs among the critics of mass society, bureacratic rationality, and consumer culture:

> Transposed into the promise of endless economic growth, the frontier theory provided the rationale for postponing internal reforms (via civil rights or welfare legislation). As the Monroe Doctrine or the Open Door Policy, it prompted repeated American interventions abroad. As the doctrine of common sense, it encouraged active, pragmatic, empirical lifestyles at the expense of contemplative, aesthetic, theoretical ones.[3]

I want to show that these critics are wrong—that the postponement of either/or choices in pragmatism is a strength, not a weakness, and that we have something to learn from its characteristically double consciousness, its "mediating way of thinking." My procedure, in keeping with the pragmatist habit of reinstating the vague, will be rather indirect. I begin by suggesting that the "Hamletism" of late-nineteenth-century intellectuals can be taken almost literally in the case of William James—that Hamlet's situation is reproduced in James's breakdown of 1868–72 and that Hamlet's solution to the epistemological crisis revealed at Elsinore is replicated in James's repeated efforts to escape, or adjourn, the dualisms of epistemology as such. I go on to suggest that the "ontological window" through which he glimpsed an alternative to his father's intellectual dominion was an answer to the "woman question." In concluding, I will suggest that if we look over his shoulder, we can see a new relation between pragmatism and feminism in the making; for the method born of James's brush with madness can accommodate the desublimation of female desire specific to the late nineteenth century, and so can articulate new models of genuine selfhood, new forms of abstract subjectivity.

Let me begin, then, with Hamlet. In characterizing his situation and his solution, I rely on two unlikely allies, Ned Lukacher and Alasdair MacIntyre. In *Primal Scenes*, Lukacher convincingly claims that the motive force of the play is Gertrude's utterly scandalous behavior in the aftermath of her husband's death: rather than observe the normal conventions of mourning, she immediately marries the king's brother. Hamlet's "psychopathic predisposition" is created by this "spectacle of feminine desire"; for his own experience of mourning, of remembering and incorporating the intangible figure of the father, cannot commence until he comes to terms with the feelings of sexual rivalry and longing triggered by his mother's intemperance. Which is to say that he cannot accredit and act on the Ghost's account of past events—he cannot become his father's son—until he understands how his mother's body could have become "sullied flesh." Lukacher summarizes the argument as follows:

> There can be no denial that Hamlet's initial response to the specta-
> cle of feminine desire is misogyny and an impulse to matricide. . . .
> [But] Hamlet's uniqueness inheres in the fact that he is not simply
> horrified by the realization that feminine desire is not synonymous
> with maternal desire. . . . What separates Hamlet from Orestes is the
> fact that the "old mole" of feminine desire burrows beyond the
> depths of Oedipal revenge and toward a new abstract subjectivity;
> for Hamlet is the first character in Western literature to be able to
> reflect upon the nature of his subjectivity, to look at it as if from out-
> side himself and reflect not simply on the content of that subjectiv-
> ity but on its capacity for self-reflection. Shakespeare goes beyond
> the Oedipal structure of revenge tragedy to ponder the relation
> between feminine desire and abstract subjectivity, for it is precisely
> in the discursive space that has been opened up by the feminine that
> Hamlet is able to represent himself to himself in an entirely new way.

For all his homage to deconstruction, Lukacher is a profoundly Hegelian thinker: the chapter in which this passage appears is called "Shakespeare in the Ear of Hegel." So it is not surprising that he concludes his reading of *Hamlet* by invoking the progress of the Spirit in history: "What *Hamlet* demonstrates above all is that the absolute spirit as will can only define itself in relation to feminine desire. The will appears in the unlikely form of unchecked female passion before passing into and thus creating the space of abstract subjectivity."4 I will be borrowing this Hegelian perspective to suggest that the progress of the Spirit in the late nineteenth century is similarly determined, or permitted, by the desublimation of female desire and by the recapitulation of Hamlet's itinerary in the thought and character of William James.

But before we follow him to the edge of the abyss, we need to let MacIntyre remind us that "an epistemological crisis is always a crisis in human relationships"; for if we cannot make ourselves intelligible to others because we have chosen to represent ourselves in terms that no one else can take for granted, as Hamlet did in pursuit of a narrative that would make sense of what happened *before* he arrived at Elsinore, we risk the diagnosis *and* the experience of madness. We risk complete isolation, that is, from the objects and the sources of our desire. According to MacIntyre, "the form of epistemological crisis encountered by ordinary agents"—by people who aren't trained in philosophy—is the result of realizing that there are rival interpretations of the *very same* events, utterances, gestures, and behaviors which yield *incompatible* accounts of what is really going on. MacIntyre specifies *Hamlet* as the "classic study" of this form of epistemological crisis. From his standpoint, the problem the prince faces is a surfeit of plausible yet mutually exclusive narratives, each of which entails deadly consequences:

> Hamlet arrives back from Wittenberg with too many schemata available for interpreting the events at Elsinore. . . . There is the revenge schema of the Norse sagas; there is the renaissance courtier's schema; there is a Machiavellian schema about competition for power. But he not only has the problem of which schema to apply; he also has the other ordinary agents' problem: whom now to believe? His mother? Rosencrantz and Guildenstern? His father's ghost? Until he has adopted some schema he does not know what to treat as evidence; until he knows what to treat as evidence he cannot tell what schema to adopt.

The resolution of this epistemological crisis is the result of a narrative that treats each schema, every existing account, as an event that can be explained. Hamlet's "solution" is then to suspend belief in these inherited schemata so that he can construct a narrative that lets us understand why he began by believing them, but also how he came to know that they had led him into error—a narrative that treats existing accounts as both plausible and inadequate. That suspension of belief is, however, rather difficult. It means, among other things, that Hamlet cannot depict himself to others in terms they will expect and understand unless he is willing to become deceitful as well as ironic almost to the point of madness, where there is no transparent relation between "seems" and "is." So he has to find a new way to *make himself intelligible*—he has to produce a narrative that contains but also exceeds existing accounts of Denmark's decay.[5]

No wonder "Hamletism" pervaded the culture of Victorian America, when every inversion of received tradition could be called progress and yet the future could not be named except by the authors of so-called utopias. According to George Cotkin, the author of an intriguing and insightful book on James as a public philosopher, "the figure of Hamlet had come to serve as a cultural commonplace" by the late nineteenth century, when the prince became "a trope expressive of the dangers of the divided self, the individual so consumed by uncertainty that he or she was incapable of sustained or directed activity." Cotkin goes even further, to claim that "Hamlet was the 'old mole' who kept resurfacing in James's reading and thought" of the late 1860s—just as the sources of the impending breakdown began to take symptomatic forms—and to conclude that James "came to construct and interpret his life along the culturally inscribed lines of Hamlet."[6]

To examine this breakdown from the standpoint provided by Lukacher, MacIntyre, and Cotkin is, I think, to see that James experienced the crisis in his relationship to his father as an epistemological crisis that demanded an answer to Hamlet's question (how can I tell what is going on here?) but more importantly that we need to notice its sexual dimensions or connotations if we are to understand its origins and effects —including its effects on epistemology, of all things. There is of course ample precedent for grasping the psychological problem of becoming William James as an intellectual and ideological agenda. Stuart Hampshire calls James the "first truly modern philosopher" precisely because he tried self-consciously and systematically to "project [his] inner conflicts and anxieties upon the universe." And yet Howard Feinstein's brilliant biography, which is the most comprehensive and sophisticated psychoanalytical treatment of James, makes no mention of sexuality or sexual anxiety in explaining the pivotal events of his breakdown. Instead it focuses on the vocational dimensions of an overtly Oedipal struggle between father and son.[7]

Father and Son

So let us see what happens when we notice the function of female sexuality or desire in the son's conflicts with his father, and in his anxieties about his mother. There are three distinct episodes in James's breakdown.[8] The first occurred in the winter of 1867–68, when by his own account, written from Germany, he was continually on the verge of suicide. The second was the "great dorsal collapse," as he called it, of early 1870, when he was back in Cambridge but still trying to evade the life of the laboratory scientist for which his Harvard education had prepared him. The third was a moment soon after, which he recounted thirty years later, in another's voice, as a case study in *The Varieties of Religious Experience*. In each instance, the struggle between James and his father is conducted obliquely, at a distance, but the point of difference between them is quite obvious: one is vigorously defending a "philosophy of marriage" in which the body of the wife, the woman, and the mother disappears, the other is inadvertently inventing a marriage of philosophies in which no body's desires can be ignored.

When I say that this difference between William and Henry Sr. is "quite obvious," I don't mean that everyone has noticed it. Two recent readings of the relevant texts conclude, in fact, by claiming that William remains faithful to his father's rendition of the female.[9] Let us turn, then, to these texts, to see where William stood, and where he was headed as a result.

We can begin to understand the differences between father and son by recalling what E. L. Godkin, the editor of the *Nation*, said about Henry James Sr. in 1870: "He has made the philosophy of marriage, one might almost say, a special study." The notoriously obscure and strenuously metaphysical father had indeed made a career of pronouncing on the moral significance of marriage, both in print and on the lecture circuit. In 1848, for example, he translated a tract inspired by Charles Fourier, the utopian socialist, called *Les Amours au phalanstère*, and added a preface in which he claimed that prevailing "erotic institutions and manners" were flawed because, as expressed in the marriage contract, they granted each party "an absolute *property* in the affections" of the other party. By 1852, Henry Sr. had relinquished his utopian credentials, but he was still defending a philosophy of marriage that sanctioned sex as the proper effect of "private affections," of immaterial bonds, not as the physical subjection of wife to husband which could be enforced by law. Then in the late 1860s, in response to increasing agitation on behalf of female suffrage, several sensational court cases, and significant new publications on the "woman question" —by John Stuart Mill, among others—he tried to clarify his doctrine of holy matrimony. This effort produced three essays for the *Atlantic Monthly* which were published in January, March, and June of 1870.[10]

In each of these essays, Henry Sr. insisted that marriage was holy because it established the kind of relation between male and female which let men rise above their bodies, to become something more than unruly, reflexive bearers of desire. Love "is the same in man as in the animal," he claimed, "so long as it remains unchastened by marriage." Here he treated the legal rights conferred by marriage contracts as civilizing forces because they routinized sexual intercourse and thus sublimated male desire:

> The only thing that degrades the relations of the sexes, or keeps it inhuman and diabolic, is, that its sensuous delights are prized above its inward satisfactions or the furtherance it yields to men's spiritual culture. And what marriage does for men, accordingly, . . . is that it dulls the edge of these rapacious delights, of these insane cupidities, by making them no more a flattering concession of privilege, but a mere claim of right or matter of course.[11]

The *Nation* noted that James could reach such conclusions only "by ignoring the existence of such a thing as sexual passion, or treating it simply as 'lust,'" that is, only by assuming that *female* desire was naturally contained by domestic or maternal functions. Henry Sr. replied in a typically apocalyptic manner: "We must either come to regard marriage as a finality—i.e., as existing solely in its own right—or else expect the hideous carnival of crime in which, so far as the sexual relations are concerned, we are now festering, to prolong itself eternally."[12]

The second son, Henry Jr., who had not yet published his first volume of stories, read his father's essays with excited appreciation, and closely followed the subsequent controversy in the *Nation*. The eldest son was no less engaged in the controversy, as we shall see, but he was much less impressed by Henry Sr.'s contributions to it. Just about the time of his "great dorsal collapse" in mid-January 1870, William wrote to his brother: "Father has been writing a couple of articles on 'woman' and marriage in the Atlantic. I can't think he shows himself to most advantage in this kind of speculation."[13] The difference between the sons might be explained by reference to the fact that Henry Sr. began his *Atlantic* series with a consideration of the same two books William had addressed in the *North American Review* of October 1869, in his first substantial publication (and his last publication as such until the recovery of 1872)—these were Horace Bushnell's *Women's Suffrage* and Mill's *Subjection of Women*. In effect, Henry Sr. was prolonging the metaphysical debate that had animated the correspondence of father and firstborn son in late 1867. But it was now a debate about the nature of the "private affections" that conjoined men and women, and it was being conducted in an unmistakably public forum, in the pages of New England's two leading literary magazines.

Let us briefly revisit the scene of the original debate, to see how it broached the question of female desire and led to a public debate that turned on what William called "the animal potency of sex." In September and October 1867, the eldest son challenged the father's metaphysical doctrine in a series of letters written from Berlin, where he hoped to repair his "shattered frame." In the opening salvo, William described himself as "more and more drifting toward a sensationalism closed in by scepticism." He wondered whether his father had anything to say about the relation between the "'natural consititution' of things" disclosed by this sensationalism and the "'spiritual' facts" disclosed by a Swedenborgian theology. Henry Sr. claimed in reply that his son's "metaphysic wit" had been blighted by the "scientific cast" of his thinking—that is, by its enslavement to Nature, its entrapment within a merely "carnal understanding." To attain the perspective of the philosopher, the son, the new man of science, would have to free himself from the bondage of the body:

> We all *instinctively* do the same thing, but the difference between the philosopher and the man of science, between the man who *reflects* and the man who simply *observes*, is, that the former outgrows his intellectual instincts or disavows the bondage of sense, and attains to the exercise of free thought. And the first postulate of free thought is that Nature ... is void of absoluteness, or has no being *in se* but only in the exigencies of our carnal understanding.

In the "puerile" stage of thinking William still indulged, Nature seemed a universal principle because it represented the intersection of subjective and objective, the creation of female and male, the issue of mother and father. "You believe in some universal quantity called Nature," Henry Sr. told his son, "[that is] able not merely to *mother* all the specific objects of sense, or give them the subjective identity they crave to our understanding, but also to *father* them or give them the objective individuality or character they claim in themselves." So the "inward movement" of return to the creator permitted by free thought was blocked by any concession to the "lower, natural, passive, subjective side" of our "natural consciousness"—by any concession to what already carried the dual connotation of embodiment and femininity. Nature was "utterly devoid of life," the father insisted, except as the setting in which "spiritual manhood" was realized: it signified not the trail of the serpent but the "descent of the creator" Himself. To leave science behind, to become a philosopher, was then to leave females behind, to assume that women could not play a role in creation as such, not even as mothers.[14]

William, who never wanted a career in science, wrote a long, thoughtful reply in which he noted the discrepancy between the imperative form and the propositional content of his father's metaphysical perorations. He was "led astray," he noted, by the "positiveness and absoluteness of expression" which animated Henry Sr.'s published essays and private letters alike: "You say that such and such *must* be the way of creation, as if there is some *a priori* logical necessity binding on the mind. This I cannot see at all in the way you seem to." William went on to ask why something could not be substantive, or real, *and* created, that is, "real *as* created," rather than "only phenomenal," merely artifical, as his father insisted it must be. He answered himself by claiming that the body was ingredient in the working of the mind, and vice versa, that nat-

ural or spontaneous consciousness did not preclude "spiritual manhood" or individuality: "Sensation, perception, and reason apparently have their roots in the life of the nervous system, yet their
form is entirely new and original."[15]

William was still apologetic in this letter of late October,
although less so than in his previous letters. He was still trying to
disagree with but not disavow his father's arguments, no matter
how ineffable or indefensible they seemed. Ralph Barton Perry, the
author of the first scholarly biography of William James, claimed
long ago that the eldest son was able to steer this "middle course"
with the help of Goethe. It is a convenient claim for my purposes
because *Wilhelm Meister's Apprenticeship*, the classical bildungsroman organized around the figure of Hamlet, is the text to
which William turned as he moved, in 1868, from Berlin to Teplitz
and then on to Dresden in search of cures for what ailed him. From
Dresden, where he attended a stirring production of *Hamlet*, he
reported to a close friend that getting a glimpse of Goethe's enthu-
siasm was "one of the most important experiences of my own
mind." To Henry Jr., he wrote that he was no longer bothered by
the "incessant cataloguing of individual details," or the "pitiless
manner of taking seriously *everything* that came along" which
characterized Goethe's way into the world. "I smile now to think of
my unhealthiness and weakness," William told his brother, as if his
"shattered frame" had been miraculously restored by reliving Wilhelm Meister's apprenticeship, by rereading *Wilhelm Meister's
Apprenticeship*; he could now profit from what had offended him
in his "raw youth"—that is, from the "objectivity or literalness"
with which Goethe had somehow positioned himself in the world,
so that "*everything* painted itself on his sensorium." Here is how
William summarized what he had learned: "Apart from that general and undefined refreshment and encouragement which accrue
to us from the sight of great resources and possibilities in human
nature of any kind, I have drawn from Goethe a special lesson
lately which is not easy for me to define in black and white, but
which might be called a lesson of theoretical patience and respect
towards the objective."[16]

Now, what distinguishes Goethe's reading of *Hamlet* via
Wilhelm Meister is an attention to the supporting cast, and to
events outside the frame of the play, as plausible sources of dramatic movement. But the *role* of Hamlet is not diminished by that

reading; it is instead magnified because it begins to appear as a kind of register in which rival accounts of the same events intersect. Questions about the prince can accordingly be framed in terms of his narrative function, rather than his "character." This narrative function is what Jacques Lacan had in mind, I think, when he claimed that "Hamlet accepts everything," that he "is constantly suspended in the time of the Other." We might say the same thing about Wilhelm Meister; for, as Friedrich Schiller noted in a letter of 1796, he is the most necessary but not the most important character in Goethe's novel: "Everything takes place around him but not *because of him*: precisely because the things which surround him represent and express energies, and he instead pliability, his relationship with the other characters had to be different from those of the heroes of other novels."[17]

Certainly there is no lack of sexual energies in the female characters Goethe assembles to illustrate his protagonist's "pliability" and, with the very same strokes, to interpret Hamlet's deferral of his desire; indeed the "time of the Other" in which both leading men are suspended is the *narrative* time created, or required, by the words and deeds of the female characters. For example, when Wilhelm Meister explains Ophelia's motivation to Aurelie, the sister of the company's director, by reference to "'ripe, sweet sensuality'"— "'her heart abandoned itself so completely to her desire that her father and her brother [had to] warn her openly'"—the poor girl practically swoons. Aurelie prolongs the original encounter, first with stories of her childhood in a brothel, then with hints at seduction and abandonment, then again with questions about the "'suggestive and indecent nonsense'" Ophelia sings in her madness. Wilhelm's answer reminds us of the source of that madness: "'We know from the very beginning of the play what her mind is full of. The dear child lives quietly for herself, but she is hardly able to conceal her desires and wishes. Lustful tones resound throughout her mind and, . . . when she has lost all control over herself and when her heart is on her tongue, this tongue betrays her.'" This is the same Wilhelm who hears his own father in the voice of the Ghost, and who claims that the marriage of Hamlet's mother "'is even more humbling and wounding'" than the death of his father: "'now he loses his mother as well, and in a fashion worse than if she had been snatched from him by death.'"[18]

Worse than death? Wilhelm's interpretation sounds plausible only if we suppose that the spectacle of female desire is more threatening to the integrity of Hamlet's character than the murder of his father the king. To rethink and remake his integrity—not to retrieve it from the moment *before* his losses—is, however, to treat this spectacle, this threat, as a novel fact that must be confronted and *incorporated* in a new subject position; it appears then as an opportunity to be exploited in the hope of a more inclusive and complex integrity, rather than an obstacle to be avoided in the hope of staying the same, of remaining intact. But it is only by suspending belief in received traditions or inherited narratives, only by deferring any definitive conclusion on the ultimate meaning of his existence, only by postponing either/or choices, that Hamlet can begin to rethink and perhaps remake himself. He is not indecisive; he is instead refusing to choose between previous truth and novel fact. He is constantly revising his own story in light of new evidence.[19]

I think that William James understood *Hamlet* in just this way, and not simply because he was still revising the story of his life long after most of his peers had settled into careers and marriages. "The endless fulness of the play never struck me so before," he told his brother in a letter of April 1868, "It bursts and cracks at every seam." He believed that it somehow contained and criticized the standards of antiquity—what he called "the Classical conception of life & art"—and that in doing so it represented, or summarized, a distinct stage of human development which, like his own age, required explanation in *historical* terms. Here is how he put it in the letter to Henry Jr.:

> The question what is the difference between the Classical conception of life & art & that of wh. Hamlet is an example besets me more & more, and I think by a long enough soaking in presence of examples of each, some light might dawn—And then the still bigger question is: what is the warrant for each? Is our present only a half way stage to another Classical era with a more complete conception of the Universe than the Greek?

So the distance between the harmonies of classical antiquity and the discontinuities of "romantic" modernity was first measured by

Hamlet, the figure who stood at the heart of the changes that eventually enlarged the scale of our cognitive map, the figure who tried—and finally failed—to bridge the gaps these changes created:

> here comes to my "realizing sense" of the chasm between them [between ancient and modern poets] this awful Hamlet, which groans & aches so with the mystery of things, with the ineffable, that the *attempt* to express it [the difference] is abandoned, one form of words [of narrative] seeming as irrelevant as another, and crazy conceits & counter senses slip and whirl around the vastness of the subject, as if the tongue were mocking itself.

This "awful" Hamlet echoes Wilhelm's Ophelia, who was betrayed by her tongue. From his standpoint, James suggested, "action seems idle, and to have nothing to do with the point." He did not doubt what he had to do, only how to do it. For the point was to change the world, but to change it was to reinterpret it.[20]

William James was fortified by his encounter with Shakespeare and Goethe; soon he would return home to "get well." So it is perhaps not accidental that in the same letters from Dresden praising the "sturdy realism" of Goethe and remarking on the genius of Shakespeare's *Hamlet*, he also represents his recovery from depression in terms of two novel facts. One was a tendency toward "an empiristic view of life," the other was a strong attraction to a "young female from New York" who moved into his boarding house and "stirred chords," as he put it, "in [his] desiccated heart." This woman, a "Miss Havens" was in a "hysterical, hypochondriac state," according to James, but she nevertheless made him feel the "hideous waste" of his own life—and not because he could easily differentiate himself from a hysterical woman. "Her mind is perfectly free from sentimentality and disorder of any sort," he reported: "What is beautiful and so to speak absolute and finished about her has struck into me so deeply as quite to rejuvenate my feeling."[21]

The empiricism by which James proposed to pilot his thinking made him uneasy; for it promised to embroil him in more debates with his father—"Already I see an ontological cloud of absolute idealism waiting for me far off on the horizon"—and it threatened to resurrect but not redeem the body. If we assume that the human species is just an agenda of appetites, he wondered, do we have to admit that the "rich and delicate overgrowth of ideas, moral, artistic, religious and social [was] a mere mask, a tissue spun in happy hours by creative individuals and adopted by other men in the interests of their sensations"? If so, how would anyone claim either that bodily urges were irrelevant to the pursuit of happiness or that they required containment in the name of a higher good? James knew these were questions the Utilitarians had raised but could not answer. That is why he he went on to ask, "How long are we to wear that uncomfortable 'air of suppression' which has been complained of in Mr. Mill?" Can we continue to ignore or repress the very sensations on which we have founded our doctrine and, for that matter, our identities? It was a question James would soon be able to address in a public forum.[22]

Difference and Equality

He returned to Cambridge in November of 1868 and completed his medical degree the following June, at about the same time that Mr. Mill's *Subjection of Women* was published simultaneously in London and Philadelphia. James read it immediately, and began writing what proved to be a review essay rather than a "notice" for the *North American Review*. Horace Bushnell's new book, *Women's Suffrage: The Reform against Nature*, became his foil in articulating a position that criticized Mill's premises but endorsed his purposes. In mapping this middle ground, James drew on the reading and thinking he had done in Europe—in March 1869, for example, he announced to a close friend that he was still "swamped in an empirical philosophy" according to which "all is nature *and* all is reason too"—and on a long review of Mill's book in the *Nation* which stressed that "the source of whatever weakness there may be in Mr. Mill's whole argument" was his refusal to acknowledge the "social force" of "sexual attraction" in determining the relations between men and women.[23]

The essay begins by examining Bushnell's rhetorical procedures. James suggests that the author's ornate style, which confounds the reader by its excess of "self-listening," is not accidental or unrelated to the argument; instead it is the form best suited to the book's deeply dogmatic content. Bushnell proposed that women should be afforded opportunities in education and occupation commensurable with their unfolding capacities, but insisted that they should not be allowed to vote or to hold political office; for the exercise of suffrage rights or political power by women would violate the "subject nature" of woman. "This weighty conclusion is derived from a conception of the essential nature of woman," James notes, and remains plausible, or at least consistent with public opinion (the "universal sense of mankind") insofar as its defenders justify it as "a matter of inexplicable sentiment." But of course Bushnell was not willing to leave it at that. He tried instead to illustrate the doctrine of woman's "subordinate nature" by appeal to arguments from what James calls "different orders of consideration"—different, that is, from "inexplicable sentiment." These arguments were themselves sentimental or irrational or "unsound," however, because according to James they ignored the ethical principles or possibilities enabled by "modern civilization"; so they merely emphasized the dogmatic quality of a doctrine that treated the "subject nature" of woman as both premise and conclusion.[24]

The familiar arguments to which Bushnell appealed were that the subjection of women made them morally superior to men, and that if granted the rights of suffrage and political office, they would inevitably forfeit this superiority by their implication in the corruptions of power. James shows that the first argument—he translates it as "suffering is a higher vocation than action"—is incompatible with the principle of *justice* specific to modern civilization, while the second argument is incompatible with the doctrine of woman's essential difference, that is, the doctrine of her natural and ineradicable subjection to man. In both cases, the time is out of joint: historical circumstances have clearly invalidated the principles Bushnell invokes either as self-evident truths, as matters of "inexplicable sentiment," or as conclusions drawn from empirical investigation. On the one hand, these circumstances have made once acceptable hierarchies look arbitrary, and on the other hand they have already projected—or will soon project—women into situations where their supposedly fixed "nature" will inevitably undergo fundamental change.

James quite clearly enjoys poking fun at the reverend Dr. Bushnell, especially when he is able to demonstrate the author's prurient premises: "Terrible hints are given, of the naughtiness to which women will resort in order to procure votes, and the demoralization which will take place in country districts, where the voters, male and female, 'will be piled in huge wagons to be carried to the polls, and will sometimes on their return encounter a storm that drives them into wayside taverns and other like places for the night; where'—but enough; the curious reader may find the rest of the passage on page 149." It seems that men educated "in the school to which Dr. Bushnell belongs" can believe in the moral superiority of woman only so long as they can confine her to places and pursuits that do not permit the expression of female desires, and thus do not require that women make choices between rival goods. James suggests as much in criticizing Bushnell's "two-stool line of argument": "first, a vociferous proclamation of the utter and radical peculiarity of the womanly nature; then a nervous terror of its being altered from its foundations by a few outward changes. Mr. Mill's belief in the power of education is timid in comparison with this."

When James turns to *The Subjection of Women*, the mocking, bemused tone disappears. No careful reader of this essay can conclude that the reviewer favors Bushnell's dogmatism over Mill's radicalism. And yet James does not simply recount and accredit Mr. Mill's beliefs. Instead he tries to show that because they grow from a "sentimental kernel," they are no less susceptible to criticism than Bushnell's "unsound" arguments about the "subject nature" of woman. That kernel, according to James, is the belief that all differences between men and women are unnatural, or artificial, and can—indeed must—be eradicated by education; the "best kind of equality" *between* men and women, or man and wife, thus appears as an "'identity of opinions and purposes,'" not an equal relation of individuals with different opinions and purposes. "This leaves altogether out of sight the mere animal potency of sex," James declares, and creates a "somewhat nervous anxiety to efface even the present distinction[s]" between men and women. Notice that James is not insisting on the validity of separate spheres—that is, on an innate and unyielding difference between the sexes, or on an essential nature of woman. In fact, he has already rejected that position in his remarks on the reverend Dr. Bushnell. He is instead resisting the reduction of female to male which Mill's logic seems to promote. It is a strikingly modern locution because it does not treat "man" as the standard of subjectivity as such, and because it postpones the either/or choice between difference and equality which Mill offers his readers.

To be sure, James invokes the "representative American," a man, in asking if Mill's "personal ideal" could be made real. If this

typical man expected "security and repose" from the marriage relation, his question would be, "Are they easily attainable without
some feeling of dependence on the woman's side, without her rely-
ing on him to be her mediator with the external world?" The
answers James gets from his imagined interlocutors graduate from
the "dogmatic"—here Dr. Bushnell is quoted—to the "half-senti-
mental" to the "skeptical." But he does not align himself with any
of the answers except to suggest, in a skeptical spirit, that Mill's
logic leads to the disturbing conclusion that "the most important
requisite in an astronomer's wife is, that she should have a passion
for astronomy"—that the purpose of marriage is to efface the differences between man and wife.

I have belabored this ten-page book review by the young William
James for two reasons. First, recent feminist readers have mistak-
enly used it to assert that he was a backward Victorian male whose
mature philosophy shows certain traces of residual misogyny; their
mistakes need to be noticed and corrected. For example, Charlene
Haddock-Seigfried, the author of a valuable new book called *Pragmatism and Feminism*, claims that "it is particularly important to
explore just how his sexism affects his appropriation of the feminine," and discovers, in her own exploration, that James "sup-
ported Horace Bushnell's more reactionary book, *Women's
Suffrage*, against John Stuart Mill's more revolutionary book, *The
Subjection of Women*." Alfred Habegger similarly claims that
"William proved himself a loyal son after all"—that he corroborated his father's "philosophy of marriage"—and "clearly sided
with Bushnell" against Mill. I do not want to suggest that there is no
warrant for criticism of James on feminist principles; but I do want
to suggest that this review essay will not serve as such a warrant.[25]

Second, I think that the essay opens up a discursive space for the
figure of the female—or rather for female desire as the source of the
narrative time in which James wants hereafter to remain suspended. In the short term, this opening leads to his breakdown; but
in the long term, I would suggest, it allows for (it does not require)
his mature philosophy, pragmatism, which he presented in lectures
as the woman who "unstiffens all our theories" and which he dedicated, on publication, to John Stuart Mill, the man who objected
to the subjection of women.

The short term was shaped by Henry Sr.'s response to his son's
review of Bushnell and Mill in another public forum, and by

William's new identification with his consumptive cousin Minny Temple. We have already visited the scene of the father's reiteration, where the "insignificance of sex" is again emphasized as the problematic premise of Mill's argument. But we should note in passing that Henry Sr.'s emphasis served a purpose very different from William's. The latter worried that to leave the "animal potency of sex" out of the picture was to permit, perhaps even to require, the erasure of all differences between men and women. The former, the father, suggested that to believe in the "insignificance of sex" was to rob marriage of its great civilizing function, which was precisely the erasure of the key *sexual* differences between men and women. As Henry Sr. put it, "the sole dignity of marriage, practically viewed, lies in its abasing the male sway in our nature, and exalting the feminine in its place." Mr. Mill and Mr. James agreed, in this sense, that the "best kind of equality" was an identity or unity secured by marriage in which any distinction—or even relation—between male and female, or man and wife, was, quite literally, repressed.[26]

William James disagreed with both, and he paid a high price for doing so. Like E. L. Godkin, he believed that sexual desire or attraction was a "social force" that could be neither ignored nor forgotten, in part at least because it was not monopolized by men. Bodies as such were the source and the site of desire, in his view, but they were also the condition—the incentive and the limit—of reason. As he put it in March of 1869, "not a wiggle of our will happens save as the result of physical laws, and yet notwithstanding we are *en rapport* with reason." A few months later, James was less confident about the continuity of body and mind; for he now worried that his own inclinations were blocked by the impending medical career he never wanted, and that his physical condition was declining because he was again "abridging" his own desires. By the end of the year, he could report to his brother that he had "been a prey to such disgust for life during the past three months as to make letter writing almost an impossibility."[27]

The "great dorsal collapse" came early the next year, at the same moment Henry Sr. published his opinions on the woman question according to Bushnell and Mill. The deepening discord between father and son was now on record. Where Henry Sr. saw evil in the selfishness of man's "sway power," and looked to woman's moral superiority for deliverance, William saw it in the form of female desire as well, and tried to make room for it in his "empirical philosophy." The question he kept asking was, if desire and reason are neither antithetical nor identical, but are rather indissoluble—if the wish must be father to the thought—how is the "moral interest" to be preserved? In a set of propositions written while he was reading *The Subjection of Women*, James equates *Man* with "a bundle of desires, more or less numerous," which "exist by mere self-affirmation." How then was any "philanthropic action," any attempt at moral improvement in the face of a real choice between good and evil, possible? "To 'accept the universe,' to protest against it, [are] voluntary alternatives," James answers, "So that in a given case of evil the mind seesaws between the effort to improve it away, and resignation." If the moral problem is that our desires divide us up in time, the solution lies "in taking neither [side] absolutely, but in making the resignation only provisional (that is, voluntary, conditional)." In other words: "Resignation should not say, 'It is good,' 'a mild yoke,' and so forth, but 'I'm willing to stand it for the present.'" This *provisional* resignation amounted to Goethe's "theoretical patience" and corresponded to Hamlet's hard-earned "readiness"; it created the discursive space in which moral progress or improvement became conceivable. As James puts it, "resignation affords ground and leisure to advance to new philanthropic action." But these were not metaphysical propositions. William was hoping to explain how the deferment of his own desires, in accordance with his father's wishes, would not disfigure his future.[28]

The Worst Kind of Melancholy

He returned to the fray in February 1870. By that time his body had betrayed him again. But emotional reinforcement in the struggle against his father had meanwhile appeared in the form of cousin Minny Temple, the orphaned daughter of Henry Sr.'s sister. She had fought openly with her uncle during her visit to Cambridge in November 1869, and this seems to have brought her friendship with cousin Willy to a new level of intimacy; in any event, William revised his opinion of her, and praised "the courage with which she [kept] 'true to her own instincts'" in a letter describing her tumultuous visit. Alfred Habegger goes so far as to suggest that perhaps cousin Willy was driven toward breakdown by the perceived contradition between the "conservative [*sic*] view of womanhood" on display in his *North American Review* essay and his admiration of Minny's "stubborn integrity" in disputing uncle Henry's ideas of spiritual regeneration. I think it is much more likely that the cousins' new intimacy derived from their shared resistance to Henry Sr.'s metaphysics. Minny was a kindred spirit; as she noted in a letter to William dated January 15, 1870, "there is an attitude of mind, (not a strength of intellect by any means) in which we are much alike."[29]

But she did give up the fight momentarily, at this very moment in fact—she decided that maybe uncle Henry was right after all. And then she reverted to her "pagan" views. William, who had identified so strongly with his cousin in her disputes with Henry Sr., reached his lowest point after learning of Minny's defection. "Today I about touched bottom," he wrote in his diary on February 1, 1870. For now there was no one to turn to for help in answering the question of how desire, reason, and morality were related. "I must face the choice with open eyes," he told himself, and then posed it: "shall I *frankly* throw the moral business overboard?" Or could he imagine a "militant existence, in which the ego is posited as a monad, with the *good* as its end, and the final consolation only that of irreconcilable hatred"? He wanted to give this militant alternative a "fair trial." But that meant believing that "though evil slay me, she can't subdue me, or make me worship her. The brute force is all at her command, but the final protest of my soul as she squeezes me out of existence gives me still in a certain sense the superiority." It meant believing that the devil could take the shape of a woman.[30]

Desire as such now began to look more deeply problematic if not dangerous. It could, for example, implicate its bearer in consanguinous relations that threatened to produce "unhealthy offspring," as William reminded his brother Robertson, who wanted, in November 1869, to marry a cousin. He almost certainly reminded himself as well over the next three months. To believe that he must have done so is not to accredit Habegger's speculation regarding the intensity or intimacy of the new relation between William and Minny Temple, although I am willing to do so; it is instead to assume that the simple, innocent embodiment of his increased affection for the female cousin who stood up (but then succumbed) to his father would cause him to think about the "social force" and moral valence of desires expressed as sexual attraction.[31]

So I am suggesting that Minny Temple's visit to Cambridge and subsequent correspondence with William is just as important to his impending breakdown as Habegger would have it, but not because Minny demonstrated how backward her cousin's views on women were; those views were not backward, and his breakdown was not a result of embarassment. I am suggesting that she elicited the sexual anxieties and represented the sexual implications of William's overtly Oedipal struggle with his father—that her ambiguous or intermediate position within and without the James family cast her as an unstable isotope of sister, mother, and wife, as a complex figure that somehow stood between the son and the father by resisting each and attracting both. To mourn for Minny after her death in early March of 1870, as William did, was to incorporate, without thinking, this ambiguity or intermediacy into a personality already riven by debilitating conflict with his father. It was also to realize, again without thinking, that the moral valence of sexual desire was perhaps as "insane" as his father had recently portrayed it.³²

At any rate, William did break down soon after, and did represent his "panic fear" in terms of the dangers of desire. That representation did not appear until 1902, with the publication of the Gifford lectures as *The Varieties of Religious Experience*; and the people who heard James deliver these lectures did not know they were listening to autobiography when he recited his own case as an instance of "the worst kind of melancholy." Howard Feinstein and John Owen King quite rightly see this recitation as a *rewriting* of the father's "vastation," which occurred in 1844; both therefore juxtapose the texts through which the two sufferers recorded their suffering. Feinstein is so insistent on the parallels—for example, Mary James, who was Henry Sr.'s wife and William's mother, "figures prominently in both crisis tales"—that he places the related accounts of father and son side by side in his own text. But he notes that while both father and son originally resisted the impulse to run to Mary James for help, "only William kept to himself to the end."³³

Let us listen to the son's account, and then ask *why* he kept to himself.

> Whilst in this state of philosophic pessimism and general depression of spirits about my prospects, I went one evening into a dressing-room in the twilight to procure some article that was there; when

suddenly there fell upon me without any warning, just as if it came out of the darkness, a horrible fear of my own existence. Simultaneously there arose in my mind the image of an epileptic patient whom I had seen in the asylum, a black-haired youth with greenish skin, entirely idiotic, who used to sit all day on one of the benches, or rather shelves against the wall, with his knees drawn up against his chin, and the coarse gray undershirt, which was his only garment, drawn over them inclosing his entire figure. He sat there like a sort of sculptured Egyptian cat or Peruvian mummy, moving nothing but his black eyes and looking absolutely non-human. This image and my fear entered into a species of combination with each other. That shape am I, I felt, potentially. Nothing that I possess can defend me against that fate, if the hour for it should strike for me as it struck for him. There was such a horror of him, and such a perception of my own merely momentary discrepancy from him, that it was as if something hitherto solid within my breast gave way entirely, and I became a mass of quivering fear. After this the universe was changed for me altogether. I awoke morning after morning with a horrible dread at the pit of my stomach, and with a sense of the insecurity of life that I never knew before, and that I have never felt since. It was like a revelation; and although the immediate feelings passed away, the experience has made me sympathetic with the morbid feelings of others ever since. It gradually faded, but for months I was unable to go out in the dark alone. In general I dreaded to be left alone. I remember wondering how other people could live, how I myself had ever lived, so unconscious of that pit of insecurity beneath the surface of life. My mother in particular, a very cheerful person, seemed to me a perfect paradox in her unconsciousness of danger, which you may well believe I was very careful not to disturb by revelations of my own state of mind. I have always felt that this experience of melancholia of mine had a religious bearing.[34]

To my ears, it is quite clear that William kept to himself because he knew that he was the source of danger to his mother. But what was the danger of which she would have become conscious had he revealed his state of mind to her? That there was a "merely momentary discrepancy," not a significant difference, between William and the black-haired, idiotic youth about whom one could not claim, here "all is nature *and* all is reason too"? "That shape am I, I felt, potentially," he says, not that patient, that person, that youth. This shape appeared "absolutely non-human" because it did not inhabit a body, it just was its body; its apparent inertia was qualified by the connotation of convulsion in the early reference to epilepsy, but its objectivity (it sat on shelves rather than benches) was confirmed by the same reference. And yet it was human after all—the distance between observer and observed was "merely momentary" because it was an *image* that arose in the observer's mind as the expression of a "horrible fear of [his] own existence," a horrible fear, that is, of *himself*. The danger to Mary James was then the possibility that her son could become "that shape" at any time. But what danger would he represent to anyone, let alone his mother, in the seemingly passive condition of an idiotic youth? Again, why would the revelation of the son's "state of mind"—the reproduction of the image produced by his fear of himself—alert her to this danger? Did he know his state of mind was dangerous to her because it contained both desire for and resentment of the figure of the mother, because it now contained matricidal as well as patricidal impulses?

I think so. The danger William James perceived in his mourning and melancholia—in the difficult work of abandoning the dead body but reincorporating the courageous spirit of Minny Temple in a new ego ideal, a new structure of identity—was that the female figure who stood between him and his father could be both the object of his desires and the subject of her own. The issue of female desire that appeared as an intellectual possibility in his writing and thinking of 1869–70, in a more or less public debate with his father on the woman question, reappeared as an emotional reality in the presence and the example of the outspoken Minny Temple, but then again as a psychological problem in the isolation occasioned by her defection to the father and the private torments of mourning that followed her death. James could not solve that problem on his own, with the resources at his command in 1870; to stay suspended in the time of the Other, in the narrative time created or required by the female figures in his life, was now too confusing, too painful, too frightening. Of course he refused the original, matricidal impulse, just as he had refused to repudiate his father's philosophy of marriage; but the "provisional resignation," the "theoretical patience" that allowed him to accept everything *except* his own desires and his own failings, divided him too deeply in 1870. He disintegrated soon after.

But this brush with madness did show James that he had to find a way to make himself intelligible, within his own family and in the broader world as well. The point, as he saw it, was not to reinstate his "abridged" desires by going back to what he was, or wanted, before his father thwarted his career choices, before Minny Temple died, before his breakdown. He tried instead to understand that our quite real losses of innocence, integrity, and loved ones are also opportunities precisely because they divide us up in time—precisely because they let us see our worlds in new ways and create the conditions for the construction of new identities. "Since tragedy is at the heart of us, go to meet it," he wrote in his diary two weeks after Minny's death, "work it in to our ends, instead of dodging it all our days, and being run down by it at last."[35] If nothing will come of ignoring or evading the divisions of time we usually experience as tragedies, there is no reason to abstain from them in the hope of somehow remaining intact, as we were *before* they intervened to obliterate the "always already" in which we still believe. But neither is there any reason to treat these tragedies as external obstacles or events that are impervious to our interpretations—impervious, that is, to our prospective purposes and our retrospective revisions. If we want to, James suggests, we can make them parts of a usable past.

To do so is, however, to defer any definitive conclusion on the ultimate meaning of our existence, to postpone either/or choices, to remain open to novel facts: "the readiness is all," as Hamlet finally put it. But this readiness, this pliability, should not be mistaken for mere uncertainty; for it requires the kind of "theoretical patience" or "provisional resignation" that lets us keep revising the narratives we take most seriously. In the case at hand, William James was able to reopen his mind to the novel fact of female desire. And so it became the "old mole" that burrowed beneath the separate spheres of male and female, beyond the notion of an essential womanly nature, toward a new abstract subjectivity convened in *and as* the changing relation between men and women. In this sense, the intellectual agenda James constructed in the aftermath of his breakdown presupposed the desublimation of female desire; which is to say that the pragmatism he gives us is improbable if not inconceivable in the absence of feminism.

Unstiffening
Our Theories

Pragmatism, Feminism, and the End(s) of Capitalism

The Gender of Modernity

Those readers who value William James are typically admirers of his rhetorical strategies—that is, of his deceptively simple language. So they tend to appreciate and emphasize the metaphors that often carry the weight of Jamesian argument. I am no exception to the rule. In chapter 2, I tried to explain his persistent use of financial metaphors as a clue to his acceptance of a "credit economy" and its (corporate) corollaries, and in other chapters I have mentioned that James pretends pragmatism is the kind of woman who can "unstiffen our theories." At the outset of this last chapter, I want to revisit these primal scenes of pragmatist metaphor. Doing so will allow me to explicate their intellectual implications and thus to introduce two related arguments. First, Judith Butler's theoretical position can best be defended by rewriting its genealogy so that William James rather than Friedrich Nietzsche appears as its locus classicus; here I am taking my cue from Butler's rewrite of Slovoj Žižek in *Bodies That Matter*. Second, the corporate "world of large-scale production" which Teresa Brennan criticizes so forcefully in *History after Lacan* can be seen as the necessary condition of pragmatism and feminism as well as socialism.[1]

We can begin to gauge the importance of gendered metaphors in *Pragmatism* by measuring the radical differences between Frank Lentricchia and Charlene Haddock-Seigfried. In *Ariel and the Police* (1987), Lentricchia argues that James resisted the absolutist urges of "rationalism"—the "totalizing" imperatives of high theory—by treating pragmatism as if it were a woman:

> In an effort to tame theory in the name of pragmatism, James seems to allow himself one theoretical moment, the sentimental essential- ization of mind as Manichean battlefield—a struggle between tradi- tional philosophy, or "theory," a male principle, and "pragmatism" (homage to Anne Hutchinson), which is a woman: the principle that "unstiffens" all theories and makes them useful, and a synonym for "himself" as woman in his untraditional philosophic activity. . . . James's figurative language tells us that pragmatism is a woman, but not identical with the female gender: pragmatism is democratic, pragmatism is Protestant, pragmatism is inseparable from the dream of America.

In *Pragmatism and Feminism* (1996), Haddock-Seigfried claims that, in a 1907 interview with the *New York Times* which summa- rized the principles of pragmatism, James "paint[ed] a picture of the philosopher as a predatory male, one whose attacks are sometimes resisted, sometimes welcomed by a world/woman who literally [*sic*] 'opens herself to others.'" She defends her claim as follows:

> Late in life James is repeating, and thus reinforcing, a masculinist insemination view of how truths are forced upon the world. He had already linked engendering to a submerged rape metaphor in *Prag- matism*, where he explained the creativity of our cognitive as well as our active life in a grammatical trope asserting that we make real additions to the subject as well as the predicate part of reality. He continued: "The world stands ready malleable, waiting to receive its final touches at our hand. Like the kingdom of heaven, it suffers vio- lence willingly. Man engenders truth upon it." From the later reap- propriation [in the interview], we know that in this passage he is also thinking of the world as a *she*, not an it.[2]

It would seem that there is no way to reconcile these readings— both Lentricchia and Haddock-Seigfried can't be right about the meanings of the metaphors deployed in *Pragmatism*. Or can they? Let us have a look at the text itself, to see whether their radical differences can be mediated after all. It is clear, to begin with, that James does designate pragmatism a woman, as for example: "Ought we ever not to believe what is better for us to believe? And can we then keep the notion of what is better for us, and what is true for us, permanently apart? Pragmatism says no, and I fully agree with her." Or again: "You see by this what I meant when I called pragmatism a mediator and reconciler and said, borrowing the word from Papini, that she 'unstiffens' our theories. She has in fact no prejudices whatever, no obstructive dogmas, no rigid canons of what counts as proof. She is completely genial. She will entertain any hypothesis, she will consider any evidence."[3]

So we have to wonder why Haddock-Seigfried ignores this personification—or impersonation—for it is at least as striking as any "submerged rape metaphor" lurking in the text. But there is another woman in the same text, and she is a woman that I, too, ignored until an undergraduate student pointed her out in a class discussion on the gender(s) of pragmatism. That woman is "rationalism," the neo-Kantian extreme of Western metaphysics: "Thus, just as pragmatism faces forward to the future, so does rationalism here again face backward to a past eternity [where truth is immutable]. True to her inveterate habit, rationalism reverts to 'principles,' and thinks that when an abstraction once is named, we own an oracular solution." I didn't know what to do with this sudden increase of metaphorical females in James's figurative language until I realized that pragmatism and rationalism represent very different women, very different discursive moments, very different attitudes toward the density and complexity of modernity.[4]

The architecture of rationalism, James notes, is "clean and noble." Indeed it is so completely "refined," "cloistered," and "spectral" that it resembles a "classic sanctuary." Thus it "is no *explanation* for our concrete universe, it is another thing altogether, a substitute for it, a remedy, a way of escape." In short, rationalism is innocent, or rather "chaste"—for she is removed from "the world of concrete personal experiences to which the street belongs." Pragmatism, by contrast, wants to stay on that busy street, to mingle with those who know that this world is "tangled, muddy, painful and perplexed," to bring out the "cash value" of every proposition, to trade on her truths. Rationalism presides over a safe haven in the heartless world of the cash nexus. Pragmatism refuses to remain in that separate sphere: she wants to be less virtuous, more worldly, more commercial. In this sense, rationalism expresses the spirit and the program of the nineteenth-century "woman movement," which proposed to reduce the reach of market values by enlarging the scope of family values, as well as the neo-Kantian movement in late-nineteenth-century philosophy. Pragmatism exhibits instead the sensibility of the New Woman who invented modern feminism by extricating herself from an *exclusive* preoccupation with domesticity, entering market society as an individual—not necessarily as a bearer of domestic roles such as mother, daughter, or wife—and redrawing the boundary between private and public enterprise, between the personal and the political. So there is nothing particularly Protestant or even American about pragmatism, unless we are willing to identify these adjectives with the complex market society that emerges in the late nineteenth century; but there is something specifically modern about it, and it speaks in the voice of a woman.[5]

This reading is, I think, corroborated by the "persistent use of financial metaphors" in *Pragmatism*. I mean that its "credit system," the site on which truths get traded, is also a woman. But to understand this figural connection between finance and females, we need to go back to the early modern period, when Machiavelli could declare that "Fortune is a woman." As J. G. A. Pocock, Hannah Pitkin, Stephanie Jed, and others have shown, Fortune represented the instability of things secular—the unpredictable and probably irrational movement of historical time—in part because she embodied or enabled the conversion of opinion, caprice, fantasy, and passion into determinants of social relations. In the eighteenth century, when the startling consequences of the "financial revolution" inaugurated in 1694 could begin to be gauged by writers such as Defoe, Addison, Steele, Bolingbroke, and Mandeville, the Machiavellian idiom once used to depict the ancient figure of Fortune was now deployed to analyze the new economics of Credit. Thus the "personification of Credit as an inconstant female figure," as Pocock puts it, was a rhetorical gesture specific to, and characteristic of, the eighteenth-century passage beyond the simple market society of the early modern period—that is, it was a gesture that recalled the figure of Fortune but also apprehended and anticipated the emergence of modern industrial (capitalist) civilizations, circa

1750–1850. For Credit embodied or enabled a new political economy of the sign in which fantasy could easily become fact, in which opinion rather than effort determined value, in which the passions and the interests were equally matched. In short, the emergence of a "credit economy" announced the arrival of a post-artisanal market society—a society in which there was no solid foundation for selfhood in work or property, and in which the "vicissitudes of the self" could therefore be registered with alarming rapidity.[6]

The American version of a "financial revolution" was postponed, as it were, until the late nineteenth century, because the "country party," the amorphous yet outspoken opposition to the "credit economy" originally designed by Alexander Hamilton, had a great deal more political leverage here than in England. To be sure, Jacksonian Democracy presided over primitive accumulation via "Indian removal," and thus enabled the so-called market revolution, but it meanwhile disavowed "public credit" by abolishing the Bank of the U.S. So it was not until the mid-1850s that banknotes in circulation regained the level of 1837, and not until the late 1860s that the exigencies of war finally caused a "financial revolution." Hereafter subaltern movements, from the Greenbackers of the 1870s to the Populists of the 1890s, would specify this moment as the source of the republic's political problems and would propose, accordingly, to repeal its social-economic consequences. The National Banking Act of 1863, the "Crime of '73"—the demonetization of silver—and the resumption of gold payments in 1879, for example, always figured prominently in the narratives through which the exploitation of the "toiling millions" was explained as a function of financial manipulation or speculation, that is, as a result of a "credit economy" in which there seemed to be no calculable relation between exertion and income, between labor-time and market value, or, as Edward Bellamy suggested in 1888, between the representations of value and the objects they were supposed to represent: "Money was a sign of real commodities, but credit was but a sign of a sign." By the 1890s, therefore, when this new economy finally became the cutting edge of historical change in the U.S. because it was the soil in which the new corporations took root, "credit" and its dangerous, post-republican connotations had become the indispensable metaphors through which the Populists and the Knights of Labor imagined an American apocalypse. "The money power on the one side and the producers and toilers on the other are marshalling their forces for the fight," as the editor of the *Populist* in Monroe, Georgia, put it in August, 1893: "The grand battle of Armageddon is close at hand."[7]

Because there is so much residual confusion attending the "money question" of the late nineteenth century, it is still worth emphasizing that the Populists did not, and could not, endorse a "credit economy." Most of that confusion is a result, or an echo, of the mistakes Lawrence Goodwyn made in defending the financial programs sponsored by the Greenbackers and their political heirs among the Populists. Goodwyn demonstrated that these subaltern movements proposed inflation of the circulating medium—of the currency—as the solution to almost every economic problem, and meanwhile believed that the value of this medium was a function of legislation or political purpose (hence their demand for banking *by* the federal government, not government regulation *of* banking). He concluded that they must have been committed to a more or less "modernist" vision of the future, a future in which the form of money and the source of value derived from social conventions or political interventions, not from "natural" laws or unplanned trends—unlike the "financial conservatives" who defended the gold standard, so the argument goes, these subaltern movements must have been committed to the fluidity and contingency of a "credit economy."[8] But let us suppose that Goodwyn et al. are correct to claim that the Greenbackers and the Populists wanted to arm themselves against the accumulation of capital by nationalizing the banks and coining more money. Do their larger conclusions about the "modernist" inclinations of these movements follow, either logically or historically?

In a word, no. The subaltern movements of the late nineteenth century wanted, above all, to reduce, or to eliminate, the symbolic surplus generated by a "credit economy," and accordingly to restore an *equilibrium,* a *correspondence*, between the useful products of labor and the monetary representations of those products. In short, they wanted enough currency in circulation to represent the quantity of goods in the market, but just enough: anything more was an invitation to "speculation," gambling, and decadence. They did not believe that property was intangible, and so could reside in "good will," or in the "probable expectation" of a "reasonable" income from the deployment of that property. Their opponents, those whom Goodwyn et al. caricature as "financial conservatives," wanted to put that symbolic surplus to work, and to regulate—not abolish—the new markets in which the new instruments of credit traded; in this sense, they agreed with the Supreme Court of the United States in assuming that property could be a thought as well as a thing, an effective claim on or about objects as well as the objects themselves. They also understood that the money supply had, in fact, increased since 1873, even though silver had been demonetized and the volume of national banknotes in circulation had declined; for the new credit instruments had made it possible to complete many transactions without currency, and many more transactions without enlarging supplies of either legal tender or specie (that is, without adding to the "foundation" of the symbolic system). They understood, in this sense, that the "cash basis" of the economy had shrunk in the late nineteenth century, but that the money supply had meanwhile grown and become much more flexible as well as efficient through the use of the new credit instruments. For good reasons, not the least of which was a severe shortage of accessible bank capital in the South and West, subaltern social movements—from the Greenbackers to the Populists—equated money supply with currency or coin in circulation, and defined the emergent "credit economy" as both cause and effect of the "trusts." So they believed that the solution to their problems was to enlarge the "cash basis" of the economy, not to enlarge upon the illusory capacities of credit and thereby expand corporate power. As the Greenbacker-cum-antimonopoly editor of the *Texas Advance* put it in September 1893: "The fact is, if there were sufficient money to do the business of the country on a cash basis absolutely, we could, and necessarily would, have the most systematic and economical financial system ever established." His opponents, the financial innovators who wanted to reform the banking system by validating and regulating the new credit instruments, believed otherwise, and eventually carried the day.[9]

I have rehearsed the "money question" at such length because doing so lets us grasp the connotations of the metaphors through which William James pressed his claims about the contingency of truth and the irrelevance of epistemology. By mobilizing the metaphor of a "credit system," he is placing pragmatism in the "court party" that accepts the post-artisanal market society determined and signified by the "financial revolution" of the late nineteenth century. So he is in effect embracing the modernist intellectual

implications of what his contemporaries called the "trust movement." He is futhermore confirming that pragmatism speaks in the
voice if not the name of the New Woman; for the metaphor of a
"credit system" deployed in the pivotal Lecture 6—"Pragmatism's
Conception of Truth"—reminds us in two ways that James is complicating the gender of modernity. We can be sure, to begin with,
that in the American idiom of 1907, Credit remained the "inconstant female figure" who made economic independence and thus
self-mastery impossible by validating the "trusts" (that is, by dri-
ving smallholders from the market) and who meanwhile allowed,
even enforced, the emergence of a "social self." But we can also
surmise that in completing the pragmatist critique of epistemology
by recourse to the same metaphor with the same connotations,
James is proposing to let the New Woman stand in for the "man of
reason."

All modern critics of epistemology—that is, of the disembodied
subject or mind or consciousness posited by traditional philosophy
("rationalism")—can be read as sympathetic to certain feminist
principles because, in treating subjectivity or consciousness as a historical artifact rather than an absent cause, they are insisting that
the condition of reason or truth or knowledge is not abstraction
from particular, historically determined circumstances, from the
locations and effects of desire, but rather immersion in them. In this
sense, they are depriving reason or truth or knowledge of an *origin*
that subsists outside of historical time: they are "de-centering" the
rational subject who is constituted by withdrawal or abstention
from all that is temporal, contingent, and sensuous. By doing so,
they are claiming that men no longer monopolize the resources of
rationality; for the subject presupposed by epistemology was the
self-mastering "man of reason," the male proprietor who typically
appeared in ancient *and* modern political discourse as the main
character in the "small holder economy" that underwrote popular
government (e.g., the yeoman, the Gothic freeholder, the artisan,
the entrepreneur).[10]

The implicit feminism that resides in every critique of epistemology is endorsed and emphasized in *Pragmatism* by the presence,
indeed the centrality, of that "inconstant female figure," Credit. But
does James mobilize this metaphor as a way of claiming that
women can be just as reasonable as men—that they can attain the
attributes of the "man of reason"? Or is he claiming that reason as

such must be reinterpreted as a function, a result, of implication or embodiment in the temporal, contingent, and sensuous world, not withdrawal or abstention from it? I think he is making the larger claim because he assumes that "chaste thinking" is impossible—that reason and desire are not antithetical modes of apprehending reality—and therefore that the relation between subject and situation, or agent and action, cannot be understood by designating the fixed dimensions of the rational subject or agent and asking what follows. Instead, he suggests, that relation must be understood almost in reverse, as if agency is a *function* of historically specific actions, as if subjectivity can be realized only in the concrete forms through which it can be expressed and so must be a *result* of the situations in which it "finds" itself in both senses. William Carlos Williams, the modernist poet who admired pragmatism, explained the reversal in this way: "No ideas but in things."[11]

So James won't let us pretend that rationality is an attribute of manhood, and won't let us forget that pragmatism speaks as a woman. But he doesn't install the New Woman as the successor to the "man of reason"—he doesn't suggest that women are more rational than men, or that subjectivity has somehow been "feminized." I mean that he doesn't merely invert the inherited conventions of Western philosophy, through which Reason was invariably aligned with "Man" and self-mastery was reserved only for men. And yet he is not suggesting that reason is *neither* male *nor* female—a calculus that is universal because it is disembodied. He is instead suggesting that we don't need to stipulate the nature of the thinker, or the process of thinking, to explain the "passing thought." In this sense, he is also blurring the distinction between male and female by suggesting that these categories are comparable to agency or subjectivity because they are functions of actions or results of situations, not ontological conditions or transhistorical presuppositions of knowledge as such. Pragmatism is *both* male and female, then, but it is the changing relation between these gendered parts rather than their straightforward sum; for by this account the parts themselves cannot be given or fixed or natural. I would conclude, accordingly, that we don't have to choose between Lentricchia and Haddock-Seigfried because they're both right. To appreciate their insights, however, is to put them to work by going beyond them, by treating their interpretations as necessary but not sufficient to the comprehension of pragmatism.

As Emile Durkheim (and others) noticed in the early twentieth century, the Jamesian rendition of subjectivity is reminiscent of the Nietzschean rendition—it was Nietzsche who claimed that "'the doer' is merely a fiction added to the deed"—because it allows for actions without agents as their *origin*. But there are significant differences between them that are worth exploring as a way of understanding those contemporary feminists who have hired Michel Foucault or Jacques Derrida as their guide to Nietzschean outposts, and as a way of seeing that James may well prove more useful than Nietszche in composing an explicitly feminist "critique of the subject." Let us begin that exploration by visiting the current scene of this critique. Judith Butler is probably the most prominent of the contemporary feminists who draw on poststructuralist positions to make subjectivity itself a political question. Here is how she poses it: "Do women want to become subjects on the model which requires and produces an anterior region of abjection, or must feminism become . . . self-critical about the processes that produce and destabilize identities?" And here is how she answers it:

> We may be tempted to think that to assume the subject in advance is necessary in order to safeguard the *agency* of the subject. But to claim that the subject is constituted is not to claim that it is determined; on the contrary, the constituted character of the subject is the very precondition of its agency. . . . My suggestion is that agency [i.e., as conceived in epistemological or phenomenological terms] belongs to a way of thinking about persons as instrumental actors who confront an external political field. But if we agree that politics and power exist already at the level at which the subject and its agency are articulated and made possible, then agency can be *presumed* only at the cost of refusing to inquire into its construction.[12]

Butler cites a Nietzschean warrant for this urgently necessary inquiry into the practices through which subjectivity and its gendered attributes are "performatively produced": "The challenge for rethinking gender categories outside of the metaphysics of substance will have to consider the relevance of Nietzsche's claim in *On the Genealogy of Morals* that 'there is no "being" behind doing, effecting, becoming: "the doer" is merely a fiction added to the deed—the deed is everything.'" She treats the theoretical position that follows, a position developed in *Gender Trouble* (1990) and elaborated in *Bodies That Matter* (1993), as a corollary of this claim: "There is no gender identity behind the expressions of gender; that identity is performatively constituted by the very 'expressions' that are said to be its results."[13]

In view of the family resemblance between the Jamesian and the Nietzschean renditions of subjectivity—and in view of the "social self" sponsored by both pragmatists and feminists since the turn of the century—it is perhaps surprising that Butler's most outspoken critics among feminists are legitimate claimants on the pragmatist tradition. Seyla Benhabib, for example, a political theorist who is no less interested in a feminist "critique of the subject" than Butler, notes that the "key insight" in the work of Jürgen Habermas is his emphasis on the "intersubjective constitution of the self," and that Habermas "often formulates this insight . . . in the language of George Herbert Mead." Nancy Fraser, a feminist political philosopher who is similarly engaged in a search for alternatives to the modern (bourgeois) individual, cites the very same intellectual lineage. But both are stridently critical of Butler's poststructuralist account of subjectivity as a function of "performativity." Benhabib responds to it by asking a series of pointed questions: "If this view of the self is adopted, is there any possibility of changing those 'expressions' that constitute us? If we are no more than the sum total of the gendered expressions we perform, is there ever any chance to stop the performance for a while, to pull the curtain down, and let it rise only if we can have a say in the production of the play itself? Isn't this what the struggle over gender is all about?" She concludes that "the very project of female emancipation" is unthinkable from the perspective Butler proposes because it provides no "regulative principle" on the basis of which we can plausibly assume that "agency, autonomy, and selfhood" are historical realities and political possibilities: "What follows from this Nietzschean position is a vision of the self as a masquerading performer, except of course we are now asked to believe that there is no self behind the mask." Fraser is less combative but equally critical of Butler—especially of her "deeply antihumanist" language, which is so far "removed from our everyday ways of talking and thinking about ourselves [as] to require some justification." The fundamental problem in the Foucauldian or poststructuralist account of subjectivity, according to Fraser, is that it "surrenders the norma-tive moment" by forgoing "critique" and settling for "resignifica-tion" as the insignia of agency. Even "foundationalist theories of subjectivity"—that is, "the view of subjectivity as possessing an ontologically intact reflexivity that is not an effect of cultural processes"—can be put to progressive use, she insists: "witness the French Revolution." But if "it is not possible to deduce a single, univocal political valence from a theory of subjectivity," Fraser concludes, Butler's repudiation of the "humanist self" is at least unwarranted and quite possibly dangerous.[14]

Both Benhabib and Fraser claim, then, that the "death of the subject" announced in Nietzschean theorems on selfhood has trou-bling *political* implications. As Benhabib puts it in protesting a strictly semiotic account of subjectivity: "Along with this dissolu-tion of the subject into yet 'another position in language' disappear of course concepts of intentionality, accountability, self-reflexivity, and autonomy." They acknowledge the need for a feminist "cri-tique of the subject," but they want somehow to preserve inherited notions of self-consciousness, self-mastery, and thus political agency; for in their view a socially determined or culturally con-structed self must be the creature as well as the creation of power. Now, I see nothing wrong with their effort to annul and preserve previous truths about genuine selfhood; indeed I will soon be argu-ing that pragmatism can help us understand why we need to recu-perate rather than repudiate the past. But I do find it intriguing that in criticizing Butler's theory of "performativity," Benhabib and Fraser sound uncannily like Anthony Giddens criticizing George Herbert Mead's concept of a "social self": "Mead's social philoso-phy, in an important sense, was built around reflexivity [that is, around what Habermas calls "intersubjectivity']. . . . But even in Mead's own writings, the constituting activity of the 'I' is not stressed. Rather, it is the 'social self' with which Mead was preoc-cupied. . . . Hence much of the possible impact of this theoretical style has been lost, since the 'social self' can easily be reinterpreted as the 'socially determined self.' " So we need to ask how Benhabib and Fraser can cite Mead's authority (via Habermas) without sub-jecting themselves to the same strictures they have aimed at Butler—in my opinion, they cannot—and, beyond that, how we might use a different variation on the theme of pragmatism *both* to strengthen Butler's position *and* to make it more acceptable to her critics. In effect this last question is how to get beyond Nietzsche without reinstating the "man of reason" as the indispensable agent or origin of intelligible action, as "'the doer' behind the deed."[15]

The variation on the theme of pragmatism that I have in mind is of course the Jamesian variation. As John Dewey noted in an essay of 1940, "The Vanishing Subject in the Psychology of James," his predecessor among pragmatists was more than skeptical of the suprahistorical subject that modern Western philosophers typically posited as the necessary condition—the origin—of knowledge, reason, and consciousness. In fact, in the studies of "radical empiricism" which fed into the later lectures on pragmatism, James suggested that consciousness was "a kind of external relation," and consequently that neither the intent nor the content of thinking as such could be known apart from its historically specific embodiment in or practical application to the world—that is, apart from its *enactment*, apart from the changes it made in the world. Thinking was an active, transitive, performative "function" in this account, a way of turning thoughts into things, and it did not, therefore, require a philosophical inquiry into its origins. So the Jamesian "critique of the subject" was just as insistent and sweeping and scandalous as the Nietzschean. But it was not, strictly speaking, a *radical* departure from the philosophical tradition it criticized because, Dewey notwithstanding, it did not repudiate the notions of subjectivity reiterated, and thus reproduced, over centuries by that tradition: unlike Nietzsche, James tried to mediate between "previous truth and novel fact." I mean that he tried to annul *and* preserve these inherited notions by changing their cognitive and cultural status, by incorporating them within a new conception of "social selfhood." He recognized, I think, that if our purpose is to explain or justify agency, accountability, intentionality, or rationality, then we should not and cannot begin by specifying, in abstract or metaphysical or "normative" terms, the dimensions of the rational subject (or of "mind," "consciousness," etc.). Instead, we should assume that individuality or subjectivity is an achievement, a *result* of historical development—"a relation that unrolls itself in time"—not a substance that somehow subsists in a pre-discursive, extra-temporal moment, or, by the same token, a discontinuous series of social roles or "pure experiences." So individuals and individualism were realities that James could acknowledge but would not presuppose as requirements, as origins, of the "moral personality" and its political capacity.[16]

It is this refusal of radicalism, this refusal to leave the past unchanged, that makes the Jamesian rendition of subjectivity more useful than the Nietzschean in clarifying and strengthening Butler's position. What James permits by refusing the either/or choice between "previous truth and novel fact"—between the "archaic" notions of subjectivity embedded in Western culture and the emergent model of "social selfhood"—is a *transformation* of the "archaic." I mean that the new model he favors is not superimposed on, or simply opposed to, the old, as if it were a naive American observer of European manners from one of his brother's novels; it stands instead in a productive, "developmental" relation to its predecessors because its articulation changes the forms in which the "archaic" notions can be enunciated, and thus influences and modulates the expression of subjectivity as such. Again, "previous truth" is annulled and preserved by allowing "novel fact" to affect it.

The advantages of this "double strategy" are obvious. To begin with, the old and the new models of subjectivity become commensurable and thus arguable: we can approach them as historical events and contemporary realities rather than mutually exclusive "normative" principles of feminist theorizing. For example, in these terms we can grasp Butler's project—an inquiry into the limits of discourse in producing gender difference and "bodies that matter"—as a consequence and a species of the "new science" that characterizes the twentieth century, through which we have come to understand that investigating a reality that exists inertly and independently of the investigation is inconceivable. We can accordingly rethink the relation between her project and its rivals. To be specific, we can see that her accomplishment is not a discovery of truths about subjectivity and agency that existed all along but a *transformation* (by "resignification") of previous truths which acknowledges the *social* sources and character of selfhood: no wonder she sounds like John Dewey, the pragmatist who insisted that "individuality is not originally given but is created under the influences of associated life," when she claims that "the constituted character of the subject is the very precondition of its agency." In this sense, her project is itself a performative speech act because it *enacts* the relation that it names: it does things *to* as well as *with* words. So the "false antitheses" that Fraser attributes to Butler and Benhabib can now begin to look like the extremities that allow the body of feminism to maintain its intellectual mobility and sustain its ethical integrity—they are indispensable parts of a larger whole. As Hegel put it, "the false is no longer false as a moment of the true."[17]

Rewriting the genealogy of Butler's "critique of the subject"—that is, installing James as its locus classicus—has other, perhaps less obvious advantages. By doing so, we can appreciate her citations of speech act theorists, particularly of Ludwig Wittgenstein, the philosopher of language who was, as we have seen in chapter 3, deeply and consciously indebted to Jamesian rather than Nietzschean ideas about "speaking subjects." In other words, we can make better sense, and better use, of the intermediate intellectual lineage Butler constructs insofar as we acknowledge its sources in and connections to the pragmatist tradition. But it is not just the past that is preserved by annulment (by "resignification") in the Jamesian variation on this theme—the impending future, what James called the "existing beyond," is also *transformed*. I mean that he lets us appreciate both "previous truth" and "novel fact" by emphasizing that we are always already in transition, indeed that we *are* the transitions, that is, the discursive efforts through which we translate our unfolding, often discontinuous moments of mere experience into coherent narrative and intelligible remembrance.

These efforts are, to be sure, retrospective, but they situate us in the present and orient us toward, or prepare us for, a certain future, *not* the future as such. For the ways in which we appropriate or narrate the past will determine the ways in which we can experience the impending future, and vice versa. "We live forward, but we understand backward," as Kierkegaard put it. Our question should then be, what future(s) does James prepare us for? Many scholars argue or assume that he was an old-fashioned "bourgeois individualist," and so could neither accept bureaucratic "bigness" nor approve the "pacific cosmopolitan industrialism," as he named it, that emerged from the social-economic crises of the 1890s—in short, these scholars suggest that he could not have abided corporate capitalism and its corollary in consumer culture. I resist this characterization of James simply because if we reduce him to a "bourgeois individualist" in any meaningful sense of the term, we cannot explain his profound effect on subsequent analysts and advocates of the "social self." I think he did see "pacific cosmopolitan industrialism" as an ambiguous promise of a better future, that is, as both condition of and constraint on a "socialistic equilibrium." So my answer to the question turns, once again, on the metaphors he mobilizes in the name of intellectual reconstruction.[18]

Here and in chapter 2, I have suggested that James's "persistent use of financial metaphors" in *Pragmatism* should be read as his acceptance of a "credit economy" and its decidedly corporate connotations. In this chapter, I have also suggested that the same metaphors imply his acceptance of the world he would later caricature in "The Moral Equivalent of War" as "a world of clerks and teachers, of co-education and zoophily, of 'consumer's leagues' and 'associated charities,' of industrialism unlimited and feminism unabashed"—that is, a world in which women's work and women's movements are immediately recognizable representations of an impending future that somehow remains "industrial." So I would now propose that the "inconstant female figure" of Credit functions as a principle of hope in James's conspectus. As the future tense of money, it "faces forward": it is the prospective middle term between the "pleasure economy" and the New Woman, between the two novel facts residing in "pacific cosmopolitan industrialism." In this sense, the metaphor of Credit signifies the connection, or rather the transactions, between the economic and the cultural dimensions of the complex market society sponsored by corporate capitalism; at any rate it reminds us that, like modern feminism, pragmatism is both cause and effect of the "socialization of industry" which emptied the home of its economic functions and extricated women from an exclusive preoccupation with domestic or familial roles.[19]

I am claiming, then, that, like pragmatism, modern feminism is at once symptom of and attempted cure for the decay of proprietary capitalism: each requires and inhabits the "credit economy" specific to what we call corporate capitalism. But if my claim is that the transition from proprietary to corporate capitalism was the enabling condition of both pragmatism and feminism, what hope is there in it? If these two modes of cognition are moments in a "managerial culture," or contributions to a "corporate-liberal ideology," how can they function as cognate critiques of modern capitalism? To reduce these questions to their political essentials, can we "speak truth to power" if we are complicit with power?

Most of my colleagues on the American Left would say no, we can't. My answer is even less complicated: we don't have a choice. Truth presupposes complicity, not because power determines all utterance but because all utterance is ideological, no matter who the "speaking subject" is, because all truths are contingent until "proven"—that is, until we can enact what they have provisionally named—and because there is no "normative moment" before or after historical time. But my answer should not be misconstrued as a "pragmatic" concession to an inherited, immutable historical reality. I mean it instead as an endorsement of Butler's position, as a way of saying that the "very condition of agency" is an acknowledgement of our prior implication in the corruptions of power and passion and interest. We can avoid or adjust to those realities that we perceive as naturally given, or as external to our desires and discourses; but we cannot change them. To change them is to grasp them as *realities that are still subject to transformation* by reinterpretation, by "resignification." In the case at hand, if we perceive the stupefying realities of corporate capitalism and consumer culture as given, as external to our desires and discourses—as a story told by others with an ending we already know—we will be unable to see any reason to hope for a future that departs from the present, unless of course we understand that departure as simple "subversion," as either a "radical" repudiation of the abiding present or a "conservative" return to the glorious past; for we will be unable to see ourselves as authors, as narrators of the required transition. If by contrast we perceive these historical realities as open to our reinterpretation and resignification *because they are not in any sense external to our desires and discourses*, we can try to retell the story as if we are characters in it, and can't yet know the ending. I don't mean that we must feign ignorance and hope for the best. Again I mean that we can't know what the future holds until we adopt an attitude toward history; for the future we can recognize and realize is revealed only in retrospect, by our reinterpretations of the past.

If, for example, we assume that the triumph of corporate capitalism required the eradication of Populism, and furthermore that the proprietary model of (male) subjectivity validated by Populist rhetoric is the paradigm of genuine selfhood in a modern market society, then we will tend to argue that corporate power was, and is, the solvent of subjectivity as such. To admit complicity with that power is to relinquish one's "critical distance," even one's identity. If we assume by contrast that alternatives to the possessive individualism of this proprietary model—alternatives like the "social self"—were produced in and by the passage beyond proprietary capitalism, we will want to argue that the triumph of corporate capitalism represents a kind of progress. We will also want to argue that changing the subject of political discourse by designing alternatives to the modern (bourgeois) individual is an urgent requirement of democratic theory and practice in a post-industrial society. To admit complicity with corporate power in this historiographical register is to acknowledge and audition for these alternatives, and to authorize oneself as an agent of its transformation.[20]

Let me cite another example of the process through which we script a future by rewriting the past. If we assume that capitalism is a closed system that by definition excludes other modes of production, particularly but not only socialism, and furthermore that the corporate (or "monopoly") form is the "highest stage" of capitalism, and finally that the financial sector—where all those incomprehensibly intangible assets get "produced" and traded—is the headquarters of corporate capitalism, we will tend to argue that corporations and social democracy are incompatible, and that "globalization" by means of international financial integration must prove a disaster. If we assume instead that both capitalism and socialism are porous and interpenetrating modes of production that have developed together since the turn of the last century as elements of hybrid social formations; furthermore, that the characteristic legal and organizational innovation of the corporation—the separation of ownership and control of productive assets—implies that the right to allocate such assets cannot be derived from its traditional source in the "natural right" of private property, and that the performance of corporate managers need not be evaluated according to strictly economic criteria such as profit and loss; and finally, that the rationalization and "socialization" of bank credit or surplus capital by means of modern financial institutions—those whose lending criteria are not limited to political connections, social standing, or inherited wealth—can animate insurgency and foster democracy at home and abroad; then we will want to argue that to posit Credit as a principle of hope is not to cede the future to the International Monetary Fund. To put this conclusion less defensively, we will want to argue that the future James prepares us for is the present.[21]

But we don't have to take his word for it. There were other advocates of a "socialistic equilibrium" who saw political promise in the "trust movement" of the late nineteenth century, that is, in the displacement of small producers by the corporations that flourished in a "credit economy." For example, the younger radicals who raised the banner of sexual emancipation in the early twentieth century differed from the older, "social-purity" majority of the Socialist Party USA because they didn't try to preserve an inherited sexual morality by designating the integrity of the household or the autonomy of the artisan as a limit to the scope of the commodity form and the development of capitalism; as Mari Jo Buhle notes, they "accepted instead the tendency of capitalism to foster new social relations among women and men as the basis of a moral system adequate to modern life." Walter Lippmann is another good example. In *Drift and Mastery* (1914), he noted that because "capital shall be impersonal, 'liquid,' 'mobile'" under the aegis of the "large-scale corporation," the civilizing "magic of property" was moot; he declared accordingly that "the trust movement is doing what no conspirator or revolutionist could ever do: it is sucking the life out of private property." He also noted that the "real news about business is that it is being administered by men who are not profiteers." He meant that the separation of corporate ownership and control had created a new social stratum, and perhaps a new political prospect: "The managers are on salary, divorced from ownership and bargaining. They represent the revolution in business incentives at its very heart."[22]

Another eminent socialist had meanwhile identified a causal relation between the modern "credit system," the creation of "stock companies"—that is, of corporations—and the "socialization" of capital. The "social character of capital," he argued, "is promoted and fully realised by the complete development of the credit and banking system." That is why he believed that this system would "serve as a powerful lever during the transition from the capitalist mode of production to the [mode of] production [organized around] associated labor." For it had already caused the "formation of stock companies," and had consequently converted "private capital" into a "form of social capital"; these corporate, "social enterprises" thus represented "the abolition of capital as private property within the boundaries of capitalist production itself." This same socialist summarized his argument on modern credit and modern corporations as follows:

> Stock companies in general, developed with the credit system, have a tendency to separate [the] labor of management as a function more and more from the ownership of capital, whether it be self-owned or borrowed. . . . Since the mere owner of capital, the money-capitalist, has to face the investing capitalist, while money-capital itself assumes a social character with the advance of credit, being concentrated in banks and loaned by them instead of by its original owners, and since, on the other hand, the mere manager, who has no title whatever to the capital, whether by borrowing or otherwise, performs all real functions pertaining to the investing capitalist as such, only the functionary remains and the capitalist disappears from the process of production as a superfluous person.[23]

The "speaking subject" here is of course Karl Marx, the most ferocious critic of capitalism until Lenin came of age. The point of citing him is not to cloak myself in the mantle of Marxism—however that is defined these days—or to align William James with that intellectual tradition. I want instead to suggest that if it is possible even for Marx to see socialism as a function or dimension of *corporate* capitalism, then we need not fear or resist implication in corporate *power*; indeed I would propose that we learn to treat this implication as the necessary condition of our criticism and contestation. I want to suggest, once again, that the "difficult labor of forging a future from resources inevitably impure," as Butler puts it, requires the "double consciousness" of pragmatism and the "double strategy" of feminism, through which we annul and preserve the past by transforming it, that is, by rewriting it.[24]

I also want to emphasize that Marx can be read against the grain, in such a way that the corporations, the creatures of the modern "credit system," are the media in which the transition from capitalism to socialism becomes both imaginable and actionable: because they "socialize" capital and regulate markets, the "world of large-scale production" over which they preside represents real progress, real movement toward a culture in which capitalists look anachronistic and in which economists accordingly get treated as J. M. Keynes hoped they would be, as "humble, competent people, on a level with dentists." But I cannot pretend that the long view of the twentieth century afforded by my appropriation of Marx is shared by many of his readers. By and large, the contemporary critics of capitalism who claim a more or less Marxist warrant see this century as a catastrophe. Unlike most of their predecessors, however, these critics typically cite environmental, cultural, and/or psychological damage rather than, or in addition to, economic inequality or exploitation, and they often enlist feminist and/or psychoanalytic theories in making their case against "late capitalism." I want, therefore, to address these critics as a way of defending my appropriation of Marx, and more importantly, as a way of reasserting my claim that corporate capitalism is the enabling condition of pragmatism and feminism as well as socialism.[25]

Marxism in Green, Feminism in Red, Populism in Drag

Teresa Brennan's forceful, funny, and fascinating book *History after Lacan* (1993) will serve as my exemplary text.[26] The aim of this book is to integrate social theory and historical method in the name of eco-feminism without apologies. Brennan treats Lacanian psychoanalysis and Marxian political economy as commensurable *historical* perspectives on the links between social psychosis and commodity fetishism because she recognizes that the key figures in the contemporary theoretical firmament (Lacan, Foucault, Derrida) are equally in debt to Martin Heidegger and Alexandre Kojeve, the renegade phenomenologists who, like Marx, were close readers of Hegel. I mean that although her arguments are deeply informed by both classical and poststructuralist theory, she is trying to explain the social-psychological sources of what Lacan called the "era of the ego"—roughly 1600 to the present—in concrete historical terms, so that her concluding indictment of the "world of large-scale production" has a practical, imperative effect. She hopes that by bridging the "applicability gap between theory and explanation," she can provide "the generality necessary for tracing a guide to action" (5; cf. 188–96).

At its most prosaic, Brennan's purpose is simply to elucidate the rigid opposition of subject and object, or mind and matter, which dominates Western culture as such, but which, as enforced and enhanced by technologies specific to modern capitalism, has erased or endangered the natural environment (the "natural living reality" beneath a "socially constructed overlay" [16, 21, 116, 146, 151]). She recognizes, however, that if this opposition, this "foundational fantasy," represents, at its apogee in our own time, a "social psychosis," she needs somehow to explain how the social is, or becomes, psychological, and vice versa. Lacan's theories are then necessary but not sufficient to the task at hand; for they can help us understand how gendered subjects are constructed through the abjection of the Other—through the "psychical fantasy of woman"—but they can't help us understand how modern subjectivity gets reproduced or why it differs from its predecessors: "the unelaborated relation between the economic dimension and the ego is the subjective [*sic*] flaw in Lacan's historical theory, because it is only through the elaboration of this relation that the mechanism by which the social psychosis could exist simultaneously in and around individuals will emerge" (44).[27]

Enter Marx, stage left. In the most original sections of the book, Brennan revisits the scene of commodity fetishism and revises the labor theory of value as a way of claiming that consumer culture enforces the "foundational fantasy" by reanimating a hallucinatory desire to immobilize and control the "mother's body, an origin before the foundation" (90–105). Here is a summary of her argument on consumer goods as the props of "social psychosis":

> Thus far it seems we have an account of a psychical fantasy which tallies with the desires encapsulated in commodities. It is this psychical fantasy I am positing as a foundational psychical fantasy. That is to say, I am positing that the desire for instant gratification, the preference for visual and "object"-oriented thinking this entails, the desire to be waited on, the envious desire to imitate the original, the desire to control the mother, and to devour, poison, and dismember her, and to obtain knowledge by this process, constitute a foundational fantasy. (101)

Hereafter Brennan takes up a study of the commodity form that echoes but also extends Marx's rhetorical procedure in the opening chapters of *Capital*, volume 1. Her basic claim throughout this exposition should be familiar to anyone who has read Carl Boggs, Carolyn Merchant, or Mike Davis on the environmental costs of capitalism: "The point here is simply that in order to satisfy the demands of large-scale production, more and more of nature has to be destroyed" (138).[28]

To get us to that point, however, and to guide us beyond it, Brennan uses a map that is almost indecipherable because it allows her to scold Marx for taking roads he never traveled, and because it lacks the very landmarks she wants us to notice. For example, in a variation on the venerable theme of fetishism, she claims that the commodity "functions analogously with hallucinations in that it binds living substances in forms which are inert, relative to the energetic movement of life." This sounds to me like Marx's claim to the effect that under the spell of alienated labor, people tend to apprehend social relations of production as relations between things. Brennan thinks not—she claims that to understand how "the fixed points of commodities" proliferate "at nature's expense," we need to dispense with the "subjective emphasis" of Marx's value theory, according to which "labour was [cast as] the subject, [and] nature was relegated to the realm of object" (118–19, 205–13). But what then are we to make of his repeated and explicit inclusion of *human* nature in the broader category of Nature? What should we do with his designation of the earth as the "extended body" of the human species? How do we acknowledge his insistence on the twofold character of the commodity, that is, on the intersection of particular, material, *use* values and universal, symbolic, *exchange* values in the commodity form? If every commodity is the site of this intersection, where thoughts and things become interchangeable parts, how can it be a "fixed point"? And how should we interpret the following passage from the *Gründrisse*? "It is not the *unity* of living and active humanity with the natural, inorganic conditions of their metabolic exchange with nature, and hence their appropriation of nature, which requires explanation or is the result of a historic process, but rather the *separation* between these inorganic conditions of human existence and this active existence, a separation which is completely posited only in the relation of wage labour and capital."[29]

My purpose in asking these questions is not to conjure a Marxian master text that has already anticipated and addressed Brennan's broadly environmental concerns. I want instead to suggest that she doesn't need to rewrite Marx's theory of value to condemn "large-scale production" and consumer culture—two sides of the same coin—as root causes of environmental degradation: she could accomplish her stated purposes by consulting and citing John Locke or Adam Smith. In other words, we don't need a specifically Marxian version of value theory, no matter how recondite, to believe that "small is beautiful": many writers and politicians who are not Marxists have criticized economic concentration or monopoly power or bureaucratic rationality in precisely the same terms Brennan derives from her exposition of Marx.[30]

Does it follow that if we favor "environmental protection" and/or feminism, we can forget Marx? Let me answer by rereading the map Brennan uses to steer us toward a post-capitalist future. In her view, a rewrite of the labor theory of value is necessary to explain "large-scale production" and its results, the most important of which are of course the degradation of the environment and the abjection of women. These related results are reproduced in, and reinforced by, "subject-object thought," that is, in and by the "foundational fantasy," because the "objectifying attitude" it permits meanwhile "severs connections to the living reality" of the (maternal) body and the earth: "the split between mind and matter, as it has been described here, is also the split between the individual and the environment" (21, 73, 116). Thus the pivot of the analysis becomes the *scale* of production. "One of the aims of this book," Brennan announces, "has been to contribute to this awareness [of structural constraints on political action] by drawing out the dialectical implications of capital's spatial expansion in relation to nature. This makes the question of economic scale paramount rather than incidental" (190; cf. 173). And indeed it must animate every claim she makes, because by her account "subject-object thought"—the paranoid style of thought that makes the degradation of nature and the oppression of women seem rational or inevitable—is itself a function of the scale of production: "An enlargement of scale does not *produce* subject-object thought, but it does enhance its dominance" (168). No wonder Brennan concludes that "the position of women invariably suffers (both in relation to their former position and in relation to men) with twentieth-century 'development' and capitalization." After all, "it is women who are most significantly affected by the scale factor" (163 n. 36, 161). Small is not only beautiful, it is necessary to the cause of feminism.

But how does a rewrite of Marx's theory of value serve this seemingly feminist purpose? A different way to pose the same question is to ask whether the empirical claims that derive from the rewrite are reliable. More specifically, can we verify the connections Brennan postulates between the enlargement of economic scale, the intensification of dualistic models of cognition ("subject-object thought"), and the *consequent* degradation of nature and women? If so, we cannot argue in good faith that corporate capitalism is an enabling condition of modern feminism. If not, we should stop restating the Populist case by arguing, as Brennan does, that the "small business mode" is "a structural and strategic basis for resistance" to capitalism, and by assuming that pure and simple opposition to corporations is the premise of political progress (189–93).

If I understand her correctly, Brennan departs from Marx by defining "natural sources apart from human labour" as substances that add (as well as have) value in the production process. As a result of that departure, she can claim to have transcended the "subject-centred" character of the theory as Marx left it—nature now appears as an agent in its own right rather than an object of human manipulation—and to have raised the issue of "real value, meaning nature overall as the source of all value" (124–33). On this basis, Brennan can also equate "real substance" with use value, and suggest that the transformation of real substances into commodities inevitably "diminishes and objectifies" nature: the materialization of energy in marketable products by the application of labor (time and energy) is "that type of transformation which diminishes, by rendering natural substances into a form in which they are no longer able to reproduce themselves" (136). Marx was wrong about the immiseration of the proletariat, but his value theory can, it seems, be revised to account for the impending immiseration of nature as such.

The "inherent dynamic" of Capital is to increase profit by reducing the costs of commodity production—that is, by reducing the exchange value of every component of every commodity, including the "value realized by all the natural substances entering into production." This dynamic in turn demands an increase in the *speed* and the *scope* of production, distribution, and exchange, which can be effected only by economies of scale. The "logic of natural substances" expressed in "reproductive or generational time" is thereby displaced by an "artificial space-time" and ultimately sacrificed to the Leviathan of "spatial centralization" (136–51). So Capital "is literally altering the *physis* of the world, adjusting the inbuilt logic of nature and the spatio-temporal continuum to suit itself. By its will, it is imposing a direction on physical processes which is other than their own.... It establishes its own foundations, but it does so by consuming the real foundations, the logic of natural substances" (151).

In effect, then Brennan has used a revised labor theory of value to analyze the depletion of natural resources as a recapitulation of proletarianization and alienation: as artisans could no longer reproduce themselves as integrated, self-determining personalities once they were separated from their customary means of subsistence and forced into the unnatural environment of the factories, so natural substances have been increasingly confined, by "large-scale production," to settings and forms "in which they are no longer able to reproduce themselves" as the unitary source and substrate of all "real value." In this sense, the revised theory does not merely inform the story of "spatial centralization," it becomes a kind of historical narrative in its own right by casting nature as the main character in the unfolding tragedy of modern capitalism. History after Lacan—that is, history in an eco-feminist key—does then require Marx.

Even so, the relation specified here between social theories, historical narratives, and political imperatives is still worth scrutiny. Brennan herself urges us to test her theses by reference to the historical record: she admits that her findings "are not based on an empirical overview" of the ego's era, but she insists that "they could be readily measured against it" (120). So let us take these measurements by returning to the empirical question of connection, by asking whether her theory of the commodity form accounts for "spatial centralization," and whether the "enlargement of economic scale" bears the explanatory weight she assigns it. We can then turn to the problem of political implication.

I have two reasons to doubt that any theory of the commodity form can account for "spatial centralization," however we may define this process. First, commodities circulate before and after "centralization" takes place as a function of industrialization under capitalist (or socialist) auspices. The household economy of which Brennan is so enamored—"Household production, or petty commodity production, as Marx and Engels termed it, accorded women a very different and generally better economic place" (160)—was constituted, as the Marxist terminology suggests, by production of goods for the market, not by abstention from the market. That production was sometimes strategic and selective, to be sure, but it was nonetheless regulated by if not organized around the production of commodities: "simple market society," as C. B. Macpherson called it, was the soil in which industrial capitalism could, and often did, take root. If we reverse the chronology, moreover, we can see that commodities still circulate in the "post-Fordist" batch production that *post-industrial* society permits, and will presumably continue to circulate in a post-capitalist society. So commodities have, or are, a history that cannot be deduced from a theoretical treatment of the commodity form as such.[31]

Second, there is no "law of motion" that tells us how petty commodity production will necessarily evolve. Macpherson showed that, in theory, even if every small producer who sold his goods in the market was satisfied with the property and income he already had, he would be forced to acquire more property just to stay competitive, and thus would undermine the *cultural* consensus that stabilized "simple market society"; in this sense, he proposed the same inescapable logic of "centralization" that animates Brennan's argument. In practice, however, that is, *in history*, what we find is a lot of "near misses"—that is, many "proto-industrial" societies or household economies that never crossed the threshold of (capitalist) industrialization or "market revolution," usually because they lacked the requisite political and intellectual resources. We also find that the transition from proprietary to corporate capitalism at the turn of the last century was by no means inevitable, not even in the extremity of bourgeois society we know as the United States; as late as 1909, the legal standing of the new industrial corporations was still a matter of serious debate among jurists, and it was not until 1914 that the Federal Trade Commission finally removed the issue of "the trusts" from normal political discourse. Again, the historical development of capitalism has not been determined by the mere existence of petty commodity production, and cannot be predicted by positing the commodity form. To put the same conclusion another way, there were (and are) many varieties of market society—while a capitalist society is by definition a market society wherein wage labor is the predominant form of producing goods, a market society is not necessarily a capitalist society.[32]

I have equally good reasons to doubt that an "enlargement of economic scale" enforces the degradation of women and the environment by enhancing "subject-object thought." Brennan claims that the "late capitalism" of the twentieth century "reveals the spatial imperative in all its munching glory, with its speedy circulation and its ever-expanding reach that cuts off the roots of reproductive time" (153). And yet she also notes that the "present period in the West" is the moment at which "the idea of the subject as a contained entity is being re-examined" (114). If "the sense of internal containment is historically inflected" because "technological shifts have energetic effects on us," and if this "sense of self-containment [is] breaking down" just now (89–90), then shouldn't she claim that the "spatial centralization" sponsored by "late capitalism" is the solvent rather than the support of "subject-object thought"? In other words, shouldn't Brennan entertain the possibility that the emergence of corporate capitalism announces the imminent end of the ego's era, and thus enables new models of cognition or subjectivity—models such as pragmatism and feminism—which militate against the degradation of women and the environment by adjourning, or at least interrogating, ontological distinctions between subject and object, male and female, mind and matter, thoughts and things, humanity and nature? Shouldn't we?

We should, I think, but we can't proceed by assuming that our task is to trace the inner, "energetic" effects of outer, "technological" shifts, that is, by treating corporate capitalism as the missing "economic dimension" of Brennan's argument. To do so is to assume that this dimension is already external to our desires and discourses, to suggest that it is somehow determinative "in the final instance," and thus to reinstate the very dualisms we criticize as pragmatists or feminists. We should instead assume that no economic event or transaction becomes a "material reality" in the absence of language, thought, or purpose. From this standpoint, we can see that a price system is a cultural system because it presupposes buyers who understand the meanings of monetary symbols and the limits of their bargaining power, or that a contract is a performative speech act because its fulfillment *creates* a truth by naming the future and reshaping reality in accordance with that provisional designation. We can see, in short, that capitalism is more than an economic phenomenon because it is an ensemble of social relations, a chain of social connections—or rather that the "economic dimension" of any mode of production, capitalism included, cannot exist apart from the representations, the discourse, through which it becomes intelligible and actionable.

Corporate Personality, Bureaucratic Rationality, and Modern Feminism

How, then, does the emergence of corporate capitalism, now construed as both a social and an intellectual movement, authorize new models of cognition or subjectivity? Let us suppose that Hegel was correct to claim that "property is the first embodiment of freedom and so is in itself a substantive end" because its articulation at the law or by the state, and its reproduction through everyday exertion, entails acknowledgment *by others* of the owner's *self*-possession. "This taking possession of oneself," he explained, "is the translation into actuality of what one is according to one's concept, i.e., a potentiality, capacity, potency"; for the conversion of thoughts into things makes one's purposes social, public, recognizable: "In that translation one's self-consciousness for the first time becomes one's own, as one's object also and distinct from self-consciousness pure and simple, and thereby capable of taking the form of a 'thing.'" Let us also suppose that J. G. A. Pocock, a more recent authority on these matters, was correct to claim that because property was the "material foundation" of personality as such in the post-feudal world ("It was common ground that the political individual needed a material anchor in the form of property no less than he needed a rational soul"), we must be "aware of the possibility that different modes of property may be seen as generating or encouraging different modes of personality." If these suppositions are plausible, we should expect to find that the redefinition of property—thus of legal personality and political capacity—which accompanied and enforced the emergence of corporate capitalism, circa 1890–1930, permitted or required a redefinition of subjectivity.[33]

We should then ask how changes in the *concept*—the idea, the law, the cultural function—of property became the premises of debate on the future of individualism. I have already mentioned the eclipse of "natural right" as the self-evident justification of private property and its disposition. By the 1890s, economists, jurists, and striking workers had begun the search for alternatives to this Enlightenment category, in the hope of explicating and modulating the rigors of modern-industrial society; that is why contemporary assertions of an absolute right of property by George Pullman or E. H. Harriman sounded so arrogant, so scandalous, to most Americans. Alfred Marshall, who inspired a whole generation of younger economists in the U.K. and the U.S., insisted, for example, that private property could not be justified by citing "natural right"; it could, however, be justified, he suggested, by demonstrating a historical correlation between secure property rights and genuine social progress. John Bates Clark, the American economist who enthusiastically admired and argued with Marshall, followed up on this suggestion in the 1890s, and, in doing so, he became midwife to the birth of marginalist theory in the U.S.[34]

Henry Carter Adams, the University of Michigan economist who served as the statistician of the Interstate Commerce Commission and who therefore witnessed at first hand the corporate consolidation of the railway system in the 1890s, was no less skeptical than Marshall and Clark of "natural right" in the age of "social production" specific to the large-scale, vertically integrated enterprise pioneered by the railroads. "The mistake of English political economy," he argued in his presidential address to the American Economic Association in 1896, "does not lie in the emphasis it gives to competition as a regulator of commercial conduct, but in its assumption that the *bourgeois* conception of property was ordained by nature and on that account, lay outside of evolutionary forces." Adams specified two such evolutionary forces as the solvent of "natural right," and with it the "individualism of the eighteenth century." The first was "the modern system of transportation that [had] revolutionized the world of morals" by destroying "localism in government, in industry, in thought and in interest"—that is, by creating and enforcing an unprecedented "interdependence among men." The second was "the appearance of corporations" in their late-nineteenth-century legal form, as "private industrial concern[s]" rather than "agencies of the state" that were chartered "for the purpose of attaining public ends"; this development demanded a new "social ethics" as well as "a new definition of liberty and the individual himself," all of which would recognize "the social interest, the social impulse, the social aim" residing in an increasingly corporate economic order.[35]

Adams worried that an eighteenth-century conception of property lacked explanatory adequacy and political force in a post-artisanal market society: "The institution of private property, as defined in the eighteenth century, worked fairly well so long as tools were an appendage to the worker, but it fails to guarantee equality in opportunity now that the worker is an appendage to the machine." To revise or revoke the "natural right" of property in view of the "social production" sponsored by the new corporations, and thus to redefine individualism, was, however, to appropriate the insights of socialists, who typically identified the "trust movement" as the origin of a collectivism congenial to democracy: "These suggestions are not new. They are, on the contrary, the common thought of socialist writers, and the fact that they are made the premise of socialist conclusions seems to have led economists who appreciate the grandeur of English jurisprudence to overlook them or to deny them." Adams nevertheless insisted that to ignore or reject this body of thought on political grounds was to rely on metaphysics—"speculation and philosophy"—as the rationale for the rights of property *and* persons: "To deny the fact of social production, and thus preclude the possibility of a development in the idea of property, is not only unfortunate, but there is no justification for it in the nature of the case. Individualism does not consist in living in isolation, but rather in dwelling in a society of recognized interdependencies. Its development is marked by the regress of self-sufficiency and the progress of association." A few of the distinguished economists who responded to Adams took issue with his particular proposals regarding the redefinition of property—he wanted to acknowledge the "workmen's property" in "the fact of social and associated production" by means of collective bargaining—but no one bothered to defend either "natural right" or, what is the same thing, the "individualism of the eighteenth century," as the bulwark of liberty in the modern-industrial world.[36]

Adams and his interlocutors understood that the "natural right" of property could not survive the emergence of corporate capitalism because it was the corollary of a labor theory of value and the predicate of an outmoded individualism. In any event, it could not explain or justify the allocation of corporate assets by salaried managers; for the political function of this right—the guarantee of each citizen's independence from the coercive powers of the state and from the general will of all other citizens—could not be deduced from the separation of ownership and control of corporate assets, or from the magnitude of corporate wealth and bureaucracies. Even when the corporation appeared in legal discourse as a "natural entity," it was usually approached as the creature of the law, and in most juridical treatments, it appeared as an "artificial person" who could not have "natural" rights that existed prior to any political community or purpose. Indeed we might say that the intellectual problem of "corporate personality," which preoccupied philosophers like John Dewey as well as jurists and politicians from the 1890s to the 1930s, was the larger problem of explaining agency or accountability in the absence of a "natural person" to whom one could ascribe these attributes. For this was the problem presented by the new forms of and titles to property organized by a corporate credit economy—the forms and titles that eventually made the individual proprietor an endangered species.37

Certainly the Populists thought so. Here is how James "Cyclone" Davis, a legendary Texas orator, put their case in 1894:

> These corporations being artificial creations invested with authority to act as natural persons, they are moved only by an exhaustless greed for lucre, without one human sympathy. . . . Being souless, artificial and intangible, they act only through created agencies. Thus natural persons who own and move their power, look to them only for an increase of gains, and feel no personal concern for the moral quality of the acts which produce money. . . . The individual is merged in the money-machine of which he is an integral part, and the morality of his action is the morality of the company, not his.

The *Platte County Argus* of Columbus, Nebraska, concurred with Davis: "No matter for what corporations were organized, nor what they have accomplished in the past, all men today know that they are great engines of oppression. They have crushed individual efforts and hopes for a competent and independent living." But one didn't have to be a Populist to believe that the moral personality residing in the individual proprietor was at risk in a society shaped by the capacities and requirements of the new corporations. Judge Peter S. Grosscup of the U.S. Circuit Court of Appeals—he issued the injunction against officials of the American Railway Union in 1894, during the Pullman strike and boycott—argued in 1905 that the "loss that republican America now confronts" as a result of the corporate reorganization and redefinition of property "is the loss of individual hope and prospect."[38]

In his own way, Dewey agreed with these assessments. In a 1926 essay for the *Yale Law Journal*, he argued that the rise of large corporations threatened the integrity, or rather the cultural utility, of the "natural person" who had served as the *sujet de droit* of modern law but also as the presupposition of metaphysical, theological, and vernacular notions of "the subject" or the "seat of personality." The "merging of popular and philosophical notions of the person with the legal notion," Dewey noted, was a consequence of the "conception that before anything can be a jural person it must intrinsically possess certain properties, the existence of which is necessary to constitute anything [as] a person." Because these properties had long been associated in both popular culture and legal doctrine with individuals, not with "group personalities," the function and the future of the individual was inevitably at issue in every discussion of the corporation as a person: "The readiest starting point is a singular man; hence there is imposed the necessity of finding some nature or essence which belongs both to men in the singular and to corporate bodies." But this false necessity only obscured the simple fact that the increasing salience of corporate "persons" required the reconsideration—and the reconstruction—of subjectivity as such: "The root difficulty in present controversies about 'natural' and associated bodies may be that while we oppose one to the other, or try to find some combining union of the two, what we really need to do is to overhaul the doctrine of personality which underlies both of them." In the end, therefore, Dewey treated the corporate threat to the "natural person" as a promise, that is, as a premise of new thinking about the *social* sources of subjectivity: "The group personality theory has been asserted both as a check upon what was regarded as [an] anarchic and dissolving individualism, to set up something more abiding and worthful than a single human being, and to increase the power and dignity of the single being as over against the state." From this standpoint, which Henry Carter Adams and his colleagues in the American Economic Association clearly shared, the "social self" looks like the cousin of the "corporate personality," or rather the offspring of those "associated bodies," those "artificial persons," whose agency and accountability are collective and bureaucratic—that is, the negation of what Dewey called the "old individualism."[39]

As Max Weber recognized, the characteristic progeny of the modern corporation was a "bureaucratic rationality" that established and enforced a new division of manual and mental labor. In most historical accounts, this rationality is synonomous with scientific management, or with the larger movement in business toward closer surveillance of the industrial workforce, or with the eclipse of entrepreneurial eccentricity. Frederick Winslow Taylor's project did of course require a small army of white-collared supervisors, and it did leave once-skilled workers with little more than their manual dexterity, and it did demote the entrepreneur from rugged individual to class clown. But we should also notice that corporate bureaucracy—the headquarters of the "world of large-scale production"—became the setting in which work as such was redefined to accommodate an educated female labor force, and therefore became the "tertiary" site on which the New Woman discovered her sisters. If "the effect of the industrial revolution was the dedomestication of women," as *Fortune* magazine claimed in 1935, that effect was not felt by native-born, *middle-class* women until the corporate reconstruction of American capitalism made paid employment a respectable and finally typical stage in their life cycle. So if the cause (in both senses) of modern feminism is the extrication of women from an *exclusive* preoccupation with domestic roles—a process that both presupposes paid employment and permits the detachment of female sexuality from familial objects or reproductive functions—and if modern feminism is by definition a cross-class social movement because it claims to speak for all women, it would seem to follow that the necessary condition of modern feminism is the rise of corporate capitalism.[40]

Let us test this proposition by first taking a look at the relevant patterns and proportions of female labor force participation. Gainfully employed women aged sixteen to forty-four comprised 21.7 percent of the labor force in 1890, 23.5 percent in 1900, 28.1 percent in 1910, 28.3 percent in 1920, and 29.7 percent in 1930. Most of these women were single, but as early as 1910, almost a quarter of them were married (in 1910, 18.6 percent of female factory operatives were married, while only 5.6 percent of female clerical workers were, but the latter proportion doubled by 1920). As with participation rates, the greatest change took place in the first decade of the century, when the proportion of married women in the labor force increased from 15.4 to 24.7 percent. During this same decade, the exodus of women from domestic service began in earnest; after 1910, the numbers of servants declined absolutely as the demand for female labor in department stores, factories, and central offices increased and as household appliances proliferated (between 1909 and 1923, household spending on "mechanical appliances" more than doubled, from $152 to $419 million). The demand from the central offices of the new corporations was especially strong. In 1890, there were about 33,000 stenographers and typists employed in the U.S.; by 1920, there were over 600,000, and 90 percent were female. In 1890, there were about 220,000 gainfully employed "clerical and kindred workers," and only 21 percent of them were female; by 1920, there were two million, and 50 percent were female. In 1890, there were about 161,000 book-keepers, accountants, and cashiers keeping tabs on American enterprise and earnings, only 17 percent of them female; by 1920, there were about 740,000, and 50 percent were female. Once again the first decade of the twentieth century appears as the watershed, whether we look at overall growth rates in the new occupations or at growth in the proportion of women in these occupations.[41]

This "feminization" of clerical work in corporate offices proceeded quite rapidly because by the end of the nineteenth century, native-born, educated, middle-class women constituted a readily available pool of underemployed labor. In 1900, for example, the number of females who graduated from high school was 50 percent greater than the number of males who graduated, but the females had far fewer opportunities in the professions. Until the central offices of the new corporations were established in the first decade of the twentieth century, demand for the skills of these educated women came largely from the elementary and secondary schools. As Grace Coyle, a lecturer in economics at Barnard whose book on clerical occupations established her as an authority on the transformation of work, noted in 1929: "While conditions within business were creating the clerical positions, circumstances outside it were producing the workers to fill them. The change in the position of women was admitting and indeed forcing them into all fields of employment." But middle-class women *chose* the clerical positions when they could because the pay, the "privileges" (vacation, sick leave, security of tenure), and the protections—particularly from unwanted male attentions—were better here than in any other line of work outside the professions, and, more importantly, because the social status associated with these positions was higher than that accruing to those those in department stores or factories despite the fact that the rapid mechanization of office work made it increasingly menial.[42]

Clerical work was a new portal between the worlds of male and female. "With men and women now working side by side," Olivier Zunz points out, "gender roles and career patterns had to be adjusted." The period of adjustment was protracted, of course, as many films of the 1920s, 1930s, and 1950s will attest, but it would have been impossible or unnecessary if corporate bureaucracies had not appeared as the horizon of white-collar work for females. Clerical work in the central offices of the large corporations was also the cultural context in which class differences were both represented and renegotiated by the juxtaposition of genders. As Coyle noted in explaining the relatively high status accorded to the clerical occupations, "there is often the possibility of contact with those in executive positions." The "social significance" of these occupations, she claimed, was then a function of the *psychological* mobility they provided to the young women who held them—the young women who perceived that, in the extra-domestic space of the office, their prospects of marriage, and of social interaction more generally, were no longer determined by their origins: "In our economic system they present the most accessible rung by which many workers may climb 'up' on the socially established ladder. The attainment of a clerical position has come to be valued, therefore, not alone for its intrinsic advantages, economic or otherwise, but also as a symbol of other less tangible benefits."[43]

It is worth emphasizing that the bureaucracies of the new corporations were not mere extensions of existing practices or enlargements of existing spaces. As Margery Davies suggests, "the expansion of capitalist firms did not entail a simple proliferation of small, 'nineteenth-century' offices," wherein male clerks had served as apprentice managers. Instead it involved a fundamental transformation of the market and the labor process, and a corresponding shift in the meanings of work and production. The "clerical and kindred" occupations grew in the bureaucratic space between mass production and mass distribution, where the large corporations thrived by integrating and centralizing functions hitherto dispersed among many firms or across economic sectors. In this sense, the rapid growth of the "feminized" white-collar workforce was an index of the extent to which managerial discretion was modifying and replacing the "invisible hand" of blind market forces in allocating resources—the extent to which prices and markets were subject to "administration," that is, to the purposes and plans of "corporate personalities." But it is perhaps more to the point to say that such growth was also an index of the extent to which the provision of technical-administrative "services" was replacing goods production as the typical setting or purpose of work. Coyle explained these new relationships as follows:

> The clerical functions serve in the essential linkage of production and distribution. The need for such a connective has been enormously increased with the development of modern business. Our large scale production, our extensive transportations, our modern high-pressure advertising all require an amount of office work per unit of goods enormously greater than in the early days of the industrial revolution. Modern business practice with its accuracy, its record keeping, and its statistical analyses would be impossible without extensive clerical forces.

Charles A. Heiss, the comptroller of AT&T, agreed with this periodization of technical and/or administrative functions. "While the art of keeping accounts of some form or other is quite old," he claimed in 1943, "accounting as a science, as a necessary aid in administration, and as a phase of productive operation is young, indeed very young. Its rise is intimately connected with the development during the past 50 years of our modern, highly developed industries and the social and economic reactions resulting from their growth."[44]

So the division of manual and mental labor inscribed in corporate bureaucracies did contribute to the "disappearance of a typically male work culture," as Zunz contends, but not merely because work rules had to change when women took over the clerical occupations. The more important cause of this redefinition of work was the rapid and universal mechanization of the labor process, which gradually but effectively undermined a sex-based division of labor. Samuel Schmalhausen, the coeditor of V. F. Calverton's *Modern Quarterly*—according to the *New York Times*, these two were "jointly the Karl Marx of the Sexual Revolution"—suggested in 1929, for example, that "the significant point, under the new mechanistic auspices, is the unprecedented mingling of the sexes within an unsentimental and comparatively objective environment, hostile to romance and the dream life, most congenial to comradeliness and a sort of flirtatious friendliness." Coyle noted that these "mechanistic auspices" had revolutionized clerical no less than factory work: "in every corner, human labor is being replaced by mechanical devices or is being used to tend machines which seem almost human in their capacities." The result, from the factory floor to the central offices, was to reverse the relation between active subject and passive objects embodied first in the artisanal experience of goods production and then in workers' control of machine production—the result, that is, was to violate the expectations of men at work. As we have seen, the skilled workers who resisted scientific management thought so: they clearly understood that their manhood and their agency as well as their wages were at stake in struggles over the content of work. The young Lewis Mumford agreed with them. In trying to explain the nature of work under the corporate regime of universal mechanization, he suggested that "the worker, instead of being a source of work, becomes an observer and regulator of the performance of the machine—a supervisor of production rather than an active agent."45

The redefinition of work in and through the central offices of the new corporations had moral implications, then, which carried sexual connotations. On the one hand, the moral significance of work became unintelligible—at least in the terms inherited from the nineteenth century—insofar as it became impossible for individuals to derive or deduce manhood, character, agency, and other attributes of the self-determining personality from their production of value through work—that is, from their participation in an increasingly bureaucratized, mechanized, and "feminized" labor process. William James recognized these implications when he proposed, in 1910, to rehabilitate manhood by making work a public virtue, a state-sponsored enterprise, a moral equivalent of war. So did Richard Hofstadter forty years later, in summarizing the difference between Progressives and New Dealers: "The generation for which Wilson and Brandeis spoke looked to economic life as a field for the expression of character; modern liberals seem to think of it as a field in which certain results are to be expected. It is this change in the moral stance that seems most worthy of remark. A generation ago, and more, the average American was taught to expect that a career . . . should be in some sense a testing and proving ground for manhood and character, and it was in these terms that the competitive order was often made most appealing."[46]

On the other hand, the redefinition of work in and through the central offices of the new corporations permitted the detachment of female sexuality from familial objects and reproductive functions, mainly by giving educated, middle-class women the chance to postpone marriage, and thus to experiment, however briefly, with their bodies and desires. At any rate we can be certain that the sexual attitudes and behavior of American women changed drastically between 1900 and 1930, and that educated, middle-class women were the rear guard of this revolution because they did not follow the sexual example of working-class women until the second and third decades of the twentieth century. By 1930, the convergence of sexual expectations across lines of both class and gender was practically complete. For example, educated middle-class women who were born in the 1890s were twice as likely to divorce their husbands or to engage in premarital sexual intercourse as those born before 1890; those born between 1900 and 1910 were again twice as likely to engage in premarital sex as those born in the 1890s. If the most serious challenge to the inherited ideal of female domesticity and its attendant allocation of female sexuality was increased labor force participation by women, as Charlotte Perkins Gilman, Rheta Childe Dorr, Linda Gordon, Kathy Peiss, and many others have suggested, we can explain the changing social composition of this staggered sexual revolution by noting that the timing of the entry of educated, middle-class women into the heterosocial world of paid employment was determined by demand for their labor from the new corporations.[47]

Now I admit that these implications of corporate-bureaucratic rationality can be read as symptoms of moral decline. But I would also insist that to arrive at this diagnosis is to assume that an artisanal or entrepreneurial model of subjectivity is the universal standard against which all other models must be judged; or that the moral personality must be grounded in the work ethic of productive labor; or that female sexuality should be regulated if not contained by marriage contracts. If we drop these assumptions, we can acknowledge that the production of value through work is not the only or even the most significant setting in which the self-determining moral personality can develop, and that the regulation of female sexuality by political and/or legal means is a moral problem which cannot be solved by reference to "family values." We can claim accordingly that the rise of corporate capitalism is more comedy than tragedy because it emptied the household of economic functions and thereby allowed the desublimation of female desire, or, to be more concrete, because the bureaucratic rationality sponsored by corporate capitalism opened up a new, extra-domestic discursive space in which the resignification of masculinity and femininity—hence the reconstruction of subjectivity as such— became both possible and necessary.

The "imaginary femininity" at the heart of *Pragmatism* was, in this historically specific sense, not accidental. It was instead the metaphorical means by which William James could most easily remove himself from the "space of representation" still guarded by metaphysical realism, and thus escape the intellectual entanglements of epistemology. His question was not, What are the rules that must govern the representation of reality?—as if that reality is already external to our desires and discourses—but, How do our representations function as realities, as causes rather than copies of something more solid or fundamental or real? Like Hamlet, then, and for that matter like Theodore Dreiser, James addressed the spectacle of female desire—the "old mole" that resurfaced in the character of Sister Carrie and in the more reputable form of the New Woman—as the occasion for a new way of thinking about our unfolding capacity for self-reflection and realization, as the warrant for a new way of narrating the future. From the standpoint he provides, we can see that if modern feminism presupposes the reconstruction of subjectivity which the original pragmatists grasped as the central fact of their times, it is also and equally true that they could not have grasped this fact unless women had been able to extricate themselves from an exclusive preoccupation with domestic roles by seizing the opportunities made available to them under the "mechanistic auspices" of corporate bureaucracy. But this is to say, once again, that the pragmatism James gives us is improbable if not inconceivable in the absence of feminism, or—to put it yet another way—that the desublimation of female sexuality enabled by the rise of corporate capitalism is the necessary condition of both pragmatism and feminism.

Afterword

No Exit

If you are by now persuaded that the meaning or content of an idea cannot be known apart from its consequences—that is, if you are thinking pragmatically about the arguments of this book—you are probably asking, What is to be done? It is not a question a professor gets asked very often. Nor is it a question that any writer can answer without the help of readers. But I think it's worth addressing here as long as we don't treat my answers as the final word.

Let me begin with what is *not* to be done. If the arguments of this book make sense, we cannot see markets as strictly economic phenomena that must undermine social democracy before, during, and after "globalization"; we cannot define consumer culture as the solvent of subjectivity as such; we cannot claim that the "social self" is the original version of the "managed self" cited, and scolded, by contemporary cultural critics; we cannot maintain that the "world of large-scale production" creates "social psychosis" or undercuts the "economic position" of women; and we cannot treat corporations as the undifferentiated, bureaucratic Other to which we are always opposed and from which we can somehow abstain.

As for what *is* to be done, I would suggest that if the arguments of this book make sense, we can look for the sources of social democracy in the here and now as well as in the habits, traditions, and movements of the past; once that search gets under way, the "Populist moment" of the 1890s and the "turbulent years" of the 1930s will no longer appear as the only democratic promises the American Left can keep. We can also grasp pragmatism and feminism as related ways of recognizing, accepting, and effecting change in the forms of human subjectivity, thus as useful ways of conducting *cultural* politics. Perhaps we can then dismantle the dualisms that still plague our thinking about politics per se—perhaps pragmatism and feminism can teach us to map the middle ground between ethical principles and historical circumstances, radicalism and conservatism, revolution and reform, socialism and capitalism, equality and difference. I am not suggesting that we should let pragmatism and feminism teach us to forfeit our principles. I am suggesting that to map the middle ground is to refuse to treat these categories as the terms of either/or choices.

For example, if we think of difference and equality as contingent moments in historical time rather than ontological dimensions of human existence, we can see that to demand equality between the sexes is not to require the denial or the erasure of all distinctions between males and females; it is instead to realize that equality pre-supposes difference—if we were all the same, what would be the point of raising the question?—and to historicize both terms, so that each can be understood as a function of historical development and political commitment rather than a natural phenomenon. Feminism then becomes the device by which these terms are contained in a productive, dialogical relation. It becomes a way of seeing that apart from childbearing capacities, the differences between males and females are culturally determined conventions: like the built landscape we inhabit, they are mostly artificial but also quite real.

An even better example might be the choice between conservatism and radicalism. The proponents of both persuasions agree that the United States is exceptional because revolution (like socialism) is a foreign import without historical roots in the American experience. Conservatives revere the American past because they believe it was never disfigured by revolution, while radicals repudiate this past because they believe it was never redeemed by revolution. They agree, then, that revolution is by definition a complete break from the past, a unique moment when the conflict between "ought" and "is"—between ethical principles and historical circumstances—is violently resolved in favor of the former, and anything becomes possible. If we refuse the either/or choice between conservatism and radicalism, by mediating between them as pragmatism and feminism teach us to, we might posit a different definition of revolution and a new attitude toward our history (and vice versa). We might define revolution as the suture rather than the rupture of past, present, and future, or as the politically synthetic effort to make the relation between these temporal moments continuous rather than incommensurable. To do so would, however, require that we follow the lead of Hannah Arendt and learn to treat the French Revolution (and its Bolshevik replicant) as just one species in a profuse and increasingly plural genus, not the prototype of revolution as such. We would also have to learn that American revolutions remain unfinished because the nation itself has always been, and will always be, a work in progress.

This redefinition of revolution could let us revise the tragic narratives that now regulate the writing of American history. For example, in place of the high modernist model that still shapes social and cultural history, through which the figure of the Gothic freeholder who speaks a populist idiom gets reinstated as the paradigm of the genuine self, the moral personality, we could install a model that comprehends historical change in the forms of subjectivity as something other than deviation from the norms generated in the early modern period. We would not then be the prisoners of the past, and could claim to be something more than romantics in flight from the reified present: our narratives would not reproduce the ironic distance from the past that keeps us in exile from the present because the stories we tell about ourselves in the form of American history would allow for a future that is neither inevitable return to nor radical break from the past. The world we have inherited from the past would appear to us as both impediment *and* means to the realization of our purposes—as both constraint on *and* condition of our political innovations. And so we might even learn to feel at home in the divisions of historical time.

Notes

1. On the "Dunning School" of Reconstruction historiography and its cousins and consequences, see W. E. B. Du Bois, *Black Reconstruction in America, 1860–1880* (1935; reprint, New York: Atheneum, 1969), chap. 17.

2. See Richard Hofstadter, *The Age of Reform: From Bryan to FDR* (New York: Vintage, 1955), esp. pp. 303–16, where Hofstadter explains how the social-democratic reforms specific to the New Deal were predicated on acceptance of the large corporations—"by 1933 the American public had lived with the great corporation for so long that it was felt to be domesticated" (p. 312)—and thus represented a departure from the early "Progressive impulse" as well as from Populism. Hofstadter and others (e.g. Daniel Boorstin, Irwin Unger, William Appleman Williams) were deemed "consensus" historians because they emphasized the cultural or ideological coherence of American civilization, that is, the tacit but nonetheless effective affirmation of possessive individualism by most Americans, even in the throes of class struggle. I follow Gene Wise (see note 3, below) in preferring the term "counter-progressive" to characterize Hofstadter et al., because none of the so-called consensus historians, with the possible exception of Boorstin, ever posited the absence of conflict among Americans.

3. On the meaning and significance of "counter-progressive" historiography, see Gene Wise, *American Historical Explanations*, 2nd rev. ed. (Minneapolis: University of Minnesota Press, 1980), chap. 4; chapters 1–2, 4, below; and James Livingston, "Social Theory and Historical Method in the Work of William Appleman Williams," forthcoming in *Diplomatic History*. On marginalism and literary naturalism, see James Livingston, *Pragmatism and the Political Economy of Cultural Revolution, 1850–1940* (Chapel Hill: University of North Carolina Press, 1994), chaps. 2–3, 6; on black nationalism, see chapter 4, below; and on the "new unionism" sponsored by the American Federation of Labor, which treated large corporations as devices for regulating markets rather than evidence of the republic's demise, which guided the labor movement and the larger culture beyond a preoccupation with goods production, as against consumption, and which contributed to the radical redefinition of politics in the Progressive Era and after, see Richard Schneirov, *Labor and Urban Politics: Class Conflict and the Origins of Modern Liberalism in*

Chicago, 1864–1897 (Urbana: University of Illinois Press, 1998); Lawrence B. Glickman, *A Living Wage: American Workers and the Making of Consumer Society* (Ithaca: Cornell University Press, 1997); Dorothy Sue Cobble, "Lost Ways of Organizing: Reviving the AFL's Direct Affiliate Strategy," *Industrial Relations* 36 (1997): 278–301, and "American Labor Politics, AFL Style," *Labor History* 40 (1999): 192–96; Rosanne Currarino, "Labor Intellectuals and the Labor Question: Wage Work and the Making of Consumer Society, 1873–1905," Ph.D. dissertation, Rutgers University, 1999; and unpublished papers by Michael Merrill and Grace Palladino.

4. See Karl Marx, *Capital: A Critique of Political Economy*, 3 vols., trans. Samuel Moore and Edward Aveling (Chicago: Charles H. Kerr & Co., 1906), 1:41–196; *Grundrisse: Introduction to the Critique of Political Economy*, trans. Martin Nicolaus (Baltimore: Penguin, 1973), pp. 103–5; Max Weber, *The Protestant Ethic and the Spirit of Capitalism*, trans. Talcott Parsons (New York: Scribner's, 1958), pp. 17–27; and Karl Polanyi, *The Great Transformation* (Boston: Beacon Press, 1944), chaps. 5–6, 14. Marx is worth quoting here as a way of elucidating the notion of abstract social labor: "Indifference towards any specific kind of labour presupposes a very developed totality of real kinds of labour, of which no single one is any longer predominant. As a rule, the most general abstractions arise only in the midst of the richest possible concrete development, where one thing appears as common to many, to all. Then it ceases to be thinkable in a particular form alone. On the other side, this abstraction of labour as such is not merely the mental product of a concrete totality of labours. Indifference towards specific labours corresponds to a form of society in which individuals can with ease transfer from one labour to another, and where the specific kind is a matter of chance for them, hence of indifference. Not only the category, labour, but labour in reality has become the means of creating wealth in general, and has ceased to be organically linked with particular individuals in any specific form. Such a state of affairs is at its most developed in the most modern form of existence of bourgeois society—in the United States. Here, then, for the first time, the point of departure of modern economics, namely the abstraction of the category 'labour,' 'labour as such,' labour pure and simple, becomes true in practice." *Grundrisse*, pp. 104–5.

5. See G. W. F. Hegel, *The Philosophy of Right*, trans. T. M. Knox (New York: Oxford University Press, 1952), par. 67, p. 54: "By alienating the whole of my time, as crystallized in my work and everything I produced, I would be making into another's property the substance of my being, my universal activity and actuality, my personality." That nineteenth-century workers taught their fellow Americans to confine market forces to certain social spaces is the import if not the argument of David Roediger, *The Wages of Whiteness: Race and the Making of the American Working Class* (New York: Verso, 1991), part 2. See also Thomas Haskell's compelling contributions to Thomas Bender, ed., *The Antislavery Debate: Capitalism and Abolitionism as a Problem in Historical Interpretation* (Berkeley: University of California Press, 1992); and Amy Dru Stanley, *From Bondage to Contract: Wage Labor, Marriage, and the Market in the Age of Emancipation* (New York: Cambridge University Press, 1998), which demonstrates, among other things, that the struggle over the meaning of contract and the scope of the market was intensified, not concluded, by emancipation.

6. Weber, *Protestant Ethic*, p. 17. See otherwise Daniel Bell, *The Coming of Post-Industrial Society* (New York: Basic Books, 1973); Stuart Hall, "Gramsci's Relevance for the Study of Race and Ethnicity," *Journal of Communications Inquiry* 10 (1993): 5–27; Martin J. Sklar, *The United States as a Developing Country* (New York: Cambridge University Press, 1992); and J. K. Gibson-Graham, *The End of Capitalism (as we knew it): A Feminist Critique of Political Economy* (London: Blackwell, 1996).

7. Proprietary capitalism is the successor to bourgeois society, the simple market (or "proto-industrial") society of early modern Europe which was exported to North America in the seventeenth century. Under proprietary capitalism in the U.S., circa 1790s-1890s, a *complex* market society emerges and evolves; its salient features are (a) the convergence of ownership and control of property in the person of the proprietor or entrepreneur, as against their division between stockholders and salaried managers (bureaucracy is therefore a "political" phenomenon, a function of government rather than a typical feature of private firms); (b) the development and institutionalization of a market in labor as well as goods; (c) the completion of primitive accumulation, that is, the "removal" of the Indians and the imposition of a unitary property system on the continent; (d) the removal of goods production from the household as machines, central shops, and factories replace artisanal forms and scenes of work; (e) the articulation of class as the regulative principle of general social relations, as the forms and scenes of work are reshaped by the relation between capital and labor; (f) the demotion of agriculture to a mere "branch of industry"; (g) the creation of a new sexual division of labor as work for wages outside the home becomes the norm for white males. For further discussion of how corporate capitalism departs from its proprietary predecessor, see Martin J. Sklar, *The Corporate Reconstruction of American Capitalism, 1890–1916: The Market, the Law, and Politics* (New York: Cambridge University Press, 1988), part 1; Livingston, *Pragmatism and Political Economy*; Livingston, "Corporations and Cultural Studies," *Social Text* 44 (1995): 61–68; and chapters 1–4, 6, below.

8. See Bell, *Post-Industrial Society*; Mills, "The New Left," in Irving Horowitz, ed., *Power, Politics, and People* (New York: Oxford University Press, 1963), pp. 247–59; Cruse, *The Crisis of the Negro Intellectual* (New York: Morrow, 1967); and chapters 2, 4, below. The "cultural apparatus" becomes the cutting edge of change insofar as the social significance and cultural salience of goods production decline, that is, insofar as the domain of "socially necessary labor" recedes. In the United States, this "post-industrial" process begins in the 1920s, when the capacity, productivity, and output of both the capital goods and the consumer goods industries increase dramatically without any net additions either to the capital stock or to the labor force in these industries: see Livingston, *Pragmatism and Political Economy*, chap. 4.

9. See Livingston, *Pragmatism and Political Economy*, chaps. 8–10, and chapters 2, 4, 6, below.

10. So there is no "American evasion of philosophy," as Cornel West would have it, but there is a pragmatist critique of epistemology. The notion that "experience" somehow exists prior to everything else, including language, and the related idea that an emphasis on this ontological priority unites pragmatists and feminists, serve as the regulative assumptions of Marjorie C. Miller, "Feminism and Pragmatism," *Monist* 78 (1992): 444–57; Char-

lene Haddock-Seigfried, "Shared Communities of Interest: Feminism and Pragmatism," *Hypatia* 8 (1993): 1–14, and *Pragmatism and Feminism: Reweaving the Social Fabric* (Chicago: University of Chicago Press, 1996); Jane Duran, "The Intersection of Pragmatism and Feminism," *Hypatia* 8 (1993): 159–71. For dissent from and criticism of this position, see Livingston, *Pragmatism and Political Economy*, chap. 10; Joan W. Scott, "The Evidence of Experience," *Critical Inquiry* 17 (1991): 773–97; Richard Rorty, "Intellectual Historians and Pragmatist Philosophy," in John Pettegrew, ed., *A Pragmatist's Progress? Richard Rorty and American Intellectual History* (Lanham, Md.: Rowman & Littlefield, 2000), pp. 207–11; and chapter 6, below.

11. The reference to "double consciousness" comes of course from W. E. B. Du Bois, *The Souls of Black Folk* (1903; Signet ed., New York: Penguin, 1995), pp. 43–46. In June of 1903, William James sent a copy of this "decidedly moving book" to his brother Henry, recommending that he read it in preparation for his trip to the U.S.: see Bruce Kuklick's "Chronology" in *William James: Writings 1902–1910* (New York: Library of America, 1987), pp. 1343–44. And see Dickson D. Bruce Jr., "W. E. B. Du Bois and the Idea of Double Consciousness," *American Literature* 64 (1992): 299–309, esp. 304, on the crucial role of William James in the development of this notion. For examples of feminist theorizing that construct or acknowledge a more or less pragmatist lineage, see Mitchell Aboulafia, "Was George Herbert Mead a Feminist?" *Hypatia* 8 (1993): 145–58; Johanna Meehan, ed., *Feminists Read Habermas: Gendering the Subject of Discourse* (New York: Routledge, 1995); Seyla Benhabib, *Situating the Self: Gender, Community, and Postmodernism* (New York: Routledge, 1992); Kaja Silverman, *The Subject of Semiotics* (New York: Oxford University Press, 1983); Teresa de Lauretis, *Alice Doesn't: Feminism, Semiotics, Cinema* (Bloomington: Indiana University Press, 1984). And see also chapter 6, below.

12. See chapters 2–4, below.

13. See chapters 2–3, 6, below, and Livingston, *Pragmatism and Political Economy*, chap. 10.

14. See chapters 3, 6, below. On the origins and implications of the "social self," see also Eldon Eisenach's important book *The Lost Promise of Progressivism* (Lawrence: University of Kansas Press, 1994), and Jeff Sklansky's provocative essay, "The Ideological Origins of the 'Social Self,'" *Radical History Review* 76 (2000): 90–114: On the question of "reification," see the seminal essay by Georg Lukacs, "Reification and the Consciousness of the Proletariat" (1922–23), in *History and Class Consciousness: Studies in Marxist Dialectics*, trans. Rodney Livingstone (Cambridge: MIT Press, 1971), pp. 83–222, discussed below in chapter 1.

15. See chapters 2–4, below. On comedy as a narrative form, see Kenneth Burke, *Attitudes Toward History* (1937; rev. ed., Boston: Beacon Press, 1961), esp. part 1, chaps. 2–4, part 2, chaps. 4–6; and Hayden White, *Metahistory: The Historical Imagination in Nineteenth-Century Europe* (Baltimore: Johns Hopkins University Press, 1973), esp. pp. 93–131. Let me quote Burke here as a way of clarifying the significance of the distinction between tragedy and comedy: "Like tragedy, comedy warns against the dangers of pride, but its emphasis shifts from *crime* to *stupidity*. . . . The progress of humane enlightenment can go no further than in picturing people not as *vicious*, but as *mistaken*. When you add that people are

necessarily mistaken, that *all* people are exposed to situations in which they must act as fools, that every insight contains its own special kind of blindness, you complete the comic circle, returning again to the lesson of humility that underlies great tragedy. The audience, from its vantage point, sees the operation of errors that the characters of the play cannot see; thus seeing from two angles at once, it is chastened by dramatic irony; it is admonished to remember that when intelligence means *wisdom*, ... it requires fear, resignation, the sense of limits, as an important ingredient. Comedy requires the maximum of forensic complexity. In the tragic plot the *deus ex machina* is always lurking, to give events a fatalistic turn in accordance with the old '*participation*' pattern whereby men anthropomorphize nature, feeling its force as the taking of sides with them or against them.... Comedy deals with *man in society*, tragedy with the *cosmic man.*" *Attitudes*, pp. 41–42. Cf. White, contemplating Hegel: "Comedy is the form which reflection takes after it has assimilated the truths of Tragedy to itself.... Tragedy approaches the culmination of an action, carried out with a specific intention, from the standpoint of an agent who sees deployed before him a world which is at once a means and an impediment to the realization of his purpose. Comedy looks back upon the effects of that collision from beyond the condition of resolution through which the Tragic action has carried the spectators, even if the action has not carried the protagonist there but has consumed him in the process." *Metahistory*, pp. 94–95.

16. John Dewey, *Reconstruction in Philosophy* (1920; Boston: Beacon Press, 1948), p. 116.

Chapter 1: Modern Subjectivity and Consumer Culture

1. I am drawing on Alasdair MacIntyre, *After Virtue* (Notre Dame: Notre Dame University Press, 1981), chaps. 4–6; Stephen Toulmin, *Cosmopolis: The Hidden Agenda of Modernity* (Chicago: University of Chicago Press, 1990), chap. 3; Charles Taylor, "Legitimation Crisis?" in *Philosophy and the Human Sciences: Philosophical Papers 2* (New York: Cambridge University Press, 1985), pp. 248–88; and Hiram Caton, *The Origin of Subjectivity: An Essay on Descartes* (New Haven: Yale University Press, 1973), esp. chaps. 2–3, 5. In "Hamlet, *Little Dorritt*, and the History of Character," in Michael Hays, ed., *Critical Conditions* (Minneapolis: University of Minnesota Press, 1992), pp. 82–96, Jonathan Arac points out that "individualism" as such is practically impossible to date; but I would insist that the belief in the ontological priority of the unbound individual is a strictly modern phenomenon, and that this belief radically reshapes inherited notions—the political forms and the cultural content—of individualism.

2. See James Livingston, *Pragmatism and the Political Economy of Cultural Revolution, 1850–1940* (Chapel Hill: University of North Carolina Press, 1994), pp. 201–7, 215–24, 247–50, 365–66 n. 42.

3. For example, see Genevieve Lloyd, *The Man of Reason: "Male" and "Female" in Western Philosophy* (Minneapolis: University of Minnesota Press, 1984); Stephanie H. Jed, *Chaste Thinking: The Rape of Lucretia and the Birth of Humanism* (Bloomington: Indiana University Press, 1989); and Carole Pateman, *The Sexual Contract* (Palo Alto: Stanford University Press, 1988).

4. See Linda J. Nicholson, *Gender and History: The Limits of Social Theory in the Age of the Family* (New York: Columbia University Press, 1986), chap. 4; Hanna Fenichel Pitkin, *Fortune Is a Woman: Gender and Politics in the Thought of Niccolo Machiavelli* (Berkeley: University of California Press, 1984), esp. chaps. 4–5; Susan Moller Okin, *Women in Western Political Thought* (Princeton: Princeton University Press, 1979), chaps. 6–8; and Jean Bethke Elshtain, *Public Man, Private Woman: Women in Social and Political Thought* (Princeton: Princeton University Press, 1981), chap. 3.

5. See Livingston, *Pragmatism and Political Economy*, part 1, "The Political Economy of Consumer Culture," pp. 3–118.

6. Georg Lukacs, "Reification and the Consciousness of the Proletariat," in *History and Class Consciousness*, trans. Rodney Livingstone (Cambridge: MIT Press, 1971), pp. 83–222, here 98–99; see the pertinent citations of Weber at pp. 95–96. Page references to Lukacs in text hereafter.

7. Richard W. Fox and T. J. Jackson Lears, introduction to *The Culture of Consumption* (New York: Pantheon, 1983), pp. ix–xvii, here xii; William Leach, *Land of Desire: Merchants, Power, and the Rise of a New American Culture* (New York: Vintage, 1993), p. 302; Jackson Lears, *Fables of Abundance: A Cultural History of Advertising in America* (New York: Basic, 1994), e.g., at pp. 142–77.

8. See the discussion of *poesis* and politics in Livingston, *Pragmatism and Political Economy*, pp. 247–55, and in chapter 2, below. At the same conference to which I presented the essay you are now reading, George Lipsitz and others argued that consumer culture is by definition the solvent of politics as such. I would suggest that they may be unconsciously equating politics as such with the "public sphere" once inhabited by the modern (bourgeois) subject, and thus may be inadvertently ignoring the new domain of *cultural* politics afforded by the rise of corporate capitalism (on which see chapter 2, below). In any event, it is worth noting that, in Lipsitz's argument, the moment of political opposition to globalized corporate capitalism arrives when consumers become producers—that is, when hip-hop artists become artisans by treating their musical sources as the raw materials of new compositions.

9. In transposing the notion of primal scene from psychoanalysis to historiography, I am taking my cue from Jean Laplanche, *Life and Death in Psychoanalysis*, trans. Jeffrey Mehlman (Baltimore: Johns Hopkins University Press, 1976), pp. 38–47, Kaja Silverman, *Male Subjectivity at the Margins* (New York: Routledge, 1992), pp. 162–66, and especially Ned Lukacher, *Primal Scenes: Literature, Philosophy, Psychoanalysis* (Ithaca: Cornell University Press, 1986), pp. 19–44, 51–58, 136–56, 237–46, as well as Freud's own ambivalence, as expressed in the story of the Wolf Man, "From the History of an Infantile Neurosis" (1918), in the *Standard Edition*, trans. James Strachey, vol. 17 (London: Hogarth, 1955), pp. 7–122, e.g. at 57 ("There remains the possibility of taking yet another view of the primal scene underlying the dream—a view, moreover, which obviates to a large extent the conclusion that has been arrived at above"), and at 120 n. 1 ("It is also a matter of indifference in this connection whether we choose to regard it as a primal *scene* or as a primal *phantasy*"). See also Susan Rubin Suleiman, *Subversive Intent: Gender, Politics, and the Avant-Garde* (Cambridge: Harvard University Press, 1990), chap. 5; Donald P. Spence, *Narrative Truth and Historical Truth: Mean-*

ing and Interpretation in Psychoanalysis (New York: Norton, 1982); and Jonathan Lear, Love and Its Place in Nature: A Philosophical Inquiry into Freudian Psychoanalysis (New Haven: Yale University Press, 1990).

10. On race and nineteenth-century American historiography, see David Levin, History as Romantic Art: Bancroft, Prescott, Motley, and Parkman (Palo Alto: Stanford University Press, 1959), chap. 6. One implication of my argument in this paragraph is that "Progressive" historiography is the setting in which class supersedes, or at least begins to compete with, race as the central category of those narratives that offer to explain the national experience of the nineteenth century.

11. See Pitkin, Fortune Is a Woman, chaps. 4–6; J. G. A. Pocock, "Modes of political and historical time in early eighteenth-century England," Virtue, Commerce, and History (New York: Cambridge University Press, 1985), pp. 91–102; Ruth H. Bloch, "The Gendered Meanings of Virtue in Revolutionary America," Signs 13 (1987): 37–58. If we are to understand Populism as the social movement convened by the idea of modern subjectivity—I mean in the late twentieth as well as the late nineteenth century—we need to pay close attention to Steven Hahn's adroit analysis in The Roots of Southern Populism (New York: Oxford, 1983), e.g. at pp. 248–53, and Lawrence Goodwyn's ferocious polemic against "counterprogressive" historiography in Democratic Promise: The Populist Moment in America (New York: Oxford University Press, 1976).

12. See Richard Hofstadter, The Age of Reform: From Bryan to FDR (New York: Vintage, 1955), and William Appleman Williams, The Contours of American History (Cleveland: World, 1961). These and other examples of "counter-progressive" historiography are placed in context by Gene Wise, American Historical Explanations, 2nd rev. ed. (Minneapolis: University of Minnesota Press, 1980), chap. 4; but see also chapter 4, below, as well as James Livingston, "Radicals All!" Reviews in American History 16 (1988): 306–12, and "Why Is There Still Socialism in the United States?" ibid. 22 (1994): 577–83. In this last essay, I argued in passing that we can treat Thurman Arnold's books of the late-1930s as the source of "consensus" historiography because Hofstadter treats them as the intellectual antecedent of his own distinction between the Progressive impulse and the New Deal sensibility.

13. See Klaus Theweleit, Male Fantasies, trans. Stephen Conway, Erica Carter, and Chris Turner, 2 vols. (Minneapolis: University of Minnesota Press, 1987–89), especially 1:63–221 and 2:3–61; Carroll Smith-Rosenberg, "The New Woman as Androgyne: Social Disorder and Gender Crisis, 1870–1936," in Disorderly Conduct (New York: Oxford University Press, 1985), pp. 245–96; and Andreas Huyssen, "Mass Culture as Woman: Modernism's Other," in After the Great Divide (Bloomington: Indiana University Press, 1986), pp. 44–62, quoted from 52.

14. The machinists are quoted and discussed in David Montgomery, The Fall of the House of Labor (New York: Cambridge University Press, 1987), pp. 220–21. The recent work of Joan Scott, among others, demonstrates that gender is always already implicated in class consciousness as a kind of enabling condition; see her Gender and the Politics of History (New York: Columbia University Press, 1988), and Wai Chee Dimock and Michael T. Gilmore, eds., Rethinking Class: Social Formations and Literary Studies (New York: Columbia University Press, 1994), especially the essays by the editors themselves at pp. 57–104, 215–38.

15. See Kaja Silverman, *The Acoustic Mirror: The Female Voice in Psycho-analysis and Cinema* (Bloomington: Indiana University Press, 1988), chap. 1; and Norman Bryson, *Vision and Painting: The Logic of the Gaze* (New Haven: Yale University Press, 1983), chaps. 3–6.

16. See Silverman, *Male Subjectivity*, pp. 151–87, 413 n. 36. See also Eve Kosofsky Sedgwick's reading of James in "The Beast in the Closet: James and the Writing of Homosexual Panic," in *Epistemology of the Closet* (Berkeley: University of California Press, 1990), pp. 182–212.

17. William James, "The Moral Equivalent of War" (1910), in Henry James Jr., ed., *Memories and Studies* (New York: Longmans Green, 1911), pp. 267–96, here 281–87; see Livingston, *Pragmatism and Political Economy*, pp. 211–14, 364–65 n. 41, for a different discussion of this text which addresses the role of Simon Patten in James's periodization of necessity.

18. Cf. the more detailed discussion of Lippmann in Livingston, *Pragmatism and Political Economy*, pp. 69–75. The real challenges to social roles allocated by gender at the turn of the twentieth century, and the *subsequent* transformation of "manhood" and "womanhood," are effectively dismissed by Gail Bederman's *Manliness and Civilization: A Cultural History of Gender and Race in the United States, 1880–1917* (Chicago: University of Chicago Press, 1995); by her account, civilization and manhood were forever fused at this tragic moment, so that both concepts must remain suspect. In my view, her account ignores plentiful evidence of continuous reconstruction of gender roles and race relations into and through the 1920s. I don't mean that she should have broadened the chronological parameters of her book to satisfy my interests—I mean that if we take her argument for granted, as sufficiently demonstrated, we cannot explain (a) the New Woman; (b) the New Negro; (c) the New Empire (that is, the regulative assumption of the American imperial design, viz., what separates the peoples and cultures of the world is not race but degrees or stages of economic development). Moreover, her reading of Charlotte Perkins Gilman is unreliable at best; for the two sources Bederman uses to convict Gilman of racism are *paraphrases* of speeches quoted from newspapers published in New Orleans on the same date, December 11, 1904; in other words, these are not Gilman's own words (see notes 73, 88 at pp. 270–71, and related text at pp. 144–52). Anyone who bothers to read what she wrote with care, and for that matter anyone who merely reads the passages Bederman cites as proof of Gilman's backwardness, will realize that when she mentioned "race," she meant what we used to call the human race. A more reliable, and more intriguing, meditation on changing gender roles in the same period is Beryl Satter, *Each Mind a Kingdom: American Women, Sexual Purity, and the New Thought Movement, 1875–1920* (Berkeley: University of California Press, 1999), the implication of which is that "new thought" was the medium in which many men and women were able to imagine the detachment of female sexuality from domestic or familial functions.

19. See Livingston, *Pragmatism and Political Economy*, pp. 273–79. I would add that, in an era that seems determined to forget modern subjectivity (except of course when Lynne Cheney and William Bennett start reminiscing), the critique of consumer culture represents a return of the repressed—that is, a healthy antidote to the radicalism of both Left and Right.

20. On comic versus tragic forms of narrative, see Hayden White's treatment of Hegel in *Metahistory: The European Historical Imagination in the Nineteenth Century* (Baltimore: Johns Hopkins University Press, 1973), pp. 93–131, and my appropriation of Kenneth Burke's "frames of acceptance" in chapter 2, below. On the implications of proletarianization, see Livingston, *Pragmatism and Political Economy*, chaps. 8–10, and again chapter 2, below; DuBois is quoted from her "Radicalism of the Woman's Suffrage Movement," in Anne Phillips, ed., *Feminism and Equality* (New York: New York University Press, 1987), pp. 127–38, here 131.

21. See, for example, Richard Rorty, *Objectivity, Relativism, and Truth* (New York: Cambridge University Press, 1991); Donna Haraway, *Simians, Cyborgs, and Women: The Reinvention of Nature* (New York: Routledge, 1991); Jane Flax, *Thinking Fragments: Psychoanalysis, Feminism, and Postmodernism in the Contemporary West* (Berkeley: University of California Press, 1990); Mary Hesse, *Revolutions and Reconstructions in the Philosophy of Science* (Bloomington: Indiana University Press, 1980); Lynda Birke, *Women, Feminism, and Biology: The Feminist Challenge* (New York: Methuen, 1986); and Judith Butler, *Gender Trouble: Feminism and the Subversion of Identity* (New York: Routledge, 1990).

22. See *Fables of Abundance*, chaps. 2–3, 12; page references hereafter in text.

23. See Teresa Brennan, *History after Lacan* (New York: Routledge, 1993), pp. 102–17.

24. In addition to the pages cited hereafter in the text, see *Fables of Abundance*, pp. 183–92.

Chapter 2: Fighting the "War of Position"

1. On irony, tragedy, and the ideological effects of historiography, see Hayden White, *Metahistory: The Historical Imagination in Nineteenth Century Europe* (Baltimore: Johns Hopkins University Press, 1973), pp. 230–33, 371–76, and James Livingston, *Pragmatism and the Political Economy of Cultural Revolution 1850–1940* (Chapel Hill: University of North Carolina Press, 1994), pp. 80–82, 323–325 at note 40.

2. Alasdair MacIntyre, *After Virtue* (Notre Dame: University of Notre Dame Press, 1981), pp. 22, 92.

3. On the "usable pasts" of the young intellectuals and their more recent echoes, see Warren I. Susman, *Culture as History: The Transformation of American Society in the 20th Century* (New York: Pantheon, 1984), part 1; Casey Nelson Blake (who studied with Christopher Lasch at the University of Rochester), *Beloved Community: The Cultural Criticism of Randolph Bourne, Van Wyck Brooks, Waldo Frank, and Lewis Mumford* (Chapel Hill: University of North Carolina Press, 1990), chaps. 2–4; and Martin J. Sklar, *The United States as a Developing Country* (New York: Cambridge University Press, 1992), chap. 5. The key texts in announcing the arrival of the young intellectuals are Van Wyck Brooks, *America's Coming-of-Age* (1915), reprinted in *Three Essays on America* (New York: Dutton, 1934), pp. 9–112, and "Young America," *Seven Arts* 1 (1916): 144–51; Harold Stearns, *America and the Young Intellectual* (New York: George H. Doran, 1921); Waldo Frank, *Our America* (New York: Boni & Liveright, 1919), and Lewis Mumford, *The Golden Day: A Study in*

American Experience and Culture (New York: Horace Liverwright, 1926).

4. See James Livingston, *Pragmatism and the Political Economy of Cultural Revolution, 1850–1940* (Chapel Hill: University of North Carolina Press, 1994), chap. 5.

5. Here is how Antonio Gramsci made the point: "The relation between common sense and the upper level of philosophy is assured by 'politics.'" *Selections from the Prison Notebooks*, ed. and trans. Quintin Hoare and Geoffrey N. Smith (New York: International, 1971), p. 331. Raymond Williams quoted from *Culture and Society* (New York: Anchor, 1958), p. 340. On the tension between intellectual history and cultural studies, see the *Intellectual History Newsletter* of 1996, in which leading practitioners from both sides of the disciplinary divide assess the difficulties and consequences of continued collaboration.

6. Wiliam James, "What Pragmatism Means," Lecture 2 of *Pragmatism* (1907), in Bruce Kuklick, ed., *William James: Writings, 1902–1910* (New York: Library of America, 1987), p. 507; John Dewey, *Reconstruction in Philosophy* (New York: Henry Holt, 1920), p. 26.

7. James, "What Pragmatism Means," pp. 509–10.

8. Kenneth Burke, *Attitudes Toward History* (1937; rev. ed., Boston: Beacon Press, 1961); page numbers in text hereafter. This book might be read as an extended meditation on the debacle of the American Writers Congress of 1935: see Frank Lentricchia, *Criticism and Social Change* (Chicago: University of Chicago Press, 1983), pp. 21–38, and, for a different but nonetheless illuminating approach to Burke, see Giles Gunn, *The Culture of Criticism and the Criticism of Culture* (Chicago: University of Chicago Press, 1987), chap. 4.

9. Compare Michael Denning's treatment of Deadwood Dick and other outlaws in *Mechanic Accents: Dime Novels and Working Class Culture in America* (London: Verso, 1987), chap. 8, against Samuel P. Huntington's treatment of insurgents, radicals, and revolutionaries in *Political Order in Changing Societies* (New Haven: Yale University Press, 1968), chap. 5.

10. G. W. F. Hegel, *The Phenomenology of Mind*, trans. J. B. Baillie (original copyright 1910; reprint, New York: Harper & Row, 1967), p. 98 (translation changed slightly). On the productive relation between falsehood and truth, which is assured by language and work—by what Hegel called the "discipline of culture"—see also Alexandre Kojeve, *Introduction to the Reading of Hegel: Lectures on the Phenomenology of Spirit*, assembled by Raymond Queneau, trans. James H. Nichols Jr. (Ithaca: Cornell University Press, 1969), pp. 186–89, and Jacques Lacan, "The Function of Language in Psychoanalysis," in *Speech and Language in Psychoanalysis*, trans. Anthony Wilden (Baltimore: Johns Hopkins University Press), pp. 3–87, esp. 55–63.

11. *The Golden Day*, pp. 188–92.

12. John Dewey, "The Scholastic and the Speculator" (1891–92), in Jo Ann Boydston, ed., *John Dewey: The Early Works*, 5 vols. (Carbondale: Southern Illinois University Press, 1969), 3:145–54, here 153; William James, "A World of Pure Experience" (1905), in *Essays in Radical Empiricism* (Cambridge: Harvard University Press, 1976), pp. 21–44, here 42–43. Cf. my treatment of these texts in *Pragmatism and Political Economy*, chaps. 8, 10.

13. James, "Pragmatism's Conception of Truth," Lecture 6 of *Pragmatism*, pp. 576–77. This was the "pivotal" lecture, according to James: see *The Meaning of Truth: A Sequel to Pragmatism* (1909), in *Writings 1902–1910*, pp. 823–978, here 823–30, 897–908, 918–36.

14. "What Pragmatism Means," p. 509.

15. Edward Bellamy, *Looking Backward, 2000–1887* (Boston: Bedford Books of St. Martin's, 1995), p. 145. On the "sound money" wars of the 1890s and the problem of a "credit economy," see my *Origins of the Federal Reserve System: Money, Class, and Corporate Capitalism, 1890–1913* (Ithaca: Cornell University Press, 1986), chaps. 3–5, and *Pragmatism and Political Economy*, chaps. 6, 8.

16. The claims of the preceding paragraphs are demonstrated in Livingston, *Pragmatism and Political Economy*, chap. 8.

17. A representative sample of works regulated by what Burke calls a tragic frame of acceptance would have to include Lawrence Goodwyn, *Democratic Promise: The Populist Moment in America* (New York: Oxford University Press, 1976); David Montgomery, *The Fall of the House of Labor: The Workplace, the State, and American Labor Activism, 1865–1925* (New York: Cambridge University Press, 1987); Michael E. McGerr, *The Decline of Popular Politics: The American North, 1865–1923* (New York: Oxford University Press, 1986); Burton J. Bledstein, *The Culture of Professionalism* (New York: Norton, 1978); T. J. Jackson Lears, *No Place of Grace: Antimodernism and the Transformation of American Culture* (New York: Pantheon, 1981), and *Fables of Abundance: A Cultural History of Advertising in America* (New York: Basic, 1994); and William Leach, *Land of Desire: Merchants, Power, and the Rise of a New American Culture* (New York: Pantheon, 1993). A comparable sample of works regulated by a comic frame of acceptance is more difficult to put together because it is only in the last ten years or so that differences among historians on the Left have been articulated in a way that makes them both arguable and productive, at least with respect to the Progressive Era. The key works here, I believe, are Richard Hofstadter, *The Age of Reform* (New York: Vintage, 1955); William Appleman Williams, *The Contours of American History* (Cleveland: World, 1961), pp. 343–425; and Martin J. Sklar, *The Corporate Reconstruction of American Capitalism, 1890–1916: The Market, the Law, and Politics* (New York: Cambridge University Press, 1988). See also my own contributions to the historiographical debates: "Radicals All!" *Reviews in American History* 16 (1988): 306–12, and "Why Is There Still Socialism in the United States?" ibid. 23 (1994): 577–84. I should note that Burke is very careful to distinguish between comedy and humor: see *Attitudes Toward History*, p. 43.

18. See Livingston, *Pragmatism and Political Economy*, chap. 9.

19. *The Golden Day*, pp. 264–65. It is worth remarking that the American literary canon was established by the young intellectuals, particularly through the influential works of Brooks and Mumford (for an example of how influential they were, see F. O. Matthiessen, *American Renaissance: Art and Expression in the Age of Whitman and Emerson* [New York: Oxford University Press, 1941], p. xvii), and that they understood their repudiation of pragmatism as the intellectual condition of their escape from what Randolph Bourne called the "cult of politics"—that is, as the condition of their cultural politics and literary authority. We might then

say that instead of C. P. Snow's "two cultures" (scientific vs. humanistic) we have at least three; for our "humanistic" culture is a divided stream, represented on the one hand by Lewis Mumford and his constituency of romantic radicals on the cultural Left and on the other hand by Kenneth Burke and his constituency of more or less pragmatist critics who worry about the limits of romantic radicalism but remain on the cultural Left. We might also say that cultural studies occupies a kind of middle ground between these streams, but tends (in the long run) to favor the latter. That is probably why its admirers and practitioners are skeptical of earnest appeals to *do something* in the "real world" of politics—the kind of appeal issued by Richard Rorty in his critique of Andrew Ross (see *Dissent*, fall 1991, pp. 483–90, but also Rorty's essay on Christopher Lasch in the *New Yorker*, January 30, 1995, pp. 86–89), and by Robert Westbrook in his remarks on the recent work of Giles Gunn (see *American Quarterly* 45 [1993]: 438–44).

20. See Blake, *Beloved Community*, pp. 226–27; Robert Westbrook, *John Dewey and American Democracy* (Ithaca: Cornell University Press, 1991), pp. 130–37, 380–87, and "Lewis Mumford, John Dewey, and the 'Pragmatic Acquiescence,'" in Thomas Hughes and Agatha Hughes, eds., *Lewis Mumford: Public Intellectual* (New York: Oxford University Press, 1990), pp. 301–22 (endnotes at 420–25), here 301, 420 n. 4.

21. See chapter 1, above, and my *Pragmatism and Political Economy*, pp. 221–23, 247–55, 275–79.

22. Goodwyn and Montgomery are cited at note 17, above; see otherwise Steven Hahn, *The Roots of Southern Populism* (New York: Oxford University Press, 1983), and Herbert Gutman, *Work, Culture, and Society in Industrializing America* (New York: Vintage, 1977). The historiographical problem I raise here is analyzed in Leon Fink, "Looking Backward: Reflections on Workers' Culture and Conceptual Dilemmas in Labor History," in J. C. Moody and A. Kessler-Harris, eds., *Perspectives on American Labor History* (Dekalb: Northern Illinois University Press, 1990), pp. 5–29.

23. Lears and Leach are cited at note 17, above; see otherwise Christopher Lasch, *The True and Only Heaven: Progress and Its Critics* (New York: Norton, 1991); Roberto Mangabeira Unger, *False Necessity* (New York: Cambridge University Press, 1987); Teresa Brennan, *History after Lacan* (London: Routledge, 1993); Juliet Schor, "An Economic Critique of Consumer Society," in *Newsletter of Committee on the Political Economy of the Good Society*, vol. 5, no. 1 (winter 1995), pp. 1, 7–12, which sharpens the argument of *The Overworked American* (New York: Basic, 1992).

24. On the problem of *poiesis*, see my *Pragmatism and Political Economy*, pp. 247–55, where I am drawing on Hannah Arendt, *The Human Condition* (Chicago: University of Chicago Press, 1958); Manfred Reidel, *Between Tradition and Revolution: The Hegelian Transformation of Political Philosophy*, trans. Walter Wright (New York: Cambridge University Press, 1984); and C. B. Macpherson, *The Political Theory of Possessive Individualism: Hobbes to Locke* (New York: Oxford, 1962).

25. See James Livingston, "*Sister Carrie*'s Absent Causes," in Miriam Gogol, ed., *Theodore Dreiser: Beyond Naturalism* (New York: New York University Press, 1995), pp. 216–46; see also John McClure on "apocalyptic modernism" in *Late Imperial Romance* (New York: Verso, 1992), pp. 49–53.

26. See Livingston, *Pragmatism and Political Economy*, chap. 10.

27. See Eli Zaretsky, *Capitalism, the Family, and Personal Life* (New York: Harper & Row, 1976), chaps. 3–4; Mary P. Ryan, *Cradle of the Middle Class: The Family in Oneida County, New York, 1790–1865* (New York: Cambridge University Press, 1981), chaps. 3, 5; Lori D. Ginzberg, *Women and the Work of Benevolence: Morality, Politics, and Class in the 19th-Century United States* (New Haven: Yale University Press, 1990), chaps. 3–6; and Ellen C. DuBois, "The Radicalism of the Woman's Suffrage Movement," in Anne Phillips, ed., *Feminism and Equality* (New York: New York University Press, 1987), pp. 127–38.

28. See Linda Nicholson's brilliant exposition in *Gender and History: The Limits of Social Theory in the Age of the Family* (New York: Columbia University Press, 1986), esp. pp. 47–56, 105–21.

29. Veblen quoted from *The Theory of Business Enterprise* (New York: Mentor, 1958), p. 11. On the completion of proletarianization under corporate auspices, see my *Pragmatism and Political Economy*, chaps. 2–4. On modern feminism and the proliferation of extra-familial roles, see Nicholson, *Gender and History*, pp. 56–66, and Nancy F. Cott, *The Grounding of Modern Feminism* (New Haven: Yale University Press, 1988), pp. 21–34. On the relation between patriarchal households and patterns of women's employment in the nineteenth-century industrial sector, see Thomas Dublin, *Women at Work: The Transformation of Work and Community in Lowell, Massachusetts, 1826–1860* (New York: Columbia University Press, 1979), esp. chaps. 3–5, 8–10; Christine Stansell, *City of Women: Sex and Class in New York, 1789–1860* (New York: Knopf, 1982), chaps. 6–7; and Julie A. Matthaei, *An Economic History of Women in America* (New York: Schocken, 1982), part 2.

30. Here I am again arguing with Jackson Lears, who claims that the "managerial culture" specific to corporate capitalism caused, or contributed to, a "devaluation of female authority" (see my discussion of his *Fables of Abundance* in chapter 1, above). At any rate, I am suggesting that he may have mistaken a relative decline of *maternal* authority for a devaluation of female authority as such. I am also suggesting that insofar as we remain attached to a tragic frame of acceptance in narrating the transition from proprietary to corporate capitalism, we will be unable to see how that transition allowed the *revaluation* of female authority by permitting the proliferation of extra-familial, extra-maternal social roles for women; in other words, we will be unable to see that modern feminism presupposes the devaluation of *familial* or *maternal* authority residing in the passage beyond proprietary capitalism which is navigated by corporate legal forms.

31. Walter Lippmann, *The Phantom Public* (New York: Macmillan, 1925); page numbers hereafter in text. On its distant echoes in the 1950s, see Livingston, *Pragmatism and Political Economy*, pp. 125, 323–24 (n. 40), 338 (n. 3).

32. Gerrard Winstanley was the leading ideologue of the Diggers, the millenarian socialists who represented the extreme left wing of Oliver Cromwell's revolutionary coalition; the dictum I quote is from *A New-Yeers Gift for the Parliament and Armie* (1650) reprinted in George Sabine, ed., *The Works of Gerrard Winstanley* (Ithaca: Cornell University Press, 1941), pp. 355–89, here 366. On the "social self" and its political

correlates, see my *Pragmatism and Political Economy*, pp. 72–75, 80–82, and Chapter 3, below.

33. Dewey's reply to Lippmann is *The Public and Its Problems* ([1927] Chicago: Gateway Books, 1946); page numbers in text hereafter. See also Dewey, *Individualism Old and New* ([1929] New York: Capricorn, 1962), for an even more explicit treatment of the problem Lippmann ponders in *The Phantom Public*. We should note, however, that in the nineteenth century, mass political parties and highly partisan newspapers constantly mediated between individual voters and policy-makers in Congress: the "omnicompetent" citizen was never left to his own devices in deciding what facts were significant and which candidates deserved his votes.

34. See, for example, Westbrook, *Dewey and Democracy*, chap. 9; John Patrick Diggins, The *Promise of Pragmatism* (Chicago: University of Chicago Press, 1994), pp. 299–304, 339–42; Lasch, *True and Only Heaven*, pp. 363–68; and Stanley Aronowitz, "Is Democracy Possible? The Decline of the Public in the American Debate," in Bruce Robbins, ed., *The Phantom Public Sphere* (Minneapolis: University of Minnesota Press, 1993), pp. 75–92.

35. G. H. Mead, "The Working Hypothesis in Social Reform," *American Journal of Sociology* 5 (1899): 367–71, here 367; Jessie Taft, *The Woman Movement from the Point of View of Social Consciousness* (Chicago: University of Chicago Press, 1916), p. 26.

36. See Gramsci, *Prison Notebooks*, pp. 210–76. My thinking on these matters was clarified by Stuart Hall, "Gramsci's Relevance for the Study of Race and Ethnicity," *Journal of Communications Inquiry* 10 (1993): 5–27; but see also Ernesto Laclau and Chantal Mouffe, *Hegemony and Socialist Strategy* (London: Verso. 1985), esp. chap. 2, which demonstrates that hegemony is both cause and effect of the socialization of the market (the "withdrawal of the category of 'historical necessity' to the horizon of the social").

37. We might think of the differences in question by comparing the readers of the *New Yorker* and the *New Republic*. See my "Corporations and Cultural Studies," *Social Text* 44 (1995): 63–70, for an early version of the argument I am making here.

38. Charles S. Peirce, "The Architecture of Theories," the first in a series of five essays published in the *Monist* between 1891 and 1893, all of which are reprinted in Edward C. Moore, *Charles S. Peirce: The Essential Writings* (New York: Harper and Row, 1972), pp. 158–260; quoted from p. 168 (cf. "what we call matter is not completely dead, but is merely mind hide-bound with habits" [p. 214], and "if habit be a primary property of mind, it must be equally so of matter, as a kind of mind" [p. 235]). On habit and its evolutionary function more generally, see also "The Law of Mind," pp. 190–216, esp. 209–11, and "Man's Glassy Essence," pp. 216–37, esp. 227–35. The "objective idealism" that Peirce establishes under the sign of habit recalls Hegel's system, in part because the rules of action which become habits can be "broken up" and recast by encounter with novel circumstances; in other words, every tried-and-true habit is a potential *mistake*: "Habits are general ways of behavior that are associated with the removal of stimuli. But when the expected removal of the stimuli fails to occur, the excitation continues and increases, and nonhabitual reactions take place, and these tend to weaken the habit.... Here

then, the usual departures from regularity will be followed by others that are very great; and the large fortuitous departures from law so produced, will tend still further to break up the laws, supposing that these are of the nature of habits" (p. 233). Compare these remarks against those of William James in *The Principles of Psychology* (1890; Cambridge: Harvard University Press, 1981), chaps. 4 and 26.

Chapter 3: The Strange Career of the "Social Self"

1. Richard Rorty, "The Priority of Democracy to Philosophy," an address of 1984, published in 1988, reprinted in Rorty, *Objectivity, Relativism, and Truth: Philosophical Papers Volume 1* (New York: Cambridge University Press, 1991), pp. 175–96, here 176.

2. Alice Jardine, *Gynesis: Configurations of Woman and Modernity* (Ithaca: Cornell University Press, 1986), e.g. at pp. 25–28, 67–102.

3. Anthony Giddens, *Central Problems in Social Theory: Action, Structure and Contradiction in Social Analysis* (Berkeley: University of California Press, 1979), pp. 3, 261 n. 4; we should also note that James doesn't appear in the index.

4. Jardine, *Gynesis*, pp. 105–6.

5. The place to begin a study of transatlantic intellectual reciprocity is James T. Kloppenberg's indispensable *Uncertain Victory: Social Democracy and Progressivism in European and American Thought, 1870–1920* (New York: Oxford University Press, 1986); my argument focuses on the period after 1920. Mannheim is quoted in Kurt Wolff, ed., *From Karl Mannheim* (New York: Oxford University Press, 1971), p. cv, Wittgenstein's student from John Passmore, *A Hundred Years of Philosophy*, rev. ed. (New York: Basic Books, 1967), p. 434 n. 2. According to Bruce Wilshire, Wittgenstein "studied James in depth": see his *William James and Phenomenology: A Study of "The Principles of Psychology"* (Bloomington: Indiana University Press, 1968), pp. 137–38; as evidence of this claim, Wilshire cites Wittgenstein's *Philosophical Investigations*, 3rd ed., trans. G. E. M. Anscombe (New York: Macmillan, 1958), pp. 124–25. I think he is quite right to do so, but I would broaden the citation to include most of part 1, or at least every paragraph from 255 to 419, pp. 91–125, all of which indicate a familiarity with the seminal essays on radical empiricism of 1904–5 as well as the *Principles of Psychology*. Cf. Passmore, who declares, in the same footnote cited above, that the books "most suitable as background reading to the *Philosophical Investigations*"—apart from Wittgenstein's earlier *Tractatus*—are "Schlick's *Gesammelte Aufsatze* (especially his lectures on 'Form and Content') and William James's *Principles of Psychology*, supplemented by his *Pragmatism.*" On Husserl's intellectual debts and larger relation to James, see Wilshire, *Phenomenology*, pp. 120–22; John Wild, *The Radical Empiricism of William James* (Garden City: Doubleday, 1969), passim, esp. pp. 128, 143–45, 160–61, 389–90; and James Edie, *William James and Phenomenology* (Bloomington: Indiana University Press, 1987), pp. 19–25, 34–36, 46–48, 67–72.

6. See my *Pragmatism and the Political Economy of Cultural Revolution, 1850–1940* (Chapel Hill: University of North Carolina Press, 1994), pp. 231–36, 371 n. 2. Durkheim's enduring influence on the members of the "College de sociologie," an informal grouping of Paris intellectuals which included Georges Bataille, Roger Caillois, Michel Leiris, and at times,

Pierre Klossowski, Denis de Rougement, and Jean Wahl ("I am the worst student of the College of Sociology, but a very assiduous one," he claimed) is traced in Michele Richman, "Anthropology and Modernism in France: From Durkheim to the College de sociologie," in Marc Manganaro, ed., *Modernist Anthropolgy: From Fieldwork to Text* (Princeton: Princeton University Press, 1990), pp. 183–214. A wider angle on the College and its project of a "sacred sociology," which in one form or another preoccupied French intellectuals of the 1920s and 30s (see notes 7 and 9 below), is provided by Denis Hollier, ed., *The College of Sociology 1937–1939*, trans. Betsy Wing (Minneapolis: University of Minnesota Press, 1988); see, for present purposes, pp. 85–93, 98–102; Wahl is quoted from p.101.

7. See George L. Kline, "The Existential Rediscovery of Hegel and Marx," in E. N. Lee & M. Mandelbaum, eds., *Phenomenology and Existentialism* (Baltimore: Johns Hopkins University Press, 1967), pp. 113–38. The distant echoes of Kojève's lectures are traced in Vincent Descombes, *Modern French Philosophy*, trans. L. Scott-Fox & J. M. Harding (New York: Cambridge University Press, 1980)—see pp. 27–48 on Kojève himself—and in Judith Butler, *Subjects of Desire: Hegelian Reflections in 20th Century France* (New York: Columbia University Press, 1987). For Kojève's reading of Soloviev, which is presumably drawn from the dissertation Kline mentions, see A. Kojevnikoff, "La Metaphysique religieuse de Vladimir Soloviev," *Revue d'histoire et de philosophie religieuses*, vol. 14 (1934): 534–54, and vol. 15 (1935): 110–52. Kojève (1902–1968), who arrived in Paris in 1928, published other items under his Russian name in the 1930s. By 1933, he was teaching in the division of religious sciences at the Ecole des Hautes Etudes as an assistant to Alexandre Koyré (on whom see note 8 below). His legendary seminar/lectures on the *Phenomenology*, which were officially devoted to "Hegel's religious philosophy," attracted an audience that included Koyré, Georges Bataille, Jacques Lacan, Jean-Paul Sartre, Emmanuel Levinas, Raymond Queneau, Maurice Merleau-Ponty, and Raymond Aron, among others. Queneau's notes from the lectures were published in French in 1947; the English translation is Alexandre Kojève, *Introduction to the Reading of Hegel: Lectures on the Phenomenology of Spirit*, assembled by Raymond Queneau, trans. James H. Nichols Jr. (Ithaca: Cornell University Press, 1969).

8. See Nicolai Hartmann, "Hegel et le problème de la dialectique du réel," translated from the German by R.-L. Klee, *Revue de métaphysique et de morale*, vol. 38, no. 3 (Juillet-Septembre 1931), pp. 285–316, esp. 308ff., and Charles Andler, "Le Fondement du savoir dans la 'Phenomenologie de l'esprit' de Hegel," ibid., pp. 317–40. Koyré's essays are reprinted in his collection, *Etudes d'histoire de la pensée philosophique* (Paris: Librairie Armand Colin, 1961): "Note sur la langue et la terminologie hegeliennes" from *Revue philosophique*, 1931, at pp. 175–204, and "Hegel à Iéna" from *Revue d'histoire et de philosophie religieuses*, 1935, at pp. 135–73 (the collection's table of contents dates the latter essay from 1934, but it appeared in 1935, in the same issue that carried part two of Kojève's essay on Soloviev [see note 7 above]). Another important essay, "Rapport sur l'état des études hegeliennes en France," from *Verhandlungen des ersten Hegel-Congresses* (1930), appears in the same collection at pp. 205–27; see pp. 222–26 for Koyré's enthusiastic praise of Jean Wahl, and pp. 225–26 for Koyré's acknowledgment of Charles Andler's pioneering courses and lectures on Hegel at the Collège de France. Hippolyte is

quoted from John Heckman's insightful introduction to Jean Hippolyte, *Genesis and Structure of Hegel's Phenomenology of Spirit*, trans. Samuel Cherniak and John Heckman (Evanston: Northwestern University Press, 1974), pp. xv–xli, here xix; in the same connection, cf. Emmanuel Levinas, who claimed that Jean Wahl caused "the renewal of the study of Hegel in France"—see "Jean Wahl: Neither Having nor Being," an essay of 1976 included in *Outside the Subject*, trans. Michael B. Smith (Stanford: Stanford University Press, 1993), pp. 67–83, here 69.

9. See Jean Wahl, *Les Philosophies pluralistes d'Angleterre et d'Amérique* (Paris: Alcan, 1920), esp. pp. 90–170, where William James is the central figure, and the relation between pragmatism and pluralism is the central issue; the range of Wahl's citations is so broad that I feel safe in designating him the foremost European authority, circa 1920, on the Jamesian variety of pragmatism. Josiah Royce is quoted from *The Spirit of Modern Philosophy* (Boston: Houghton Mifflin, 1892), pp. 203–16, 496–503; quoted passages from pp. 214–15, 207. On Royce and the "social self" more generally, see R. Jackson Wilson, *In Quest of Community: Social Philosophy in the United States* (New York: Oxford University Press, 1968), chap. 6; James Harry Cotton, *Royce on the Human Self* (Cambridge: Harvard University Press, 1954), chaps. 2, 7–8; and Bruce Kuklick, *Josiah Royce: An Intellectual Biography* (New York: Bobbs-Merrill, 1972), chaps. 4–5. See also Gabriel Marcel, *Royce's Metaphysics*, trans. Virginia Ringer and Gordon Ringer (Chicago: Regnery, 1956), pp. 103–14; the papers that comprise this book (they were written in 1917–18 but not published in French until 1945) reflect the fascination with the politico-philosophical implications of religious revelation which led many French intellectuals of the 1920s and 1930s to Royce and, through him, to Hegel (or vice versa). In view of this fascination, we should ask what the idea of a "sacred sociology" has in common with the "natural supernaturalism" of romantic poetics, and in answering we should note the pivotal role M. H. Abrams assigns to Hegel's *Phenomenology* in explicating the agendas of Wordsworth and Coleridge: see his *Natural Supernaturalism: Tradition and Revolution in Romantic Literature* (New York: Norton, 1971), pp. 217–52. For recent evidence that Royce's emphasis on the social character of the "absolute self" in Hegel's *Phenomenology* was not misplaced, see Robert B. Pippin, "'You Can't Get There from Here': Transition Problems in Hegel's *Phenomenology of Spirit*," Frederick C. Beiser, ed., *The Cambridge Companion to Hegel* (New York: Cambridge University Press, 1993), pp. 52–85.

10. See Royce, *Lectures on Modern Idealism* (New Haven: Yale University Press, 1919): on the *Phenomenology* in general, pp. 136–231; on Goethe, Novalis, and romance as narrative form in the *Phenomenology*, pp. 136–37, 147–51; on the "unhappy consciousness," pp. 180–86. In the preface to the first edition of *Modern Classical Philosophers* (Cambridge: Riverside Press, 1908), Benjamin Rand makes it clear that the volume was planned around 1900, and that James and Royce were the key figures in steering it toward completion: see pp. vii-viii, and, for Royce's translation of the selection from the *Phenomenology*, pp. 614–28. Otherwise see Jean Wahl, *Le Malheur de la conscience dans la philosophie de Hegel* (Paris: Presses Universitaires de France, 1929), pp. 69–118; on Hegel and Nietzsche, compare Wahl, *Le Malheur*, pp. 8, 73 (quoted passage from p. 8), to Royce, *Modern Idealism*, pp. 68–69. And in the same spirit, see also Karl Lowith (he too lived and studied in Paris in the early 1930s), *From*

Hegel to Nietzsche: The Revolution in Nineteenth-Century Thought, trans. David E. Green (New York: Holt, Rinehart & Winston, 1964), pp. 31–51, 152–200, 263–70, 286–94, 303–10, 321–33.

11. Anthony Giddens, *New Rules of Sociological Method: A Positive Critique of Interpretive Sociologies,* 2nd ed. (Stanford: Stanford University Press, 1993), pp. 26–27; cf. *Central Problems,* pp. 120–23, 253–57.

12. See Livingston, *Pragmatism and Political Economy,* pp. 80–83, 323–24 at n. 40; and Wilfred McClay, *The Masterless: Self and Society in Modern America* (Chapel Hill: University of North Carolina Press, 1994), pp. 194–222; quoted passage from p. 222. My only criticism of McClay is that he ignores the central role of the "young intellectuals"—especially Lewis Mumford, Waldo Frank, and Van Wyck Brooks—in discrediting pragmatism, and thus in precluding serious discussion of the "social self," long before the arrival or appropriation of the Frankfurt School. On these issues, see Livingston, *Pragmatism and Political Economy,* chap. 9; Robert Westbrook, *John Dewey and American Democracy* (Ithaca: Cornell University Press, 1991), chap. 11; and Casey Nelson Blake, *Beloved Community: The Cultural Criticism of Randolph Bourne, Van Wyck Brooks, Waldo Frank, and Lewis Mumford* (Chapel Hill: University of North Carolina Press, 1990), chap. 6. In his comment on the paper that was the original draft of the chapter you are reading, Casey Blake quite rightly insisted that because the political import of alternatives to bourgeois individualism is not necessarily pluralist or progressive (as witness the post-liberal political subjectivity promoted by fascist ideology), the mere invocation of the "social self" will not serve as useful criticism of corporate capitalism or corporate liberalism. I believe that the "double strategy" of pragmatism and feminism—that is, their capacity and their tendency to include modern subjectivity within a new model of selfhood—precludes the reactionary results of certain anti-liberal sensibilities, but Blake's doubts are well worth pondering.

13. McClay, *The Masterless,* chaps. 7–8; quoted passage from p. 233.

14. Jane Flax, *Thinking Fragments: Psychoanalysis, Feminism, and Postmodernism in the Contemporary West* (Berkeley: University of California Press, 1990), p. 232.

15. I will be citing page numbers in the text from Jane Addams, "A Modern Lear," as reprinted in Christopher Lasch, ed., *The Social Thought of Jane Addams* (Indianapolis: Bobbs-Merrill, 1965), pp. 105–23; Addams, *Democracy and Social Ethics* (New York: Macmillan, 1902); Jessie Taft, *The Woman Movement from the Point of View of Social Consciousness* (Chicago: University of Chicago Press, 1915); and John Dewey, *Individualism Old and New* (original copyrights 1929, 1930; reprint, New York: Capricorn Books, 1962).

16. On the Pullman strike and ARU boycott, see Jeremy Brecher, *Strike!* (San Francisco: Straight Arrow Books, 1972), pp. 78–96, and Nick Salvatore, *Eugene V. Debs: Citizen and Socialist* (Urbana: University of Illinois Press, 1982), pp. 126–37.

17. My arguments here are based on what I have learned from Harry V. Jaffa, *Crisis of the House Divided: An Interpretation of the Lincoln-Douglas Debates* (Garden City: Doubleday, 1959), esp. chap. 17; from Hegel's preoccupation with the French Revolution, for example in *The Phenomenology of Mind,* trans. J. B. Baillie (original copyright 1910; reprint, New York: Harper & Row, 1967), pp. 559–610; and from two books that situ-

ate Hegel in the political convulsions and debates of his time: Joachim Ritter, *Hegel and the French Revolution: Essays on the Philosophy of Right*, trans. Richard Dien Winfield (Cambridge: MIT Press, 1982), and Manfred Riedel, *Between Tradition and Revolution: The Hegelian Transformation of Political Philosophy*, trans. Walter Wright (New York: Cambridge University Press, 1984).

18. An earlier expression of my worries about radicalism pure and simple is James Livingston, "Radicals All!" *Reviews in American History* 16 (1988): 306–12.

19. See Mary Jo Deegan, *Jane Addams and the Men of the Chicago School, 1892–1918* (New Brunswick: Transaction, 1988), especially chaps. 8–11; Charlene Haddock-Seigfried, *Pragmatism and Feminism: Reweaving the Social Fabric* (Chicago: University of Chicago Press, 1996), especially chaps. 2–4; Katherine Kish Sklar, "Hull House in the 1890s: A Community of Women Reformers," *Signs* 10 (1985): 658–77; Allen F. Davis, *American Heroine: The Life and Legend of Jane Addams* (New York: Oxford University Press, 1973); Robyn Muncy, *Creating a Female Dominion in American Reform, 1890–1935* (New York: Oxford University Press, 1991), chap. 1; and M. Regina Leffers, "Pragmatists Jane Addams and John Dewey Inform the Ethic of Care," *Hypatia* 8 (1993): 38–77. See also Christopher Lasch's insightful essay on Addams in *The New Radicalism in America* (New York: Vintage, 1965), pp. 3–37.

20. See Rosalind Rosenberg, *Beyond Separate Spheres: Intellectual Roots of Modern Feminism* (New Haven: Yale University Press, 1982), chap. 5.

21. See my reading of Lippmann on the New Woman in *Pragmatism and Political Economy*, pp. 69–77; for contemporary examples of the comparison between the woman movement and the labor movement, see Charlotte Perkins Gilman, *Women and Economics* (Boston: Small, Maynard & Co., 1898), p. 138, and Margaret Dreier Robins, "Need of a National Training School for Women Organizers," the Presidential Address to the Fourth Biennial Convention of the National Women's Trade Union League, St. Louis, June 2, 1913, a pamphlet preserved in the George Herbert Mead Papers, Special Collections, Regenstein Library, University of Chicago, Box 4, Folder 9, p. 14.

22. We should note that Taft's criticism of Royce sounds very much like Giddens's criticism of Mead in *Central Problems*, p. 121. In support of her position, Taft cites three of Mead's essays: "What Social Objects Must Psychology Presuppose?" *Journal of Philosophy, Psychology and Scientific Methods* 7 (1910): 170–80; "The Mechanism of the Social Consciousness," ibid. 9 (1912): 401–6; and "Social Consciousness and the Consciousness of Meaning," *Psychological Bulletin* 7 (1910): 397–405. In adjudicating the disagreement between Mead and Royce, we should remember that the former was the latter's student at Harvard in the late 1880s. In any event, Mead's debts to Hegel (and Royce) are clearly displayed in a 1921 lecture course on the *Phenomenology*, the notes from which are preserved in the Mead Papers, Box 4, Folder 4; moreover, if we may judge from these notes, Mead was trying to sketch an intellectual lineage that connected contemporary pragmatists to Hegel's original system, e.g., on April 28, he declared, "Hegel is dealing with the problem which the pragmatist tries to meet by saying that immediate experience is not knowledge."

23. See Jardine, *Gynesis*, pp. 81–85, on the "three epochs" and an impending

fourth, which I read as a speculative recapitulation of Taft's periodization; Alasdair MacIntyre, *After Virtue* (South Bend: Notre Dame University Press, 1981), chaps. 4–6, 11; Charles Taylor, *Sources of the Self* (Cambridge: Harvard University Press, 1989), chaps. 13–19; and Anthony Giddens, *Modernity and Self-Identity: Self and Society in the Late Modern Age* (Stanford: Stanford University Press, 1991).

24. I follow Bruce Kuklick in designating Royce a pragmatist. On Cooley and Baldwin, see Taft's citations at pp. 37, 48; Wilson, *In Quest of Community*, chap. 3; and Marshall J. Cohen, *Charles Horton Cooley and the Social Self in American Thought* (New York: Garland, 1982).

25. *Outlines of a Critical Theory of Ethics* (1891), in Jo Ann Boydston, ed., *The Early Works of John Dewey*, 5 vols. (Carbondale: Southern Illinois University Press, 1971), 3:239–388, here 335, 326.

26. Dewey cites James on the "uselessness of an ego outside and behind" the scene of action: see Dewey, "The Ego as Cause" (1894), *Early Works*, 4:91–95, here 95 n. 4. See otherwise "Self-Realization as the Moral Ideal" (1893), in *Early Works*, 4:42–53 (quoted passages from pp. 50, 44), and, on Dewey's continuing engagement with James's *Principles of Psychology*, see Wayne A. R. Leys's introduction to volume 4 of *Early Works*, pp. ix–xx, as well as the two-part essay "The Theory of Emotion" (1894–95), ibid. at 152–88. The last-quoted passage in this paragraph is from John Dewey, *Lectures on Ethics 1900–1901*, ed. Donald F. Koch (Carbondale: Southern Illinois University Press, 1991), p. 314.

27. *Lectures on Ethics*, pp. 292–96.

28. Ibid., pp. 312, 282–86, 267–70, 302, 296.

29. John Dewey, *Reconstruction in Philosophy* (Boston: Beacon Press, 1920), p. 187. Page references hereafter in text.

30. On Burke and "frames of acceptance," see chapter 2, above. We should note also that Burke was a close reader of Dewey in the 1930s; see, for examples, *The Philosophy of Literary Form*, 3rd ed. (original copyright 1941; Berkeley: University of California Press, 1973), pp. 184–85, 382–91.

Chapter 4: Narrative Politics

1. Derek Nystrom and Kent Puckett, *Against Bosses, Against Oligarchies: A Conversation with Richard Rorty* (Charlottesville: Prickly Pear Pamphlets, 1998), p. ii.

2. Richard Rorty, "Intellectuals in Politics," *Dissent* (fall 1991): 483–90, and *Achieving Our Country: Leftist Thought in 20th Century America* (Cambridge: Harvard University Press, 1997); page references hereafter in text.

3. See James Livingston, "Marxism, Pragmatism, and the American Political Tradition," *Intellectual History Newsletter*, vol. 20 (1998), pp. 61–67.

4. Quoted from the first debate with Stephen A. Douglas at Ottawa, Illinois, August 21, 1858, in Roy P. Basler, ed., *The Collected Works of Abraham Lincoln*, 8 vols. (New Brunswick: Rutgers University Press, 1953), 3:27.

5. Rorty cites Todd Gitlin, *The Sixties: Years of Hope, Days of Rage* (New York: Bantam Books, 1987), at p. 146 nn. 16–17; and Nelson Lichtenstein, *The Most Dangerous Man in Detroit: Walter Reuther and the Fate*

of American Labor (New York: Basic Books, 1995), at pp. 141 n. 7, 146 n. 15, 147 n. 28. See also Alan Brinkley, *The End of Reform: New Deal Liberalism in Recession and War* (New York: Vintage, 1995), and the other works cited at note 31, below.

6. Rorty's critics on the Left take issue with his call for "American national pride," in part because they confuse nationalism as such with recent episodes of "ethnic cleansing," in part because they believe that the erasure of the difference between "American national pride" and missionary faith in a "gunfighter nation" caused the Vietnam War. But the value of Rorty's argument does not lie in the particular way he narrates the history of the Left; it lies instead in his attempt to connect the Left to the history of the United States, and thus to rid us of the idea that either is exempt from the corruptions of historical time. I mean that the historical consciousness informing his argument is more important than the story he tells about the twentieth-century American Left. He names this consciousness "American national pride," but in doing so he is trying, I think, to say that a radical without a country—without some attachment to a political tradition that acknowledges but also transcends ethnic and class divisions—will inevitably sound like a tourist or a terrorist. He is claiming that intellectuals on the Left cannot realistically project their potential constituents into a better future without some knowledge of *and respect for* the many pasts of their fellow citizens. He is claiming that unless we can show how the ethical principles of the Left reside in and flow from these pasts, from the historical circumstances we call the American experience, we have no good reasons to hope for that future. So he is reminding us of what John Dewey said in his first major work, *Outlines of a Critical Theory of Ethics* (1891): "An 'ought' which does not root in and flower from the 'is,' which is not the fuller expression of the actual state of social relationships, is a mere pious wish that things should be better." Jo Ann Boydston, ed., *The Early Works*, 5 vols. (Carbondale: Southern Illinois University Press, 1969) 3:335–36.

7. On Hegel's intellectual itinerary in general, see Charles Taylor, *Hegel* (New York: Cambridge University Press, 1975). On Hegel's engagement with political economy, aside from the relevant paragraphs in *The Philosophy of Right*, trans. T. M. Knox (New York: Oxford University Press, 1952), e.g. par. 189, where he cites Smith, Say, and Ricardo, see Raymond Plant, *Hegel* (Bloomington, Indiana University Press, 1973), pp. 64–72, 87–94, 107–20; Joachim Ritter, *Hegel and the French Revolution: Essays on the Philosophy of Right*, trans. Richard Dien Winfield (Cambridge: MIT Press, 1982), pp. 63–79, 121–23, 137–42; and Manfred Riedel, *Between Tradition and Revolution: The Hegelian Transformation of Political Philosophy*, trans. Walter Wright (New York: Cambridge University Press, 1984), pp. 108–24. On the "discipline of culture," see *The Phenomenology of Mind*, trans. J. B. Baillie (New York: Harper & Row, 1967), pp. 509–48. On the origins and early development of Marxism, see George Lichtheim, *Marxism: An Historical and Critical Study*, 2nd rev. ed. (New York: Praeger, 1965), pp. 3–62, 133–200; and Herbert Marcuse, *Reason and Revolution: Hegel and the Rise of Social Theory* (Boston: Beacon Press, 1960), pp. 251–322. Marx is quoted from "Economic and Philosophic Manuscripts of 1844," trans. Jack Cohen et al., in Marx and Engels, *Collected Works* (New York: International, 1975), vol. 3, pp. 229–346, here 333.

8. See, for example, Karl-Otto Apel, *Charles S. Peirce: From Pragmatism to*

Pragmaticism, trans. J. M. Krois (Amherst: University of Massachusetts Press, 1981), p. 201 n. 35.

9. On radical empiricism, see James Livingston, *Pragmatism and the Political Economy of Cultural Revolution, 1850–1940* (Chapel Hill: University of North Carolina Press, 1994), pp. 256–73, 377–78 n. 3, and the monumental analysis of John Wild, *The Radical Empiricism of William James* (Garden City: Doubleday, 1969), parts 3 and 4; notice the comparison of Marx and James vis-à-vis Hegel at p. 352. For the "Theses on Feuerbach," see *Writings of the Young Marx on Philosophy and Society*, trans. and ed. Lloyd D. Easton and Kurt H. Guddat (Garden City: Doubleday, 1967), pp. 400–2. Marx meticulously analyzes Smith in *Theories of Surplus Value* (Moscow: Progress Publishers, 1963), part 1: see, e.g. pp. 69–174, 251–64, 300–4. Sidney Hook quoted from Christopher Phelps, *Young Sidney Hook: Marxist and Pragmatist* (Ithaca: Cornell University Press, 1997), p. 212.

10. See Brian Lloyd, *Left Out: Pragmatism, Exceptionalism, and the Poverty of American Marxism, 1907–1922* (Baltimore: Johns Hopkins University Press, 1997), which exhaustively demonstrates, to the author's dismay, the interpenetration of Marxism and pragmatism on the American Left before the Great War.

11. See Phelps, *Young Sidney Hook*, pp. 211–12.

12. On French debts to American pragmatists, see chapter 3, above; see otherwise Frank Lentricchia, *Ariel and the Police* (Madison: Universty of Wisconsin Press, 1987), chap. 2.

13. But because Rorty assumes that the spread of markets must mean the demise of democracy, he produces a narrative of the American future—a fascist nightmare (see *Achieving Our Country*, pp. 84–90)—that has nothing to do with what we actually know about the recent effects of creating more open and flexible markets in Latin America, in Asia, or for that matter in the United States. Useful correctives to such hysteria, which is by now quite common on the American Left but especially prevalent among those who, like Rorty, want to reinstate the class politics of the New Deal coalition, are J. K. Gibson-Graham, *The End of Capitalism (as we knew it): A Feminist Critique of Political Economy* (Cambridge: Blackwell, 1996), chap. 6, "Querying Globalization"; and the recent unpublished work of Jeffrey A. Frieden, whose "Economics of Intervention: American Overseas Investments and Relations with Underdeveloped Areas, 1890–1950," *Comparative Studies in Society and History* 31 (1989): 55–80, should have already caused the Left to rethink its position on the political effects of "globalization."

14. Page references to Nystrom and Puckett, *Against Bosses*, hereafter in text.

15. Dewey, *The Public and Its Problems*, p. 48.

16. See Antonio Gramsci, *Selections from the Prison Notebooks*, ed. and trans. Quintin Hoare and Geoffrey N. Smith (New York: International, 1971), pp. 210–76; Stuart Hall, "Gramsci's Relevance for the Study of Race and Ethnicity," *Journal of Communications Inquiry* 10 (1993): 5–27; and Ernesto Laclau and Chantal Mouffe, *Hegemony and Socialist Strategy* (London: Verso, 1985), chap. 2.

17. John Dewey, *Reconstruction in Philosophy* (Boston: Beacon Press, 1920), pp. 185, 203–5. Bruce Robbins reminds me that Dewey's sanguine view of an internally articulated civil society has recently been challenged by

communitarians who believe that the atomization of life under the regime of a cybernated consumer culture has left Americans "bowling alone," that is, without organized, purposeful contacts with their fellow citizens. Robbins and I agree that the communitarians conveniently ignore precisely what bothers Rorty so much—the "group identities" created by cultural politics—and that the only people who bowl alone are practicing for league play.

18. See Livingston, *Pragmatism and Political Economy*, pp. 66–83, 172–80, 353 n. 12; and Daniel Bell, *The Coming of Post-Industrial Society* (New York: Basic Books, 1973), p. 115. John Dewey clearly grasped that the expansion of "socially necessary labor" under modern-industrial capitalism meant that "economic relations became dominantly controlling forces in setting the pattern of human relations"; in 1930, when he uttered this phrase, he was not yet in a position to see that the tide was turning, or to realize that once it did, his ideas about the scope and purposes of politics would become even more compelling.

19. Harold Cruse, *The Crisis of the Negro Intellectual* (New York: Morrow, 1967). For the antecedents of Cruse's arguments, see Alain Locke, "The Concept of Race as Applied to Social Culture," *Howard Review* 1 (1924): 290–99, and "The Contribution of Race to Culture," *The Student World* 23 (1930): 349–53. For evidence of renewed interest in Cruse's arguments, see Van Gosse, "Locating the Black Intellectual: An Interview with Harold Cruse," *Radical History Review* 71 (1998): 96–120; Scott Sherman, "After the Crisis," *Lingua Franca* 9 (fall 1999): 12–13; and James A. Miller and Jerry Watts, eds., *The Crisis of the Negro Intellectual Revisited,* forthcoming from Routledge.

20. Cruse, *Crisis*, pp. 3–111, 147–89, 451–97, 544–65.

21. Cruse, *Crisis*, pp. 474, 64–65. On the significance of new media in this impending cultural revolution, see also Ann Douglas, *Terrible Honesty: Mongrel Manhattan in the 1920s* (New York: Noonday Press, 1995), and George Hutchinson, *The Harlem Renaissance in Black and White* (Cambridge: Harvard University Press, 1995); unlike Cruse, both Douglas and Hutchinson celebrate the interracial institutional sources of intellectual innovation and cultural reception in the 1920s.

22. Cruse, *Crisis*, pp. 174, 557, 188–89.

23. See Rorty, "Postmodernist Bourgeois Liberalism" (1983), in *Objectivity, Relativism, and Truth: Philosophical Papers Volume 1* (New York: Cambridge University Press, 1991), pp. 197–202, here 200.

24. On the periodization of modern feminism, see Nancy Cott, *The Grounding of Modern Feminism* (New Haven: Yale University Press, 1987); Linda J. Nicholson, *Gender and History: The Limits of Social Theory in the Age of the Family* (New York: Columbia University Press, 1986); Anne Phillips, ed., *Feminism and Equality* (New York: New York University Press, 1987); and Sara Evans, *Personal Politics: The Roots of Women's Liberation in the Civil Rights Movement and the New Left* (New York: Vintage, 1979).

25. Anne Phillips, *Engendering Democracy* (University Park: Penn State Press, 1991), p. 41.

26. See, for example, Nicholson, *Gender and History*, chaps. 3–6; Judith Butler, *Gender Trouble: Feminism and the Subversion of Identity* (New York: Routledge, 1990), esp. chap. 2; and Seyla Benhabib, *Situating the Self:*

Gender, Community, and Postmodernism in Contemporary Ethics (New York: Routledge, 1992), esp. chap. 6.

27. See, for example, Carole Pateman, *The Sexual Contract* (Stanford: Stanford University Press, 1988); Mary Lyndon Shanley and Carole Pateman, eds., *Feminist Interpretations and Political Theory* (University Park: Penn State Press, 1991); and Genevieve Lloyd, *The Man of Reason: "Male" and "Female" in Western Philosophy* (Minneapolis: University of Minnesota Press, 1984).

28. See chapter 3 above on the double strategy of feminist theory. Rorty is quoted from "The Priority of Democracy to Philosophy," an essay of 1988 reprinted in *Objectivity, Relativism, and Truth*, pp. 175–96, here 176.

29. See Daniel Aaron, *Writers on the Left* (New York: Avon, 1965), part 2.

30. *New York Times*, October 18, 1998, section 4 ("The Week in Review"), p. 6.

31. In addition to the works cited at note 5 above, see Steve Fraser and Gary Gerstle, eds., *The Rise and Fall of the New Deal Order, 1930–1980* (Princeton: Princeton University Press, 1989), wherein the new diagnostic consensus was first enunciated; Gary Gerstle, *Working Class Americanism: The Politics of Labor in a Textile City, 1914–1960* (Urbana: University of Illinois Press, 1989); Steve Fraser, *Labor Will Rule:Sidney Hillman and the Rise of American Labor* (Urbana: University of Illinois Press, 1991); and Michael Kazin, *The Populist Persuasion: An American History*, rev. ed. (Ithaca: Cornell University Press, 1998).

32. Brinkley, *The End of Reform*, pp. 10, 113–16. I do not want to be misunderstood here. I do not object to making "the institutions of the economy"—these would presumably include the large corporations—"accountable and responsive to popular needs and desires." But I do object to the assumption that the "populist persuasion" derived from the "anti-monopoly tradition" is the only viable means to this end. Let us not forget that since the 1890s, social movements inspired by the "anti-monopoly tradition" have insisted on statist command of the market economy as the necessary means to their populist ends: in effect these movements have claimed, contrary to the available historical evidence and to the American political tradition, that the cause of democracy can and will be served by subordinating society to the state, that is, by revoking the founding principle of the sovereignty of the people.

33. Richard Hofstadter located the origins of his own counter-progressive sensibility in Thurman Arnold's debunking essays of the late 1930s, but I would add Kenneth Burke and Irving Howe to the pantheon of the writers who steered us beyond the "anti-monopoly" tradition as all-purpose intellectual device, political compass, and moral calendar. In any event, Hofstadter and William Appleman Williams were the key figures in articulating a counter-progressive historiographical alternative to the neo-progressive mainstream, circa 1955–65. For further discussion, see James Livingston, "Why Is There Still Socialism in the United States?" *Reviews in American History* 22 (1994): 577–83, and chapters 1–2, above.

34. See Joseph Schumpeter, *Capitalism, Socialism, and Democracy*, 3rd ed. (New York: Harper, 1950), and Martin J. Sklar, *The United States as a Developing Country* (New York: Cambridge University Press, 1992), chaps. 1, 7. Marx is quoted from *Capital*, 3 vols., trans. Samuel Moore and Edward Aveling (Chicago: Charles H. Kerr Co., 1906) 3:516–19, 456.

35. Kazin quoted in Andrew Delbanco, "On Alfred Kazin (1915–1998)," *New York Review of Books*, July 16, 1998.

36. See Livingston, *Pragmatism and Political Economy*, chap. 8.

37. James Kloppenberg, "Knowledge and Belief in American Public Life," *The Virtues of Liberalism* (New York: Oxford University Press, 1998), pp. 38–58, here 58.

38. Arjun Appadurai, *Modernity at Large: Cultural Dimensions of Globalization* (Minneapolis: University of Minnesota Press, 1996), pp. 172–77, quoted from 176.

39. On the *Dred Scott* decision, see David M. Potter, *The Impending Crisis, 1848–1861* (New York: Harper & Row, 1976), chap. 11; on the Fourteenth Amendment and its malleable meanings, see Eric Foner, *Reconstruction: America's Unfinished Revolution* (New York: Harper & Row, 1988), pp. 251–71; Harold H. Hyman, *A More Perfect Union* (New York: Henry Holt, 1973), chaps. 17–19, 23–28; and Howard J. Graham, *Everyman's Constitution: Historical Essays on the Fourteenth Amendment* (Madison: University of Wisconsin Press, 1968).

40. See esp. the *Federalist*, no. 10: "The Utility of the Union as a Safeguard against Domestic Faction and Insurrection," conveniently reprinted in Marvin Meyers, ed., *The Mind of the Founder: Sources of the Political Thought of James Madison* (Indianapolis: Bobbs-Merrill, 1973), pp. 122–31.

41. On these crucial issues, see Hannah Arendt, *On Revolution* (New York: Viking, 1963), chaps. 4–5, and J. G. A. Pocock, *The Machiavellian Moment: Florentine Political Thought and the Atlantic Republican Tradition* (Princeton: Princeton University Press, 1975), pp. 63–78.

42. Madison quoted from "Remarks on Mr. Jefferson's Draught of a Constitution," October 1788, in Meyers, ed., *Mind of the Founder*, pp. 56–66, here 58–59, and from his speech in convention, August 7, 1787, Max Farrand, ed., *The Records of the Federal Convention of 1787*, 4 vols. (New Haven: Yale University Press, 1911), 2:203–4.

43. Cf. the "Remarks on Mr. Jefferson's Draught," *Mind of the Founder*, p. 58: "The first question arising here is how far property ought to be made a qualification [for voting]. There is a middle way to be taken which corresponds at once with the Theory of free Government and the lessons of experience. A freehold or equivalent of a certain value may be annexed to the right of voting for Senators, & the right left more at large in the election of the other House. . . . This middle mode reconciles and secures the two cardinal objects of Government; the rights of persons and the rights of property. The former will be sufficiently guarded by one branch, the latter more particularly by the other." And see also the addendum, circa 1821, which Madison attached to his speech in convention of August 7, 1787, in ibid., pp. 502–9.

44. Benedict Anderson, Imagined Communities (New York: Verso, 1995), p. 149; John Dewey, "America in the World" (1918), *Characters and Events*, 2 vols. (New York: Holt, Rinehart and Winston, 1929), 2:642–44.

45. Slovoj Žižek, "Enjoy Your Nation as Yourself!" in *Tarrying with the Negative: Kant, Hegel, and the Critique of Ideology* (Durham: Duke University Press, 1993), pp. 200–37, here 220.

Chapter 5: Hamlet, James, and the Woman Question

1. "What Pragmatism Means," in *Writings 1902–1910* (New York: Library of America, 1987), p. 510.

2. See my *Pragmatism and the Political Economy of Cultural Revolution, 1850–1940* (Chapel Hill: University of North Carolina Press, 1994), chap. 10.

3. Robert B. Ray, *A Certain Tendency of the Hollywood Cinema, 1930–1980* (Princeton: Princeton University Press, 1986), pp. 63, 74–75. Cf. Lewis Mumford, *The Golden Day: A Study of American Experience and Culture* (New York: Horace Liverwright, 1926), pp. 188–92.

4. Ned Lukacher, *Primal Scenes: Literature, Philosophy, Psychoanalysis* (Ithaca: Cornell University Press, 1986), pp. 215–16, 223.

5. Alasdair MacIntyre, "Epistemological Crises, Dramatic Narrative and the Philosophy of Science," *Monist* 60 (1977): 453–72, here 454–59.

6. George Cotkin, *William James: Public Philosopher* (Baltimore: Johns Hopkins University Press, 1990), chap. 3, "From Hamlet to Habit," esp. pp. 40–53, 58–59.

7. Howard M. Feinstein, *Becoming William James* (Ithaca: Cornell University Press, 1984), chaps. 12–15; but see chap. 17 on the "erotic tensions" between Alice James and her brother William. Hampshire quoted in Cotkin, *Public Philosopher*, p. 78.

8. See esp. Feinstein, *Becoming*, chap. 15, but also Cotkin, *Public Philosopher*, pp. 48–53; John Owen King III, *The Iron of Melancholy* (Middletown: Wesleyan University Press, 1983), pp. 154–70; and Alfred Habegger, "New Light on William James and Minny Temple," *New England Quarterly* 60 (1987): 28–53.

9. See Charlene Haddock-Seigfried, *Pragmatism and Feminism: Reweaving the Social Fabric* (Chicago: University of Chicago Press, 1995), chap. 6, and Alfred Habegger, *Henry James and the "Woman Business"* (New York: Cambridge University Press, 1989), chap. 2. I will have more to say about these readings below.

10. Godkin quoted from "Society and Marriage," *Nation*, May 26, 1870, p. 332, which was his reply to Henry Sr.'s first two essays in the *Atlantic Monthly*. See otherwise Habegger, *"Woman Business,"* pp. 29–36, 47–54.

11. Henry James Sr., "'The Woman Thou Gavest with Me,'" *Atlantic Monthly* January 1870, pp. 66–72, here 68–69.

12. "Society and Marriage," *Nation*, May 26, 1870, p. 332, and "Mr. Henry James on Marriage," a letter in response to Godkin's "Society and Marriage," *Nation*, June 9, 1870, p. 367.

13. On Henry Jr.'s response to his father's essays, see Habegger, *"Woman Business,"* pp. 49–52. William quoted from his letter to Henry Jr., January 19, 1870, in *The Correspondence of William James, Volume 1: William and Henry, 1861–1884* (Charlottesville: University of Virginia Press, 1992), p. 141. Cf. William to Henry Jr., October 2, 1869: "Father's book is out 'The Secret of Swedenborg' and is selling very fast, partly I suppose by virtue of the title to people who won't read it. I read it, and am very much enlightened as to his ideas and as to his intellectual rank thereby. I am going slowly through his other books. I will write you more when I have read more. Suffice it that many points which before were incomprehensible to me because doubtfully fallacious—I now definitely

believe to be entirely fallacious—but as this pile accumulates on one side there is left a more and more definite residuum on the other of great & original ideas, so that my respect for him is on the whole increased rather than diminished. But his ignorance of the way of thinking of other men, and his cool neglect of their difficulties is fabulous in a writer on such subjects." Ibid., 102. Also William to Henry Jr., November 1, 1869: "Father is a genius certainly—a religious genius. I feel it continually to be unfortunate that his discordance fm. me on other points in wh. I think the fault is really his—his want or indeed absence of *intellectual* sympathies of any sort—makes it so hard for me to make him feel how warmly I respond to the positive sides of him." Ibid., 120.

14. See William James [WJ] to Henry James Sr. [HJ Sr.], September 5, 1867, and HJ Sr., to WJ, September 27, 1867, in Ralph Barton Perry, *The Thought and Character of William James*, 2 vols. (Boston: Little, Brown & Co., 1935), 2:705–11.

15. WJ to HJ Sr., October 28, 1867, ibid., 711–13.

16. Perry, *Thought and Character* 1:278; WJ to Tom Ward, May 24, 1868, in ibid., 159–61, 276–77, here 160; WJ to Henry James Jr. [HJ Jr.], June 4, 1868, ibid., 278–80, here 279, and *Correspondence*, pp. 49–52, here 50–51; and again WJ to Tom Ward, May 24, 1868, in Perry, *Thought and Character*, 1:159. In mid-October, 1867, while still in Berlin, William had discussed *Hamlet* with Wilhelm Dilthey at the home of Herman Grimm, an art historian and novelist (William's first publication was a review of Grimm's novel, *Unüberwindliche Machte* [*Invincible Powers*] which appeared in the *Nation*, November 28, 1867); see Cotkin, *Public Philosopher*, pp. 43–44, and R. W. B. Lewis, *The Jameses: A Family Narrative* (New York: Farrar, Straus and Giroux, 1991), pp. 186–87.

17. Books Four and Five of Goethe's *Wilhelm Meister's Apprenticeship*, which comprise about a third of the novel, are dominated by discussions of *Hamlet*. See otherwise Jacques Lacan, "Desire and the Interpretation of Desire in *Hamlet*," in Shoshana Felman, ed., *Literature and Psychoanalysis* (Baltimore: Johns Hopkins University Press, 1982), pp. 11–82, here 17–18. Schiller is quoted from his letter to Goethe dated November 28, 1796, in Franco Moretti, *The Way of the World: The Bildungsroman in European Culture*, trans. Albert Sbragia (New York: Verso, 1987), p. 20. William James recommended this very correspondence between Schiller and Goethe to his brother: "in their aesthetic discussions you will find a particular profit I fancy." WJ to HJ Jr., June 4, 1868, *Correspondence*, pp. 49–52, here 50.

18. Johann Wolfgang von Goethe, *Wilhelm Meister's Apprenticeship*, trans. Eric A. Blackall (New York: Suhrkamp, 1989), pp. 146, 152, 195, 145. It is worth noting, in view of Lacan's reading of Hamlet, that Wilhelm's peroration on Ophelia is interrupted by a physical struggle between Aurelie and her brother over ownership of a "naked dagger," which she calls a "trusty friend" and a "precious talisman." Having won the struggle, Aurelie asks, "Must everything be harmful that looks dangerous?" She cuts Wilhelm with this same weapon at the end of Book Four, as a ritual confirmation of his vow "to withstand all fleeting attractions," and then inexplicably dies in Book Five. See ibid., pp. 152, 166–68.

19. My argument here owes a great deal to Moretti, *The Way of the World*, pp. 42–49, and probably even more to Albert Murray, *The Hero and the Blues* (Columbia: University of Missouri Press, 1973), a brilliant book

that, for all its ranting about the baleful influence of Marx and Freud on modern "protest fiction," is indispensable reading for students of American history.

20. All quotations in preceding paragraphs from WJ to HJ Jr., April 13, 1868, in *Correspondence*, pp. 46–48.

21. See Lewis, *Family Narrative*, pp. 192–95. Quotations in order from WJ to Oliver Wendell Holmes Jr., May 15, 1868, in Perry, *Thought and Character*, 1:512–18, here 516, 513; and WJ to Tom Ward, May 24, 1868, ibid., 276–77.

22. WJ to Holmes, May 15, 1868, in Perry, *Thought and Character*, 1:516.

23. See Habegger, "*Woman Business*," pp. 47–49; WJ to Tom Ward, March [?]1869, in Perry, *Thought and Character*, 1:471–73, here 473; *Nation*, July 22, 1869, pp. 72–73.

24. The review of Bushnell and Mill appeared in *North American Review* 109 (October 1869): 556–65.

25. See Haddock-Seigfried, *Pragmatism and Feminism*, pp. 115–19; Habegger, "*Woman Business*," pp. 47–48, and "New Light on William James and Minny Temple," p. 31.

26. Henry James [Sr.], "'The Woman Thou Gavest with Me,'" p. 69.

27. See generally Feinstein, *Becoming*, chap. 13. Quotations in order from WJ to Tom Ward, March [?] 1869, in Perry, *Thought and Character*, 1:472, the "Pomfret" memorandum, circa August 1869, printed in ibid., 301–2, and WJ to HJ Jr. December 29, 1869, ibid., 320–21.

28. Perry, *Thought and Character*, 1:301–2.

29. Habegger, "New Light," pp. 30–38.

30. Habegger, "New Light," pp. 41, 46–50; Perry, *Thought and Character*, 1:322–23.

31. See Habegger, "New Light," p. 42 n. 29.

32. Sigmund Freud, "Mourning and Melancholia" (1917), *Standard Edition* (London: Hogarth, 1953 and following), vol. 14, pp. 243–58, to which I was reintroduced by Judith Butler, *Gender Trouble: Feminism and the Subversion of Identity* (New York: Routledge, 1990), chap. 2, esp. pp. 43–65, 160 n. 19. As Butler points out, there are useful remarks on mourning, identification, and melancholia in *The Ego and the Id* (1923), in *Standard Edition*, vol. 19, pp. 12–59, esp. chap. 5; I would also cite *Group Psychology and the Analysis of the Ego* (1921), in *Standard Edition*, vol. 18, pp. 65–143, esp. chaps. 7 and 11. See also Peter Osborne, *The Politics of Time* (New York: Verso, 1995), pp. 91–96, on why the division of the mother's desire—the diversion of that desire from the infant to others—will be perceived by the infant as loss, and Jonathan Lear, *Love and Its Place in Nature: A Philosophical Interpretation of Freudian Psychoanalysis* (New Haven: Yale University Press, 1990), pp. 158–68, on how identification as such is predicated on loss and mourning (e.g., "Psychic structure, Freud realizes, is created by a dialectic of loss and love" [p. 160]).

33. See King, *Iron of Melancholy*, pp. 154–64; Feinstein, *Becoming*, pp. 241–45.

34. From William James, *The Varieties of Religious Experience* (1902), in *Writings 1902–1910*, Lectures 6–7, "The Sick Soul," pp. 149–50. I now think that Feinstein must be wrong about the timing of this breakdown,

mainly because James started teaching (at Harvard) and writing for publication in the fall of 1872. A more likely moment is some time between the spring of 1870 and the spring of 1872.

35. Quoted in Habegger, "New Light," p. 51.

Chapter 6: Unstiffening Our Theories

1. See Judith Butler, *Bodies That Matter* (New York: Routledge, 1993), chap. 7, esp. pp. 188–89; Teresa Brennan, *History after Lacan* (New York: Routledge, 1993), pp. 136, 138, 143, 149–50, 159–61, 168, 173, 184, 188, 190–92.

2. Frank Lentricchia, *Ariel and the Police* (Madison: University of Wisconsin Press, 1987), pp. 125–26; Charlene Haddock-Seigfried, *Pragmatism and Feminism: Reweaving the Social Fabric* (Chicago: University of Chicago Press, 1996), p. 136. On the significance of James's rhetoric, see H. S. Thayer, *Meaning and Action: A Critical History of Pragmatism* (New York: Bobbs-Merrill, 1968), p. 145, section 29, "James and Language: A Word about the Use of Words." Here Thayer notes that "since much of philosophic theory-making and all theory-stating goes on in language, the linguistic medium itself, taken as an object of study, often repays scrutiny by bringing us closer to the fuller gist of intended meaning.... For phrasings, while ordinarily passing for clues to the meaning of theory, are in fact usually contrived according to antecedent promptings of theory itself and are embodiments of it. The articulations of unburdening thought, e.g., a metaphor, while said to be 'expressive of' thought—on subsequent examination as to how and why just *that* metaphor was chosen as expressive—may tell us more than its prosaic counterpart or literal transcript."

3. William James, *Pragmatism* (1907), Lecture 2, "What Pragmatism Means," in *Writings 1902–1910* (New York: Library of America, 1987), pp. 520–22.

4. Ibid., Lecture 6, "Pragmatism's Conception of Truth," p. 585.

5. Ibid., Lecture 1, "The Present Dilemma in Philosophy," pp. 495–96; cf. James's depiction of Walt Whitman as the flaneur of Broadway, the busiest of streets, in "On a Certain Blindness in Human Beings," *Talks to Teachers on Psychology* (New York: Henry Holt, 1899), pp. 229–64, here 251. On the figure of the prostitute—the woman of the streets—as the farthest outpost of "reification," the "ultimate symbol of the commodification of eros," the exemplar of modernity, etc., see Ruth Rosen, *The Lost Sisterhood: Prostitution in America, 1900–1918* (Baltimore: Johns Hopkins University Press, 1982), pp. 41–46; Christine Stansell, *City of Women: Sex and Class in New York, 1789–1860* (Urbana: University of Illinois Press, 1987), pp. 125–29, 139–40, 171–92; Timothy J. Gilfoyle, *City of Eros: New York City, Prostitution, and the Commercialization of Sex, 1790–1920* (New York: Norton, 1992), chap. 7; Amy Dru Stanley, *From Bondage to Contract: Wage Labor, Marriage, and the Market in the Age of Emancipation* (New York: Cambridge University Press, 1998), chap. 6; Rita Felski, *The Gender of Modernity* (Cambridge: Harvard University Press, 1995), chaps. 1–3, esp. pp. 19, 64; Kathy Peiss, *Cheap Amusements: Working Women and Leisure in Turn-of-the-Century New York* (Philadelphia: Temple University Press, 1986), chaps. 3–4, esp. pp. 66, 98; Rachel Bowlby, *Just Looking: Consumer Culture in Dreiser, Gissing, and Zola* (London: Methuen, 1985), pp. 10–11, 26–29.

6. See J. G. A. Pocock, *The Machiavellian Moment: Florentine Political Thought and the Atlantic Republican Tradition* (Princeton: Princeton University Press, 1975), chaps. 13–14, esp. pp. 426, 437, 448, 452. On the Renaissance transformation of *Fortuna*, see Hannah Fenichel Pitkin, *Fortune Is a Woman: Gender and Politics in the Political Thought of Niccolo Machiavelli* (Berkeley: University of California Press, 1984), chap. 6, esp. pp. 144, 153, 169; and on incidents of sexual offense as "necessary markers" of legal-political change in both the ancient and the early modern world, see Stephanie H Jed, *Chaste Thinking: The Rape of Lucretia and the Birth of Humanism* (Bloomington: Indiana University Press, 1989), pp. 2–5, 41–50. See also the works cited at note 31 below on the correlation between legal misogyny and household economies.

7. See Edward Bellamy, *Looking Backward 2000–1887* (Boston: Bedford Books of St. Martin's, 1995), p. 149; James Livingston, *Origins of the Federal Reserve System: Money, Class, and Corporate Capitalism, 1890–1913* (Ithaca: Cornell University Press, 1986), chaps. 3–4; Ann Fabian, *Card Sharps, Dream Books, and Bucket Shops: Gambling in 19th Century America* (Ithaca: Cornell University Press, 1990), chap. 4; Gretchen Ritter, *Goldbugs and Greenbacks: The Antimonopoly Tradition and the Politics of Finance in America* (New York: Cambridge University Press, 1997), chap. 5; Elizabeth Sanders, *Roots of Reform: Farmers, Workers, and the American State, 1877–1917* (Chicago: University of Chicago Press, 1999), pp. 109–17, 125–26, 138–40, 146, 236–59; and Bruce Palmer, *"Man over Money": The Southern Populist Critique of American Capitalism* (Chapel Hill: University of North Carolina Press, 1980), chaps. 7–10, from which the *Populist* is quoted at p. 130.

8. The confusions begin with Lawrence Goodwyn, *Democratic Promise: The Populist Moment in America* (New York: Oxford University Press, 1976); but they are compounded to the point of absurdity by Ritter, *Goldbugs and Greenbacks*; Michael O'Malley, "Specie and Species: Race and the Money Question in nineteenth-Century America," *American Historical Review* 99 (1994): 369–95; and Elizabeth Sanders, *Roots of Reform*, pp. 109–10.

9. See Livingston, *Origins of the Fed*, chap. 3; *Texas Advance* quoted from Palmer, *"Man over Money,"* p. 93.

10. On epistemology and gender, the key works are Genevieve Lloyd, *The Man of Reason: "Male" and "Female" in Western Philosophy* (Minnesota: University of Minnesota Press, 1984); Luce Irigaray, *Speculum of the Other Woman*, trans. Gillian C. Gill (Ithaca: Cornell University Press, 1985); Michele Le Doeuff, *The Philosophical Imaginary* trans. Colin Gordon (Stanford: Stanford University Press, 1989); and Mary Lyndon Shanley and Carole Pateman, eds., *Feminist Interpretations and Political Theory* (University Park: Pennsylvania State University Press, 1991). But see also Renata Salecl, *The Spoils of Freedom: Psychoanalysis and Feminism after the Fall of Socialism* (New York: Routledge, 1994), chap. 8, for an important dissent from the notion that "modern subjectivity," as imagined and enfranchised by philosophers from Descartes to Kant, must be construed as intrinsically male.

11. See Bruce Wilshire, *William James and Phenomenology: A Study of "The Principles of Psychology"* (Bloomington: Indiana University Press, 1968) ; James Livingston, *Pragmatism and the Political Economy of Cultural Revolution, 1850–1940* (Chapel Hill: University of North Carolina Press,

1994), chap. 10; and on Williams, see Alec Marsh, *Money and Modernity: Pound, Williams, and the Spirit of Jefferson* (Tuscaloosa: University of Alabama Press, 1998).

12. See Emile Durkheim, *Pragmatism and Sociology*, trans. J. C. Whitehouse, ed. John B. Allcock (New York: Cambridge University Press, 1983); Friedrich Nietzsche, *On the Genealogy of Morals*, trans. Walter Kaufmann and R. J. Hollingdale (New York: Vintage, 1989), pp. 45–46; Judith Butler, "Contingent Foundations," in Seyla Benhabib et al., *Feminist Contentions* (New York: Routledge, 1995), pp. 35–57, here 48, 46.

13. Judith Butler, *Gender Trouble: Feminism and the Subversion of Identity* (New York: Routledge, 1990), p. 25; cf. *Bodies That Matter*, esp. chaps. 2–3, 7–8.

14. Seyla Benhabib, *Situating the Self: Gender, Community, and Postmodernism in Contemporary Ethics* (New York: Routledge, 1992), p. 71; "Feminism and Postmodernism: An Uneasy Alliance," in *Feminist Contentions*, pp. 17–34, here 20–22; Nancy Fraser, "False Antitheses," ibid., pp. 59–74, here 67–69; and see also Fraser, "The Uses and Abuses of French Discourse Theories for Feminist Politics," in Nancy Fraser and Sandra Bartky, eds., *Revaluing French Feminism* (Bloomington: Indiana University Press, 1991), pp. 177–94.

15. Benhabib, "Feminism and Postmodernism," p. 20; Anthony Giddens, *New Rules of Sociological Method*, 2nd ed. (Stanford: Stanford University Press, 1993), pp. 26–27.

16. See John Dewey, "The Vanishing Subject in the Psychology of James," *Journal of Philosophy* 37 (1940): 589–99; William James, "Does Consciousness Exist?" (1904) and "A World of Pure Experience" (1905), in *Essays in Radical Empiricism* (Cambridge: Harvard University Press, 1976). For commentary on these essays, see my *Pragmatism and the Political Economy of Cultural Revolution, 1850–1940*, pp. 263–73, and John Wild, *The Radical Empiricism of William James* (Garden City: Doubleday, 1969), chaps. 14–15. On the "passing thought" rather than the nature of the thinker as the proper object of intellectual inquiry, see William James, *The Principles of Psychology* (1890; Cambridge: Harvard University Press, 1983), chaps. 9–10.

17. I am borrowing and bending Jonathan Lear's insights into the relation between the "archaic" knowledge of bodily states and the narrativized knowledge of psychoanalytical explanation: see his *Love and Its Place in Nature: A Philosophical Interpretation of Freudian Psychoanalysis* (New Haven: Yale University Press, 1990, 1998), chaps. 2–4.

18. In resisting the reduction of James to an "individualist" pure and simple, I am arguing with, among others, Cornel West, *The American Evasion of Philosophy: A Genealogy of Pragmatism* (Madison: University of Wisconsin Press, 1987), pp. 54–68; and Deborah J. Coon, "'One Moment in the World's Salvation': Anarchism and the Radicalization of William James," *Journal of American History* 83 (1996): 70–99. Coon goes so far as to make the absurd claim that Frank Lentricchia and I characterize William James as a Marxist. But see note 24, below.

19. "The Moral Equivalent of War" (1910), in *Writings 1902–1910*, pp. 1281–93, here 1285. As I suggest in the last section of this chapter, the "credit economy" that finances the corporate "age of surplus" is the solvent of the "natural person"—the self-contained male proprietor—who sustained the "homoerotic unconscious of the phallogocentric economy." In other

words, the consumer culture underwritten by corporate capitalism permits a polymorphous perversity that was inconceivable under the early modern "regime of the brother"; for, Luce Irigaray notwithstanding, it does not require "that men be exempt from being used and circulated like commodities." Cf. Irigaray, "Women on the Market," in *This Sex Which Is Not One*, trans. Catherine Porter (Ithaca: Cornell University Press, 1985), pp. 170–97, (quoted from 172).

20. See chapters 2–3, above.

21. A representative example of mainstream "left" thinking on globalization is Leo Panitch, "Globalisation and the State," in Ralph Miliband and Leo Panitch, eds., *Between Globalism and Nationalism: Socialist Register 1994* (London: Merlin Press, 1994), pp. 60–93; see pp. 89–90 for the bizarre programmatic implications of this critique of globalization. Much more useful meditations on the question are Doug Henwood, "Antiglobalization," *Left Business Observer* #71 (January 1996) and Bruce Robbins, *Feeling Global: Internationalism in Distress* (New York: New York University Press, 1999). On the interpenetration of capitalism, socialism, and other modes of production, see J. K. Gibson-Graham, *The End of Capitalism (as we knew it): A Feminist Critique of Political Economy* (Oxford: Blackwell, 1996), esp. chaps. 1–4, 9–10; Martin J. Sklar, *The United States as a Developing Country* (New York: Cambridge University Press, 1992), chaps. 1, 7, and "Capitalism and Socialism in the Emergence of Modern America: The Formative Era," in Elizabeth Fox-Genovese and Elisabeth Lasch-Quinn, eds., *Reconstructing History* (New York: Routledge, 1999), pp. 304–21; and Stuart Hall, "Gramsci's Relevance for the Study of Race and Ethnicity," *Journal of Communications Inquiry* 10 (1993): 5–27.

22. Walter Lippmann, *Drift and Mastery: An Attempt to Diagnose the Current Unrest* (1914; reprint, Madison: University of Wisconsin Press, 1985), pp. 45–47; Mari Jo Buhle, *Women and American Socialism, 1870–1920* (Urbana: University of Illinois Press, 1981), p. 249; cf. Linda Gordon, *Woman's Body, Woman's Right: Birth Control in America*, rev. ed. (New York: Penguin, 1990), chap. 9.

23. Karl Marx, *Capital: A Critique of Political Economy*, 3 vols., trans. Samuel Moore and Edward Aveling (Chicago: Charles H. Kerr and Co., 1906), 3:515–19, 549, 712–13.

24. Butler, *Bodies That Matter*, p. 241. In chapter 4, above, I argue that Marxism and pragmatism are, in fact, compatible and commensurable moments in the Western intellectual tradition; cf. also Linda Nicholson, *Gender and History: The Limits of Social Theory in the Age of the Family* (New York: Columbia University Press, 1986), pp. 171–72, 228 n. 9, where she cites works by Sidney Hook, Richard Bernstein, Jürgen Habermas, and Shlomo Avineri to validate her comparison of Marxism and pragmatism.

25. See, for example, David Harvey, *The Condition of Postmodernity* (Oxford: Blackwell, 1990), esp. chaps. 5, 14; and Mike Davis, *Ecology of Fear* (New York: Henry Holt, 1999).

26. Page references to *History after Lacan* hereafter in text.

27. I have work in progress that examines the intersections of pragmatism, feminism, and psychoanalysis, through which I hope both to summarize and to criticize the theoretical models of Jacques Lacan, Juliet Mitchell, Jacqueline Rose, Jane Gallop, Rachel Bowlby, Judith Butler, Jessica Ben-

jamin, Jane Flax, and many others. But, like Mari Jo Buhle in her insightful and indispensable new book, *Feminism and Its Discontents: A Century of Struggle with Psycho- analysis* (Cambridge: Harvard University Press, 1998), I will be treating theoretical models as historical artifacts.

28. See, for example, Carl Boggs, *Social Movements and Political Power: Emerging Forms of Radicalism in the West* (Philadelphia: Temple University Press, 1986); Carolyn Merchant, *The Death of Nature: Women, Ecology, and the Scientific Revolution* (New York: HarperCollins, 1990); and Davis, *Ecology of Fear.*

29. See Karl Marx, *Capital* 1:41–96, 197–206; "Economic and Philosophic Manuscripts of 1844," in *Karl Marx–Frederick Engels Collected Works, Volume 3,* trans. Jack Cohen et al. (New York: International Publishers, 1975), pp. 229–346, here 275–76; and *Grundrisse,* trans. Martin Nicolaus (Baltimore: Penguin, 1973), p. 489.

30. The "anti-monopoly tradition" that informs the anti-trust urges of Anglo-American law and that animates the "new institutionalism" in contemporary Political Science and History departments (cf. Gretchen Ritter as cited in this chapter at notes 7–8 and Alan Brinkley as cited in chapter 4, note 31) does not entail a commitment to equality between men and women, either in theory or in practice. As I suggest in chapter 4, however, and as Martin J. Sklar explains in *The Corporate Reconstruction of American Capitalism, 1890–1916: The Market, the Law, and Politics* (New York: Cambridge University Press, 1988), pp. 127–45, this tradition does imply a statist resolution to the problem of market regulation.

31. C. B. Macpherson, *The Political Theory of Possessive Individualism: Hobbes to Locke* (New York: Oxford University Press, 1962), pp. 46–61. It is worth noting here that when Brennan defends "household production" against its "large-scale" successors because the former "accorded women a very different and generally better economic place," she cites Louise A. Tilly and Joan W. Scott, *Women, Work, and Family,* 3rd ed. (New York: Routledge, 1989). My claim is of course that Brennan is wrong about women's "place" under the regime of "household production," in part because such regimes, from the ancient to the modern world, typically confined female sexuality to domestic, familial, and/or reproductive functions by means of legal and cultural misogyny, as a way of maintaining the continuity of claims to property from generation to generation and *thus grounding the identity of the male proprietor* by securing the self-sufficiency of the citizen. Insofar as Tilly and Scott's work validates Brennan's position—there is room for disagreement here—I am claiming that they, too, are wrong to suggest that women's "place" in the early modern period was better than it has since become. On the strong correlation between household or "smallholder" economies and the near-hysterical fear of female sexuality, see Nicholson, *Gender and History,* pp. 115–21, where Marilyn Arthur's seminal essay, "'Liberated Women': The Classical Era," in Renate Bridenthal and Claudia Koonz, eds., *Becoming Visible: Women in European History* (Boston: Houghton Mifflin, 1977), pp. 60–89, is put to good use also; Ellen Meiksins Wood, *Peasant-Citizen and Slave: The Foundations of Athenian Democracy* (New York: Verso, 1988), pp. 74–75, 102–4, 108, 114–21, 155–60; Walter Beringer, "Freedom, Family, and Citizenship in Early Greece," in John Eadie and Josiah Ober, eds., *The Craft of the Ancient Historian* (New York: University Press of America, 1985), pp. 41–56; L. Foxhall, "Household, Gender and

Property in Classical Athens," *Classical Quarterly* 39 (1989): 22–44; J. P. Gould, "Law, Custom, and Myth: Aspects of the Social Position of Women in Classical Athens," *Journal of Hellenistic Studies* 100 (1980): 38–59; Jane F. Gardner, "Aristophanes and Male Anxiety: The Defence of the Oikos," and Peter Walcot, "Greek Attitudes towards Women: The Mythological Evidence," in Ian McAuslan and Peter Walcot, eds., *Women in Antiquity* (London: Oxford University Press, 1996), pp. 146–57, 91–102. Most of these writers note the strong resemblance between the misogyny of the classical and the early modern periods in Western history.

32. Macpherson, *Possessive Individualism*, pp. 41, 57–59. There is nothing inevitable about the "market revolution" that announces and enforces the transition from a "proto-industrial," household economy—that is, a simple market (bourgeois) society—to a modern-industrial (capitalist) society; nor are the effects of this revolution predictable, as the Civil War era in the U.S. might suggest: see E. A. Wrigley, "The Process of Modernization and the Industrial Revolution in England," *Journal of Interdisciplinary History* 3 (1972): 225–59; Thomas Bender, ed., *The Antislavery Debate: Capitalism and Abolitionism as a Problem of Historical Interpretation* (Berkeley: University of California Press, 1992); and Livingston, *Pragmatism and Political Economy*, chap. 2.

33. G. W. F. Hegel, *The Philosophy of Right*, trans. T. M. Knox (New York: Oxford University Press, 1952), par. 45, 57 at pp. 42, 47–48; J. G. A. Pocock, "The Mobility of Property and the Rise of 18th-Century Sociology," in Anthony Parel and Thomas Flanagan, eds., *Theories of Property, Aristotle to the Present* (Waterloo: Wilfrid Laurier University Press, 1979), pp. 141–66, here 150–51, 141. Cf. also Marx on the ambiguities of property, in "Manuscripts of 1844," pp. 290–306.

34. See Alfred Marshall, *Principles of Economics*, 2 vols. (1890; Variorum edition, London: Macmillan, 1961) 1: 48. On Clark and marginalist theory, see Livingston, *Pragmatism and Political Economy*, pp. 49–62. On the redefinition of property and liberty (of contract) at the law and in the larger culture, see Thorstein Veblen, *The Theory of Business Enterprise* (New York: Scribners, 1904), chap. 8; Richard T. Ely, *Property and Contract in Their Relations to the Distribution of Wealth*, 2 vols. (New York: Macmillan, 1914), 1:165–99, 268–70, 2:586–626; John R. Commons, *Legal Foundations of Capitalism* (New York: Macmillan, 1924), passim, esp. pp. 11–64, 173–86, 211–13, 246–73; J. Willard Hurst, *The Legitimacy of the Business Corporation in the Law of the United States, 1780–1970* (Charlottesville: University of Virginia Press, 1970), pp. 65–68; Morton J. Horwitz, "*Santa Clara* Revisited: The Development of Corporate Theory," *West Virginia Law Review* 88 (1985): 173–224; and Sklar, *The Corporate Reconstruction of American Capitalism*, part 1.

35. Henry Carter Adams, "Economics and Jurisprudence [1896]," in Joseph Dorfman, ed., *Two Essays by Henry Carter Adams* (New York: Columbia University Press, 1954), pp. 137- 62, here 150–51, 143–48. On the corporate consolidation of the railway system in the 1890s, see esp. E. G. Campbell, *The Reorganization of the American Railway System, 1893–1900* (New York: Columbia University Press, 1938), but also Alfred D. Chandler Jr., *The Visible Hand: The Managerial Revolution in American Business* (Cambridge: Harvard University Press, 1977), chap. 5.

36. Adams, "Economics and Jurisprudence," pp. 155, 159. The "Discussion of President Adams' Address" is at pp. 163–72; the respondents were

Arthur T. Hadley and Henry W. Farnham of Yale, Franklin H. Giddings of Columbia, C. S. Walker of the Massachusetts Agricultural College, Leo S. Rowe of the University of Pennsylvania, George Gunton of the Institute of Social Economics, and Edward Cummings of Harvard. For a representative example of socialist thinking on the collectivizing tendencies of "the trusts," see Laurence Gronlund, *The New Economy: A Peaceable Solution of the Social Problem* (Chicago: Charles H. Kerr, 1898): "Now the Trust is the womb that has conceived Collectivism. . . . Now comes Collectivism, and it once more revives the conviction of men's solidarity" (pp. 35, 62).

37. See, for example, A. W. Machen Jr., "Corporate Personality," *Harvard Law Review* 24 (1911): 253–67, 347–65. More recent studies that analyze the changing relation between property and legal personality after 1890 are Herbert J. Hovenkamp, *Enterprise and American Law, 1836–1937* (Cambridge: Harvard University Press, 1991), chap. 4; Margaret Jane Radin, "Property and Personhood," *Stanford Law Review* 34 (1981–82): 957–1015; Kenneth J. Vandevelde, "The New Property of the Nineteenth Century: The Development of the Modern Concept of Property," *Buffalo Law Review* 29 (1980): 325–67; and J. Allen Douglas, "Property and Personality in the Culture of Corporate Capitalism," Ph.D. dissertation, Rutgers University, 2001.

38. Quoted passages from Norman Pollack, ed., *The Populist Mind* (Indianapolis: Bobbs- Merrill, 1967), pp. 28–29, 43, and Richard Hofstadter, *The Age of Reform: From Bryan to FDR* (New York: Vintage, 1955), p. 223.

39. John Dewey, "The Historic Background of Corporate Legal Personality," *Yale Law Journal* 35 (1926): 655–73, here 657–59, 670.

40. See Max Weber, "Bureaucracy," in Hans Gerth and C. Wright Mills, eds., *From Max Weber* (New York: Oxford University Press, 1946), pp. 196–244. *Fortune* magazine cited in Margery Davies, "Woman's Place Is at the Typewriter: The Feminization of the Clerical Labor Force," in Zillah R. Eisenstein, ed., *Capitalist Patriarchy and the Case for Socialist Feminism* (New York: Monthly Review Press, 1979), pp. 248–66, here 257.

41. See Davies, "Clerical Labor Force," table 2 at pp. 260–61; Joseph A. Hill, *Women in Gainful Occupations, 1870 to 1920*, Census Monographs IX (Washington: GPO, 1929), pp. 32- 45, 75–77; James McGovern, "The American Woman's Pre–World War I Freedom in Manners and Morals" *Journal of American History* 55 (1968): 315–33; Peiss, Cheap *Amusements*, chap. 2; Julie A. Matthei, *An Economic History of Women in America* (New York: Schocken, 1982), chaps. 10–12; Alice Kessler-Harris, *Out to Work: A History of Wage-Earning Women in the United States* (New York: Oxford, 1982), chaps. 5–6, esp. pp. 112–19, 142–51; Leslie Woodcock Tentler, *Wage-Earning Women: Industrial Work and Family Life in the United States, 1900- 1930* (New York: Oxford, 1979), chap. 3; Olivier Zunz, *Making America Corporate, 1870–1920* (Chicago: University of Chicago Press, 1990), pp. 116–21, 133, 138–48; Angel Kwolek-Folland, *Engendering Business: Men and Women in the Corporate Office, 1870–1930* (Baltimore: Johns Hopkins University Press, 1994), pp. 28–40, 63–69, 113–28, 165–92; Ileen DeVault, *Sons and Daughters of Labor: Class and Clerical Work in Turn-of-the-Century Pittsburgh* (Ithaca: Cornell University Press, 1990); Carole Srole, "'A Blessing to

Mankind, and Especially to Womankind': The Typewriter and the Feminization of Clerical Work, Boston, 1860–1920," in Barbara Drygulski Wright, ed., *Women, Work, and Technology: Transformations* (Ann Arbor: University of Michigan Press, 1987), pp. 84–100; Sophonisba P. Breckenridge, *Women in the Twentieth Century* (New York: McGraw-Hill, 1933), part 2, "Women and Gainful Employment," esp. chaps. 7–9, 11 (this book was written for the President's Research Committee on Social Trends, which was chaired by Wesley C. Mitchell, a founder of the National Bureau of Economic Research); Jurgen Kocka, *White Collar Workers in America, 1890–1940*, trans. Maura Kealey (London: Sage, 1980), pp. 42–74, 92–117, 155–86; Dorothy M. Brown, *Setting a Course: American Women in the 1920s* (Boston: Twayne, 1987), chap. 4; William D. Jenkins, "Housewifery and Motherhood: The Question of Role Change in the Progressive Era," in Mary Kelley, ed., *Woman's Being, Woman's Place: Female Identity and Vocation in American History* (Boston: G. K. Hall, 1979), pp. 142–53.

42. See Davies, "Clerical Labor Force," pp. 251–52; and Grace L. Coyle, "Women in the Clerical Occupations," *Annals of the American Academy of Political and Social Science* 143 (May 1929): 180–87 (an article drawn from her book *Recent Trends in Clerical Occupations* [New York: Woman's Press, 1928]). The theme of this special issue of the *Annals* was women and the family construed principally as a problem of political economy; cf. Emilie J. Hutchinson, "The Economic Problems of Women," ibid. at 132–36. See also Mary Ross, "The New Status of Women in America," in Samuel D. Schmalhausen and V. F. Calverton, eds., *Woman's Coming of Age: A Symposium* (New York: Horace Liverwright, 1931), pp. 536–49, e.g. at 549: "The change which is molding the lives of millions is a later chapter in the history of that industrial revolution which began to shift the workplace of men so radically a century ago. For women as for men, the shift has brought 'freedom' in a negative way: no longer is it necessary to work as a member of a family group in order to hold an economic footing." The editors' introduction at pp. xi–xx makes a similar argument, as does Iva Lowther Peters, "The Psychology of Sex Differences" at pp. 163–86. Among other contributors to *Woman's Coming of Age* were Margaret Mead, Charlotte Perkins Gilman, Rebecca West, Havelock Ellis, Dora Russell, and Alice Beal Parsons. The editors of this collection (and the one cited at note 44) are placed in cultural context by Mari Jo Buhle, *Feminism and Its Discontents*, pp. 93–99.

42. Zunz, *Making America Corporate*, p. 138; Gordon, *Woman's Body, Woman's Right*, pp. 200–1; Coyle, "Clerical Occupations," pp. 182, 180–81.

43. Davies, "Clerical Labor Force," pp. 251–54; Coyle, "Clerical Occupations," p. 181. Charles A. Heiss quoted from *Accounting in the Administration of Large Business Enterprises* (Cambridge: Harvard University Press, 1943), p. 10; cf. Seymour Melman, "The Rise of Administrative Overhead in Manufacturing Industries in the United States, 1899–1947," *Oxford Economic Papers* n.s. 3 (1951): 62–112.

44. Samuel D. Schmalhausen, "The Sexual Revolution," in V. F. Calverton and Samuel D. Schmalhausen, eds., *Sex in Civilization* (Garden City: Garden City Publishing Co., 1929), pp. 349–436, here 359; in his hilarious endnotes, Schmalhausen quotes from his correspondence with Havelock Ellis (who wrote an introduction for the volume) and Aldous Huxley, and approvingly cites the work of Sigmund Freud, Margaret Mead, Bronislav

Malinowski, and Horace M. Kallen, the pragmatist who celebrated consumer culture in the U.S. Among other contributors to *Sex in Civilization* were Harry Elmer Barnes, Waldo Frank, Margaret Sanger, and Charlotte Perkins Gilman. Coyle quoted from "Clerical Occupations," p. 182, Mumford from *Technics and Civilization* (New York: Harcourt Brace and Co., 1934), p. 227. On the pace, pattern, and implications of mechanization, automation, etc., in the 1920s, see Livingston, *Pragmatism and Political Economy*, chap. 4.

45. Hofstadter, *Age of Reform*, pp. 315–16.
46. See Katherine Bement Davis, *Factors in the Sex Life of Twenty-Two Hundred Women* (New York: Harper and Brothers, 1929), chap. 12; Ben B. Lindsey, "The Promise and Peril of the New Freedom," *Woman's Coming of Age*, pp. 447–71 (Lindsey, an authority on juvenile delinquency and the author of a book on "companionate marriage," argued that the detachment of female sexuality from its reproductive function was the key to the New Woman's new freedom: "Back of the new freedom is the frank admission that erotic passion is far greater in the sex life of civilised men and women than it was among primitive peoples and that it plays a double role to-day. Reproduction of the species, once its sole function, is now generally recognised as a secondary purpose."); V. F. Calverton, "Are Women Monogamous?" in ibid., pp. 475–88; Christina Simmons, "Modern Sexuality and the Myth of Victorian Repression," in Kathy Peiss and Christina Simmons, eds., *Passion and Power* (Philadelphia: Temple University Press, 1989), pp. 157–77; Daniel Scott-Smith, "The Dating of the American Sexual Revolution," in Michael Gordon, ed., *The American Family in Social-Historical Perspective*, 2nd ed. (New York: St. Martin's, 1978), pp. 321–35; John C. Burnham, "The Progressive Era Revolution in American Attitudes Toward Sex," *Journal of American History* 59 (1973): 885–908; Charlotte Perkins Gilman, *Women and Economics* (Boston: Maynard, 1898), pp. 99–153; Rheta Childe Dorr, *What Eight Million Women Want* (Boston: Small Maynard, 1910), pp. iv–xii; Gordon, *Woman's Body, Woman's Right*, pp. 189–203 ("Over the long run probably no single factor did more to change the sexual behavior of unmarried women than their entrance into the labor market, especially if it meant living away from home" [p. 200].); Peiss, *Cheap Amusements*, pp. 35–41.

Index